LOST CITY, FOUND PYRAMID

LOST CITY, FOUND PYRAMID

Understanding Alternative Archaeologies and Pseudoscientific Practices

EDITED BY JEB J. CARD AND DAVID S. ANDERSON

THE UNIVERSITY OF ALABAMA PRESS
Tuscaloosa

The University of Alabama Press
Tuscaloosa, Alabama 35487-0380
uapress.ua.edu

Hardcover edition published 2016.
Paperback edition published 2025.
eBook edition published 2016.

Typeface: Minion and Helvetica Neue

Cover image: The Great Sphinx; courtesy of David S. Anderson
Cover design: Michele Myatt Quinn

Paperback ISBN: 978-0-8173-6223-2

A previous edition of this book has been cataloged by the Library of Congress.
ISBN: 978-0-8173-1911-3 (cloth)
E-ISBN: 978-0-8173-8980-2

Contents

Illustrations

FIGURES

TABLES

Acknowledgments

We would like to thank all of the contributors to the volume for creating an important work on an underaddressed and controversial topic. We extend the same thanks to those who participated in the 2012 Society for American Archaeology session on this topic but were unable to include their work in this volume. Our thanks go to Ken Feder not only for his discussion of the contributions to this volume but also for acting as an inspiration for many of the authors represented in these pages. We would also like to thank Daniel Waterman, Wendi Schnaufer, and everyone at the University of Alabama Press for their tremendous assistance in supporting this volume and making it a reality.

LOST CITY, FOUND PYRAMID

Alternatives and Pseudosciences

A History of Archaeological Engagement with Extraordinary Claims

JEB J. CARD AND DAVID S. ANDERSON

Promotion, Engagement, Denial, and Understanding of Alternative Archaeology

This volume examines and critiques practices of archaeologists, alternative researchers, religious performers, media producers, and the public in relation to what has been called "pseudoscience" and especially pseudoarchaeology. The "pseudo" modifier is polarizing, leading some archaeologists and other commentators to other presumably more democratic labels, the most popular being "alternative archaeology." Nevertheless, even most of these critics would consider the topics under discussion to be outside of scholarly archaeology and generally outside of mainstream science altogether. A number of the contributors to this volume examine the nature and history of current unscientific practices, including alternative forms of field archaeology and use of archaeological remains in heterodox religious and magical rituals. These practices have directly impacted the authors' archaeological work or have had a negative impact on the archaeological record. Other contributors examine the nature of nonscientific or pseudoscientific practices for potential lessons for archaeology. Much of the volume examines how archaeologists react to such practices and offers critiques and suggestions for more productive strategies for engagement.

To introduce these contributions, we offer a brief history of the ways in which archaeologists have engaged with less-than-scientific approaches to remains of the past. Exploring possible approaches professional archaeology can take in engaging with "alternative archaeology" or "pseudoarchaeology" requires understanding what paths we have taken in the past. Initially, investigating and evaluating ideas and evidence that today are considered pseudoscientific or simply outlandish was a significant part of archaeology. As the discipline professionalized it increasingly rejected or outright ignored alternative or pseudoscientific claims. The controversy over how to engage with "alternatives" stems in large part from a reaction to this professionalization, occurring against the backdrop of widespread interest in both archaeology and nonscientific constructions of the past by a public.

Crafting the history of a scholarly field is fraught with difficulties. Who becomes a titan who influenced the discipline? Which innovator created seminal methodological techniques? And how do we decide whom to forget? Even delimiting disciplinary boundaries is controversial. The roots of knowledge can spring from fields that today are rigidly divided or from intellectual pursuits not considered scholarly or scientific. Copernicus, for example, drew influence from alchemy (Fara 2009:124) and Newton spent tremendous efforts on it as well (Burton and Grandy 2004:85). Galileo's foundational knowledge of astronomy originated in medical school where he taught students to cast the astrological charts of their patients (Sobel 2000:29). Likewise, many early archaeologists expressed theories and ideas that today would be roundly dismissed as pseudoarchaeology.

We also admit to a bias toward the Western hemisphere because of the background of most of the contributors to this volume and because similar efforts (Clack and Brittain 2007; Holtorf 2007) have been focused on Europe. However, we have found organizational inspiration in the periods offered in both a history of American archaeology (Willey and Sabloff 1993) and a more Eurocentric history of media and archaeology (Kulik 2007).

Sensational ideas about the past were initially a significant part of the early field, in an era of Romantic archaeology, a barely professional discipline that housed quests for myth, countercultural religious experience, and racist pseudoscience in service of nationalist projects. As archaeology became a more established discipline, professionals began their Initial Engagement with extreme claims on a methodological basis. The first generations of professional archaeologists applied new and more rigorous investigatory standards to old fantasies and contemporary hoaxes. This era was arguably archaeology's most successful period of both combating pseudoarchaeology and engaging proactively with a larger public. Initial Engagement ended, however, with the institutional maturation of the professionalized university-based discipline of academic archaeology. Absolute chronologies differ by region, but broad social and political changes by approximately 1960 led academic archaeology to largely dismiss the problematic roots of the discipline

(Rowe 1966) and focus on internal conversation and debate more than public outreach. This turn away from public outreach coincided with the first example of an internationally successful pseudoarchaeological claim originating entirely from outside the profession, the "ancient aliens" meme. This claim first began generating interest in the 1950s as documented in works such as *The Morning of the Magicians* (Pauwels and Bergier 1963) but is best marked by the 1968 volume *Chariots of the Gods?* It seems more than coincidental that as archaeology was no longer engaged in controlling the public discourse and symbols of its profession (Toumey 1996:164–65), pseudoscientists were happy to sell under our brand (after Holtorf 2007).

Pseudoarchaeological theories with a religious bent even emerged in the 2016 US presidential race when Dr. Ben Carson reiterated his belief that the Great Pyramid of Khufu at Giza, Egypt, was actually built by Joseph of the Old Testament as a granary. While condemnations of these statements quickly came from journalists, archaeologists, and Egyptian government officials, the polling impact on Dr. Carson's supporters was minimal.[1]

The subsequent proliferation of pseudoarchaeology eventually led to a new engagement. We value the methods professional archaeologists have developed for investigating, caretaking, and educating the public about cultural heritage too much to watch that heritage become fodder for poorly considered methods that are often in the service of radical ideologies of race, religion, nationalism, or other causes. At the same time, we have also realized that engagement with more nuanced yet nonacademic community-based approaches to cultural heritage can enrich our practices. The stakes are too great to ignore claims that run contrary to accepted knowledge. Engagement with a greater public, as an open but principled discipline, is necessary to maintain public acceptance of archaeology as an important and relevant discipline.

Romantic Archaeology

In the latter half of the nineteenth century, two men separately announced that they had uncovered evidence of lost cities described in Classical Greek histories of shadowy ancient times. One of these men, Heinrich Schliemann, is regularly cited in archaeology texts as a founder of the discipline as a result of his work at Troy (Fagan 2005:88; Renfrew and Bahn 2012:32; Trigger 1996:234), while the other, Ignatius Donnelley, is considered a pseudoscientific crank of relevance only to the history of the myth of Atlantis (Jordan 2001). Well into the early twentieth century archaeology was replete with adventurers seeking ancient mysteries and inspired by myth, legend, and history. Their curiosity and romantic sense of wonder were a significant stimulant in archaeology's early years. But this wonder was not always matched by the ability to discern between fact and fantasy.

Some claims about the past that are today considered extraordinary or pseudoscientific were once widely believed and propagated by archaeologists. "Moundbuilder" lore was common and orthodox in the United States for much of the nineteenth century (Williams 1991:61–76). Pioneering Egyptian archaeologist Sir Flinders Petrie first went to Egypt to research the mystical idea that history was encoded in the dimensions of ancient architecture and could be deciphered using a "pyramid inch" (Drower 1999:223). Petrie's careful documentation of the monuments of Giza convinced him the idea was bunk, but he took up the cause of protecting Egyptian antiquities, invented seriation, and trained a generation of archaeologists as the first endowed professor of Egyptology. Sir Arthur Evans carved the Minoan culture of ancient Crete out of a blend of archaeological discoveries, Greek myth, and the tabula rasa of an undeciphered writing system (Bintliff 1984).

Several early and important researchers of Mesoamerican and Andean archaeology either conducted their work in outlandish interpretive frameworks or were inspired by or involved in Theosophy, a spiritual movement following ethereal enlightened masters who channeled information about root races and sunken continents. Though they would come to be considered eccentric or worse, these Romantic archaeologists surveyed, photographed, and excavated major early sites (Scarborough 2008:1092–1096; Wauchope 1962:44–48, 1965:220, 227); discovered vital historic documents; had influential if frustrated roles in the decipherment of Maya writing; and helped found important research institutions.

The Abbé Charles-Etienne Brasseur de Bourbourg's archival work had profound effects on Maya archaeology, epigraphy, and history including early work on the K'iche' manuscript of the Popol Vuh and finding fragments of the pre-Hispanic Madrid Codex (Mace 1973). He also uncovered a copy of Bishop Diego de Landa's description of Yucatan that included a bilingual "alphabet" of Maya hieroglyphs, which would not be fully understood until the 1950s (Coe 2012:100–106, 135–139). Brasseur misapplied the text in an obsessive search for memory of the fiery destruction of Atlantis and the diffusion of high civilization to Mesoamerica (Brasseur de Bourbourg 2001 [1869]; Mace 1973:319–320).

One of Brasseur's "translations" yielded the "word" of Mu, a strand that was picked up by Augustus and Alice Le Plongeon. This pioneering pair carried out and recorded important excavations of archaeological sites in Yucatan. But they are more infamous for their reconstruction of lost continents ruled by princes and queens who were former lives for the reincarnated Le Plongeons (Desmond and Messenger 1988:25–39, 102–103, 111–115;

Ellis 1998:68; Wauchope 1962:8–10, 19–21). This endeared them to H. P. Blavatsky, the lead figure in the Theosophical movement that underpins much of modern alternative archaeology (Colavito 2005; Wauchope 1962), who repeatedly mentioned the Le Plongeons and their work in her most influential book, *The Secret Doctrine* (Blavatsky 1893:38; Desmond and Messenger 1988:106–107).

Three followers of Blavatsky or other Theosophists were Benjamin Lee Whorf, William E. Gates, and James Churchward. Whorf is most famous for his work on linguistic relativity, but he was significantly influenced by Theosophy (Lee 1996:37–40; Roth 2005:72–73), published in Theosophical venues (Lee 1996:21–22), and like Brasseur tried and failed to produce a phonetic decipherment of Maya glyphs, ending attempts at a phonetic decipherment for a generation (Coe 2012:136–138). Gates was a self-taught scholar of Mesoamerican historical documents and amassed an important library on the topic. He helped create the first catalogue of Maya glyphs in 1931 (Gates 1978) and attracted outside funding to become the first director of Tulane University's Department of Middle American Research (later the Middle American Research Institute). He was also a Theosophist searching for Atlantis (Brunhouse 1975:129–133). Churchward was not an archaeologist or a scholar but a follower of Blavatsky's who took Brasseur's "Mu," transferred Le Plongeon's sunken Mu/Atlantis into the Pacific (Desmond and Messenger 1988:125), and declared it the homeland of an Aryan empire. He further collaborated with archaeologist William Niven to create evidence for Mu. Niven had excavated over 2,000 "glyph stones" at Azcaptozalco, a discovery considered dubious by the rest of the archaeological community. Churchward claimed the glyphs as Muvian Naacal and with Niven's aid published the most complete record of the glyphs and then "deciphered" them (Wicks and Harrison 1999:213–219, 237–253).

Early archaeology's search for the mystical and the numinous is openly cited by more recent pseudoarchaeologists to support their use of mythology to explain the past (Hancock and Bauval 1996:197–198). Given the way Romantic archaeology could bleed into outright pseudoarchaeology, the later disavowal of the Romantic period by academic archaeology is not mysterious. For those not sympathetic to such "alternatives," the professionalization of archaeology is in part defined by the discrediting of lost races, sunken continents, and hyperdiffusion.

Initial Engagement

Romantic archaeology set much of the early profession's tone, especially in the eyes of the public. With growing professionalization, and the emergence of innovators and professionals like Kidder, Gamio, Childe, Wheeler, and Petrie, sensationalism began to diminish. Nonetheless, Romantic sentiments could still be found at the forefront of the profession (witness Sir Leonard Woolley's careful archaeological work at "Ur of the Chaldees," including the discovery of a supposed Deluge stratum [*New York Times* 1931a, 1931d]), while more colorful characters such F. A. Mitchell-Hedges (of crystal skull infamy) continued to persist on the edges of the profession not only because they provided good press but also because they provided good artifacts. Mitchell-Hedges continued to provide thousands of archaeological and ethnographic artifacts in return for support by the British Museum and the Heye Foundation's Museum of the American Indian even after he had been called a charlatan in a libel case he lost (*New York Times* 1928, 1930, 1931b).

Yet with professionalization, we see the new techniques and approaches of professional archaeology being applied to extreme cases. A number of these cases are not the "debunking" of outside claims but debate within archaeology, suggesting a resemblance to Holtorf's (2005, 2012) scenario of alternatives as part of a larger archaeology. The watershed moment was the overturning of the popular Moundbuilder myth by Cyrus Thomas (1894). Working with considerable support from the American Bureau of Ethnology, under the direction of John Wesley Powell, Thomas carried out a comprehensive study of earthen mounds in the eastern United States. He concluded that they had in fact been built by the ancestors of contemporary Native Americans. Thomas's efforts were not in praise of Native Americans and the mounds lost much of their prestige and interest for Americans (Pauketat 2004; Trigger 1996:185), but this investigation is an important landmark in American archaeological method and theory.

Examples of debunking deliberate hoaxes can also be found throughout North American archaeology in this era, particularly of inscribed objects such as rune stones or glyph stones. In some cases these objects were initially accepted by archaeologists as part of the Moundbuilder culture or as examples of contact with nonindigenous civilizations (Williams 1991 provides numerous examples). It was ultimately epigraphers, linguists, and other scholars of writing systems and art history that demonstrated that most, if not all, of these stones were deliberate hoaxes. For example, the Kensington Rune Stone of Minnesota, a supposed grave marker for medieval Norse explorers, was criticized by linguists and epigraphers shortly after it became known to the public, a line of argument that has continued to the present in the Kensington case (Kehoe 2005; Wahlgren 1958) and in others (Lepper and Gill 2000; Mainfort and Kwas 2004).

A later example involves the "Acambaro figurines" (Figure I.1). In the 1950s, the Amerind Foundation and the University of Pennsylvania Museum of Archaeology and Anthropology investigated ceramic figurines col-

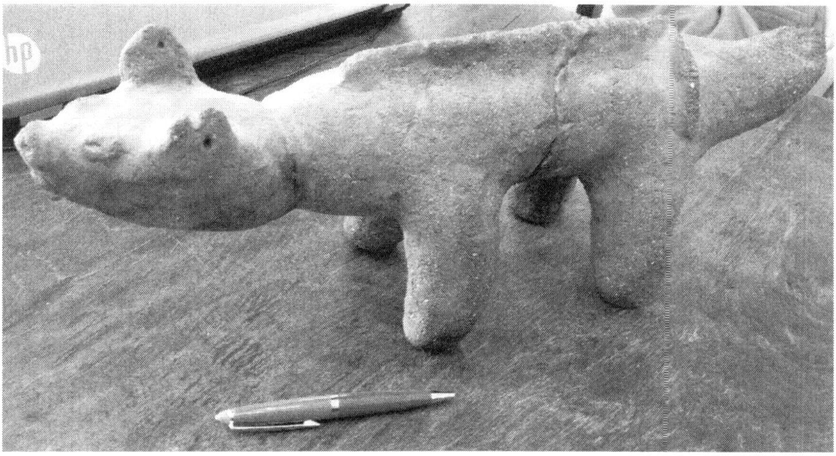

Figure I.1. Possible Acambaro figurine. Photograph by David Anderson.

lected by Waldemar Julsrud depicting Egyptian motifs as well as humans and dinosaurs as contemporaries. Julsrud's large collection of figurines was mostly purchased from the inhabitants of the village of Acambaro, Guanajuato, Mexico. The Amerind Foundation sent Charles di Peso (1953) to Mexico, where he examined a number of the figurines and watched an excavation in progress. Di Peso noted that the figurines, in a context including fresh horse manure, had obviously been planted prior to the excavation, and he found a family in Acambaro that admitted to making the figurines to sell to Julsrud. Julsrud continued to insist on their authenticity and hired his own expert, Charles H. Hapgood (2000), who disputed Di Peso's findings and argued the figurines were pre-Columbian. Ultimately the University of Pennsylvania, at the request of one of their prominent donors, commissioned thermoluminescence dating that confirmed the modern origin of the figurines (Pezzati 2005).

Archaeologists and other professional scientists also began conducting excavations to test extraordinary claims. One such case was the Michigan Relics. For decades beginning in 1889, inscribed artifacts evoking Old World civilizations were found in what has been called the "longest running hoax" perpetrated in the United States (Williams 1991:176–186). James Talmage, director of the Deseret Museum, visited these excavations and saw artifacts in situ, but, troubled by the physical characteristics and the context of the artifacts, he conducted his own quiet and fruitless excavations. Talmage's excavations and an investigation by University of Chicago archaeologist Frederick Starr effectively debunked the Michigan Relics, driving their proponents to angry words and legal threats (Ashurst-McGee 2001). The "Roman" artifacts of Tucson likewise involved professional archaeologists excavating in response to discoveries that turned out to be hoaxes (Burgess 2009).

Such efforts became more formal as this period progressed, such as in the case of the Newport Tower (Figure I.2). Since the early nineteenth century persistent beliefs in Newport, Rhode Island, suggested that a masonry "tower" was not a windmill built by colonial governor Benedict Arnold in the 1670s but a much older structure associated with pre-Columbian visitors from the Old World such as Norse explorers (Williams 1991:189–191). The tower and other supposed evidence of Norse colonization of New England provided a northern European fictive ancestry for nineteenth-century descendants of colonial settlers, faced with increasing immigration from southern Europe (Godfrey 1951:120). Mainstream historians agreed on the Arnold origin, but the old folklore was revived in 1942 by South American archaeologist Philip Means's book *Newport Tower*. Means offered to dig the tower with private funds but was refused by Newport's Park Commission (Williams 1991:217–218) and Means died soon after. Claims by Means and others led to deliberation within the Society for American Archaeology. Some committee members thought that investigation would be a pointless waste of money on a settled question (Godfrey 1951:123). Despite this, Peabody Museum graduate student William S. Godfrey, Jr., a lineal descendant of Arnold, excavated in 1948–1949 and found artifacts and features dating the Newport tower to the mid-seventeenth century, thus confirming the tower was in fact built during Arnold's lifetime (Godfrey 1951; Williams 1991:219).

A similar project was undertaken a few years later at "Pattee's Caves" in southern New Hampshire. Beginning in 1935 colonial-era constructions have been "reconstructed" into "Celtic" or other pre-Columbian European architecture by one owner after another and the site has since been marketed as "Mystery Hill" and "America's Stonehenge." Excavations in 1956 only produced nineteenth-century artifacts (Vescelius 1956). The continuing interest in such sites pushed Vermont State archaeologist Giovanna Neudorfer (1980) to undertake a study on the poorly documented rural colonial structures, a case in which alternative archaeological concerns pushed mainstream archaeology to fill a real hole in its research.

This period also featured archaeological engagement with the public through mass media. Sir Leonard Woolley (1960 [1954]) appeared in the 1920s and 1930s on BBC radio programs popularizing archaeology and wrote popular accompanying books. Archaeologists of the Engagement generations likewise adapted to the new medium of television. One of the most successful examples was *Animal, Vegetable, Mineral*, a BBC program featuring some of the biggest names in archaeology, including Sir Mortimer

Figure I.2. The Newport Tower, Newport, Rhode Island. Photograph by Jeb J. Card.

Wheeler and Glyn Daniel, attempting to identify mysterious objects selected by the show's producers for dramatic effect (Kulik 2007:117). The show was a rousing success, and both Wheeler and Daniel were named "TV personalities of the year" in 1954 and 1955 (Holtorf 2007:42). In the United States, the University of Pennsylvania Museum of Archaeology and Anthropology followed suit with their own television show, *What in the World?* While the format was similar, this program did not meet with success, highlighting a long-term difference in European and American popular archaeology. The success of the British *Time Team* franchise, the hosts of which are celebrities in the U.K., vs. the valiant struggles of the American *Time Team* (Schuldenrein 2014) echoes the failure of *What in the World?* In the early twenty-first century, America's most recognizable "archaeologist" is Giorgio Tsoukalos, a producer of *Ancient Aliens* and host of *In Search of Ancient Aliens*.

One volume stands out near the end of the period of Initial Engagement. When Robert Wauchope's *Lost Tribes and Sunken Continents* was published in 1962, it was the first book-length critique of pseudoarchaeology written by a professional archaeologist. It examines a number of alternative claims and their shortcomings, though it served primarily as a rebuttal of Harold Sterling Gladwin's *Men out of Asia* (1947), a primer on race and transoceanic contact theories that featured a foreword by eugenicist E. A. Hooton (Gould 1981:111). Gladwin is a fundamentally important figure to the archaeology of the American Southwest, but one with a distaste for professional academic archaeology (Lekson 2008:52–54), which is on display in *Men out of Asia*. Another accessible volume aimed at the broad phenomenon of pseudoarchaeology would not be produced by professional archaeologists for over 20 years, despite the dramatic success of new "alternatives" to professional archaeology.

Academic Archaeology and the Growth of Pseudoarchaeology

A recounting of the well-known post–World War II arc of an increasingly scientific archaeology, the rise of the "New Archaeology," and the subsequent theoretical diversity and conflict within the profession is not possible here. However, it is noteworthy that with the rise of a more middle-class archaeology in the "publish or perish" universities rather than in museums or private foundations, in an era of national funding for science, and at a time when new technologies such as radiocarbon were truly revolutionary, the attitude toward sensational claims changed. The New Archaeology had little time for the old myths and eccentricities of an era of dilettantes and colonialists, who were to some degree whitewashed or erased from the history of the field. The post-Processual theoretical schools of Marxist, structuralist, and symbolic archaeology were likewise far too engaged with the older New Archaeology in a struggle for the future of the profession.

This period of intense theoretical advancement and turmoil was largely unnoticed by the public. They were too busy reading books or watching television programs about "ancient astronauts," psychic archaeology, ley lines, and other New Age–infused made-over versions of the old Theosophical tenets of ascended masters, hidden symbols, and lost civilizations (Colavito 2005). The most successful example of this era was Erich von Däniken's runaway best seller *Chariots of the Gods?* This book inspired the television documentary *In Search of Ancient Astronauts* that launched an entire genre of television: the paranormal documentary. This effect was so pronounced that when a public survey was held in England in 1984 asking respondents to name an author of archaeological works, the most common response was Erich von Däniken (Kulik 2007).

Following on the success of Von Däniken, many new pseudoarchaeological authors launched onto the scene (Argüelles 1987; Fell 1976; Sitchin 1976;

Van Sertima 1976). This new wave also swept up Pacific experimental sailor Thor Heyerdahl. *Kon-Tiki* had been a tremendous success, though it was consumed by the public more as a love letter to the Pacific, part of the larger "Tiki" movement (Kirsten 2003:114–121), rather than as a work of alternative archaeology. Heyerdahl's racialist pseudohistorical motivations were downplayed in some editions of the book (Andersson 2010:84–88), but with Von Däniken's success, Heyerdahl returned to prominence with his hyperdiffusionist *The Ra Expeditions* (1971).

As we have moved into the twenty-first century, the popular appeal of pseudoarchaeological books and television shows has managed to reenter archaeology through an unexpected venue: for-hire cultural resources management and nonacademic archaeology. The Newport Tower continued to be a magnet for hyperdiffusionist and esoteric claims, despite the archaeological investigation by the Peabody. In 2003 the Chronognostic Research Foundation (CRF), arguing that the tower was a medieval astronomical structure, hired a cultural resources management (CRM) firm to conduct excavations. These professional excavations found no evidence that challenged the seventeenth-century date (Barstad 2007) yet the CRF continued to suggest a medieval date based on supposed astronomical alignments (CRF 2008a). The excavations instead served as a focus for media attention on the more exotic claims of the CRF and coincided with media opportunities for promoting the "mystery" of the tower (CRF 2008b) (Figure I.3). A similar use of CRM occurred outside Roswell, New Mexico, in 2002. With backing from the Sci-Fi (today SyFy) Channel, two UFO investigators used eyewitness testimony to locate the likely site involved in the Roswell incident legend of a UFO crash in the New Mexico desert in 1947. The project contracted with the cultural resources management office associated with the University of New Mexico, and despite dramatic television presentation of the investigation final analysis found no anomalous features or artifacts (Doleman et al. 2004), though this did not stop the ufologists in question from continuing with other lines of investigation (Carey and Schmitt 2009). Contract archaeology provides the tools and the prestige of archaeological science to anyone with a hypothesis to test, but hypothesis testing does not seem to necessarily be the goal of some alternative claims and claimants. Instead, the fact of professional archaeologists working on research designed by outsiders with extraordinary claims had significant media appeal (see Shinn 2004 for another example) even though their analysis contradicted the claims of their clients (see Beisaw's chapter in this volume on the rhetorical power of archaeological practice and comparisons with media-driven paranormal investigation).

Figure I.3. The Newport Tower used in an advertisement, Oxford, Ohio. Photograph by Jeb J. Card.

A New Era of Engagement?

By the end of the 1970s the first serious professional critiques of the growth of pseudoarchaeology began to emerge (Cole 1980; Daniel 1979; Feder 1980, 1984; McKusick 1982). These critiques began to expand to several book-length examinations of the issue (Feder 2014; Williams 1991). Feder's *Frauds, Myths, and Mysteries* has been the most successful of these efforts, used in Introduction to Archaeology classes and in other fields because of its use of "fun" topics to teach critical thinking and the scientific method. The audience for this volume has always been popular: undergraduate students or other interested nonprofessionals. It repurposes the popular appeal of extraordinary claims, using myth, mystery, and adventure as hooks to educate the reader. The book celebrates the value of scientific archaeology and the information it has produced about the past.

Wauchope's volume and the works of Feder and others that appeared a generation later differed from the works published during Initial Engagement by being embedded in a thoroughly professional archaeology. They specifically pointed out how pseudoarchaeological practices differed in method and theory from professional archaeology (Fagan 2006b; Kosso

2006; Stiebing 1995; Wauchope 1962:125–137; Williams 1991:11–27) and have sometimes more broadly addressed the nature of science and pseudoscience (Feder 2014:18–46). These discussions largely critiqued either the earliest "eccentric" archaeologists or antiquarians or increasingly later outsiders (often a difficult line to define).

Academic archaeology particularly embraced historical critiques of ideological archaeology in service of nationalist, racist, and/or religious causes and regimes. Many "normal" pseudoarchaeological efforts are tied to such causes with race and religion particularly integral to many "alternative" archaeologies (Orser 2004:62–74). Yet these examinations have focused on the practices of professional archaeologists in societies (most infamously Nazi Germany) that created a politically favorable past by bending and breaking scientific or scholarly standards (Arnold 2006; Hubbard and Burrett 2012; Humes 2012; Lewis 2012; Trigger 1984; Witzel 2006). In such cases, mysticism, the occult, and political "science" often intermingle (Pringle 2006:48–50, 79–81, 286–287). The theme of ethnic or religious construction of the past through pseudoscientific practice is addressed in three chapters in this volume (Anderson; Bielo; Pruitt).

But more recent discussion of extraordinary claims has been less about such claims or claimants and more aimed at archaeologists as both subject and audience. Some efforts have continued in the vein of seeing pseudoarchaeology as a serious problem for professional archaeology but go beyond a simple description of the problem and why such claims are wrong and either explore case studies in pseudoarchaeology as inherently interesting or devise professional strategies of reaction (Fagan 2006a). Related to this work has been more visible investigation of sensational claims (Mainfort and Kwas 2004; Sax et al. 2008; Stamps 2001).

Another tack has seen commonalities between the conflict-laden relationship "alternatives" have to professional archaeology in light of contested heritage, concerns about multivocality, community-based archaeology, and critiques of the role of power in an archaeology that may be accused of polarizing scientism (Andersson 2012:126–127; Simandiraki-Grimshaw and Stefanou 2012:9). Strong negative reactions from academia against nonscientific alternatives strike some within the profession as being too harsh (Derricourt 2012a), akin to crusades against religious heresy (Cusack 2012:145; Holtorf 2005), and being so vociferous in defense of a data-based Enlightenment paradigm that archaeology becomes patronizing and elitist in the eyes of the public (Cusack 2012:151). This perspective describes a more democratic archaeology that includes highly nonscientific constructions using the past as colors or flavors of archaeological practice and experience (Holtorf 2012). It does not necessarily advocate nonscientific archaeologies, though in some cases it has engaged at a peer level with archaeologies that are based at least in part on the nonmaterial (Cremo 2012).

Approaches in This Volume

Among the authors represented in the following pages we can find those who openly critique pseudoarchaeology and those who examine the relationship between mainstream archaeology and other alternatives. No chapters support non-science-based archaeologies, but a number critique the standard practices of archaeology or how archaeology relates to nonmainstream claims. What unites these chapters is an emphasis on the practices of those engaging with the archaeological and pseudoarchaeological.

In this introduction, we have briefly referred to controversy over the use of the terms "pseudoarchaeology" and "pseudoscience" and the calls for other less polemic approaches. Kenneth L. Feder, one of those most commonly cited in this controversy, addresses labels in the final chapter. Part of the complicated aspect of this controversy is that it reflects larger concerns about outreach, heritage, representation, power, and the very mission of archaeology itself. In the first chapter of the volume, "Steampunk Inquiry: A Comparative Vivisection of Discovery Pseudosciences," Jeb J. Card steps back from archaeology specifically and examines "discovery" fields (Bader et al. 2010:12–13) that are routinely labeled as pseudoscientific. These are practices with at least some relation to an existing scientific field but undertaken by amateurs or lone/rogue professional scholars. Cryptozoology deviates from normal field biology by searching for "monstrous" animals of myth and legend, ufologists scan the memories of eyewitnesses rather than the astronomical skies in search of extraterrestrials, and parapsychologists look to external rather than internal psychological mechanisms to explain phantasms and psychic abilities. These methods reflect obsolete research techniques and priorities from foundational periods in the "parent" fields, such as Victorian zoological expeditions. The similarities of these "fields" expose the basic operating principles of some alternatives to archaeology and their anti-authoritarian stance.

The chapters in part 1, "Case Studies in Alternative Constructions of the Past: Methods, Ideologies, and Practitioners," present examples of the nature and culture of pseudoarchaeologies and related alternative constructions of the past. Chapters 2 and 3 are by archaeologists who have witnessed firsthand how the archaeological record is reframed as myth and legend. In "The Lost White City of the Honduras: Discovered Again (and Again)," Christopher Begley explores the multiple readings surrounding tales of Ciudad Blanca, a lost city of Honduras's Mosquito Coast, and maps out the long history of stories about the city. He finds that there is indeed more to the legend than appears at first glance, arguing that both the material remains of pre-Hispanic settlements and the remembered environment of indigenous habitants, including the Pech and Tawahka, were reshaped after collision with the European colonial trope of the Lost City. This story has taken an intriguing twist with the announcement (in conjunction with a forthcoming television documentary) in 2013 and 2015 of LiDAR remote sensing results indicating that Ciudad Blanca, as a "lost city," had been discovered. Begley argues that such "discoveries" not only miss the point of the relationship people have with their past and ancestors but in fact create legendary topics such as "lost cities."

Stacy Dunn, in "Witches, Shamans, and Looters: Alternative Uses and Contemporary Ritual Reuse of Archaeological Remains in the North-Central Coast of Peru," takes us to the arid Andean coast of South America, where pre-Hispanic heritage collides directly with postcontact ideologies of capitalism, archaeology, and *brujeria* magic, and examines how the activities of archaeologists produce both monetary and spiritual value that makes archaeological sites vulnerable targets. Dunn focuses on the multiple ways in which the pre-Hispanic dead are treated in the Norte Chico region of Peru. Some local inhabitants simply use archaeological sites as convenient corrals or trash dumps. Families casually collect artifacts as part of leisure outings informed by broader constructions of the Peruvian past, while professional *huaqueros* loot sites for profit. Archaeologists, and those who work for them, dig into ancient settlements to explore a scientific past, while *brujos* and other ritual magicians undertake their darkest or most powerful magics within archaeological sites in part because of the emphasis archaeology has placed on them.

Begley's and Dunn's chapters raise an important point that needs to be addressed, the cultural context not only of "pseudoscience" but of those who pass positive or negative judgment on these practices. Many of the magical practices described in Dunn's chapter would not typically be described as "pseudoarchaeological" because they are not explicitly framed within a scientific paradigm. Yet they are entangled with the archaeological. At a minimum, they involve physical manipulation and in many cases destruction of the archaeological record. A number of these practices do indeed form part of the Peruvian engagement with heritage and the archaeological, such as nonprofessional looting for recreational and personal reasons. Some of those engaged in these practices are also directly engaged in scientific archaeology, with practice and lore from both worlds blending together. With regard to the magical practices, a number of commenters on Dunn's work and similar situations in Latin America have lumped these practices in with "indigenous knowledge" as an "alternative" approach to archaeology. But as Dunn points out, these practices are largely European/African in origin, or are blended with indigenous elements, and are practiced by many in Latin America including those who do not identify as indigenous. Similarly, Begley's direct engagement with the archaeology of the Mosquitia allowed him to interact with indigenous knowledge about the archaeological record that is radically different from imposed "lost city" myths. Yet such stories, like the "reconstructed" tales of cryptids discussed by Card, are often given a legitimacy as "local" or "indigenous" legend when they may be nothing of the kind. These two chapters suggest two questions. Are outsiders from a predominantly Euro-American background, when viewing practices from across a cultural divide, missing important differences about how heritage, science, ethnicity, and power may interact in other societal contexts? And is the notion of pseudoscience itself contextually specific, reflecting local constructions of science and what is considered outside of those constructions?

The next three case studies directly examine the production and maintenance of alternative ideologies of the past. In "Black Olmecs and White Egyptians: A Parable for Professional Archaeological Responses to Pseudoarchaeology," David S. Anderson examines the racial recasting of two "mother cultures" as the valued ancestors of fringe ethnic movements. The African Olmec equation emerged in a Victorian era when race was commonly used in both popular and scholarly approaches to human variation and history, hyperdiffusion was mainstream, and indigenous Americans were believed too primitive to produce "civilization." Later politics of liberation led some authors to revitalize African Olmecs as a legacy for the African Diaspora. This reversal emphasizes both the continuing importance of archaeology's preprofessional image and the ability of alternative beliefs to easily flip across political boundaries. Anderson compares this with the racial casting and recasting of ancient Egypt as an esoteric root for European identity (despite ample evidence from ancient Egypt of a locally complex phenotypical history), using much of the same data as the African Olmec revisionists.

"Creationist History-Making: Producing a Heterodox Past," by James S. Bielo, examines an alternative creation of the past through a lens of play that is well suited to early twenty-first-century America and its economically and culturally important creation and consumption of entertainment and simulation. Through ethnographic study, Bielo chronicles the practice and theory of "imagineers" creating a Creationist theme park. This creative team moves between personal faith, the ideological goals of the park, and the techniques most suited for entertaining their audience. Bielo critically discusses the issue of anti-science that has come to dominate discussions of pseudoarchaeology and alternative approaches. By moving past the Science vs. Anti-Science frame some of the parallels (and differences) between Creationism and professional archaeology become more distinct.

The examination of ideological pseudoarchaeology as practice is also at the heart of Tera C. Pruitt's "Creating Pyramids: Participation, Performance, and Pseudoarchaeology in Bosnia-Herzegovina." Pruitt examines how the belief and "excavation project" were and are accepted by locals as well as national government authorities. The motivations found in this case include national pride, identity, and tourism. How the project operates, including how it legitimizes itself, is an important aspect of how history is rewritten not just by esoteric authors but in public performance supported by influential institutions.

The chapters in part 2, "How Archaeologists Should or Should Not Engage with Pseudoarchaeology," approach the other side of the coin: how archaeologists should, and in some cases should not, engage with these communities. Denis Gojak's chapter, "The Central Australian Face: A Study of Archaeological Responses to a Pseudoarchaeological Claim," is a fascinating study of how archaeologists largely refuse to engage with extraordinary claims. Most archaeologists declined or refused to interact with an individual asking about a supposedly man-made landform in central Australia. Not only does Gojak's survey investigation reveal this startling fact but it uncovers reasons why archaeologists may be loath to respond to, never mind attempt to challenge or educate, members of the public who subscribe to ideas not supported by science.

The remaining chapters in this part examine directly or tangentially the power television has in shaping the public perceptions of history and science. Evan A. Parker's "The Proliferation of Pseudoarchaeology through 'Reality' Television Programming" notes how recent trends in reality television are particularly relevant and problematic for archaeology. In addition to the success of directly pseudoarchaeological television shows such as *Ancient Aliens* and *America Unearthed*, a major trend in reality television has been the proliferation of object-oriented shows where objects from the past are identified and appraised primarily for their market value. Parker examines how this genre taps into core aspects of early twenty-first-century American media and particularly examines the collision between professional archaeology, avocational artifact prospectors, and two reality shows, not only engaging in the excavation of archaeological artifacts to sell for profit but framing themselves as a populist contrast to elitist professionals. Parker offers some suggestions for archaeologists to take media production into their own hands.

An even closer engagement between archaeology and media is chronicled in "Lessons Learned from *Lost Civilizations*" by Kenneth L. Feder, Terry Barnhart, Deborah A. Bolnick, and Bradley T. Lepper. The authors describe how, individually, they participated in a documentary in which they intended to educate the public about North American prehistory, only to find that they had been used to increase the respectability of a religiously inspired work of pseudoarchaeology. Alongside the recounting of this case of media gone horribly wrong, the authors provide hard-learned concrete guidelines and suggestions for how archaeologists should, and should not, interact with media production companies.

April M. Beisaw's "Ghost Hunting as Archaeology: Archaeology as Ghost Hunting" is not primarily about television media, but her topic of inquiry—avocational paranormal investigation—has been dramatically impacted by the success of television shows about ghost hunting. Beisaw recognizes that ghost hunters are engaged, as archaeologists are, in telling stories about the past in relation to the material record and the built as well as imagined environment. In recent decades ghost hunters have had more success in attracting public interest in the past than has archaeology. Beisaw describes how she has used ghost hunting as a pedagogical tool in teaching college students about archaeology and history, emphasizing that an archaeological audience is typically expected to listen to a professional lecture, while a ghost-hunting audience is invited and encouraged to explore the past themselves through investigation, data collection, and elements of hypothesis testing. While there are some clear differences between archaeology and ghost hunting, it does seem that archaeology could learn practical pedagogical techniques from ghost hunting about how people engage with the past and with science.

Kenneth Feder concludes the volume by examining the broader issues of critical thinking, science education, and the responsibilities of professional educators and scholars in engaging with the public. He focuses on the history of approaches archaeologists have taken to pseudoarchaeology and the nature and nomenclature of this subject. In addition, through examination of the chapters in this volume, he identifies potential ways forward.

Note

1. For more on Ben Carson's pseudoarchaeological ideas and his presidential run, see: Erica Brown and Ellen Uchimiya, "Ben Carson's Unusual Theory about Pyramids," *CBS News*, November 4, 2015, and Michael E. Miller, "Ben Carson Believes Joseph Built Egypt's Pyramids to Store Grain—and It Just Might Get Him Some Votes," *Washington Post*, November 5, 2015.

1
Steampunk Inquiry
A Comparative Vivisection of Discovery Pseudosciences

JEB J. CARD

Pseudoarchaeology, Pseudoscience, and the Victorians

In the introduction to this volume, David Anderson and I have chosen to examine the archaeological engagement with and reactions to alternative archaeology, pseudoscientific practices, and hoaxes. This is in part due to the useful definitions and explorations of pseudoarchaeology undertaken by others (Feder 2014). Garrett Fagan (2006b) provides a good overview of tactics and themes found in pseudoarchaeology. Among these, he notes that pseudoarchaeology has a "dogged adherence to outdated theoretical models" because "pseudoarchaeologists are forced to plunder outdated scholarship" (Fagan 2006b:30–31). A comparison with other forms of pseudoscience, particularly "discovery" activities that seek to pursue evidence of the paranormal rather than follow a path to personal enlightenment (Bader et al. 2010:12–13), suggests that outdated methods and theories are a symbolically important feature, not an incidental bug, of the popular appeal of pseudoarchaeology. These anachronisms reflect key powerfully appealing aspects of the image or brand (Holtorf 2007) of archaeology, aspects diminished by the professionalization of the field. Some of the characteristics that persist and thrive in pseudoarchaeology (race-inflected hyperdiffusion, strong interest in early state monuments and royal regalia, extensive use of nonprovenienced materials, an emphasis on texts and iconography) stem from a founder's effect in the practices of an archaeology that emerged during the era of European colonialism and nationalism, as well as from inherent aspects of the profession and how humans view physical remains of the past (an emphasis on discovery and mystery, supernatural reconceptualization of physical remains, etc.) (Card n.d.).

Fagan (2006b:31–34) discusses the paradoxical relationship outside theorists have with academic authority. On the one hand, professional archaeologists are disparaged as rigid and timid dogmatists conspiring to suppress important truths of humanity's past. On the other hand, alternative texts cite academic works, often outdated ones, as major authorities in a "kitchen-sink" mode of argument, drawing on data from numerous disciplines, including "art history; ancient epigraphy; comparative global mythology; comparative religion; philology; linguistics; mathematics; astronomy; and geophysics" (Fagan 2006b:36–37). Feder (2014:8–9), Fagan, and others emphasize the tactical component of this paradox, of dazzling one's audience with information from a broad range of sources they are unlikely to fully understand. Careful inventory of the sorts of sources Fagan notes suggests an alternative explanation. It is no coincidence that pseudoarchaeologists not only reach for older discarded theories and ideas but also utilize a "jack of all trades" approach that strongly resembles preprofessional archaeology and anthropology, particularly the emphasis on art and text (e.g., Fell 1989:12–13 bemoaning the lack of Classical epigraphers in North American archaeology) that marked the most popular fields of preprofessional archaeology: Classical, Near Eastern, Egyptian, and Mesoamerican archaeology, and European antiquarianism before that.

There are various reasons for the paradoxical embrace of "long nineteenth-century" (beginning with the Napoleonic era, ending with World War I) archaeology by pseudoscientists: public domain material; the ability to co-opt the work and degrees of the dead; a popular image of archaeology influenced by the field's media popularity in the early twentieth century. But an additional reason, perhaps the most important of them, is the anti-professional stance the symbols of this period evoke. Determined and/or wealthy amateurs and antiquarians dominated archaeology in this period. The first professionally trained archaeologists only began to be trained in the mid- to late nineteenth century. The Disney Chair in archaeology was endowed at Cambridge in 1851. Flinders Petrie had no academic background when he was appointed in 1893 as the Edwards Chair at University College London, the first professorship dedicated to teaching Egyptology, where he (with significant help from Margaret Murray) trained many of Britain's archaeologists (Drower 1999:225–228). Professional archaeologists today understandably see colonialism, racism, sexism, and other structural ills in depictions of the "bad old days" of pith helmets, safari jackets, dodgy artifact exports, collection of "primitive" human remains and sacred relics, "native" guides, and other tropes of pulp adventure archaeology. It is certainly no accident that the commercial model of partitioning artifact hauls to stock museums, or the cavalier treatment of ancient remains such as Heinrich Schliemann's dynamiting of Troy or Giovanni Belzoni's crushing of mummies, mirrored the extraction industries practiced in colonial contexts. While professional archaeologists use these abuses and excesses as teaching moments, some pseudoarchaeologists laud the likes of Schliemann for his recovery of "myth" from the archaeological record. Archaeology has its roots in antiquarianism and in a number of cases was integral to the creation of national identity. But the heyday of archaeology in the late Victorian era was an archaeology of an exotic Other that was excavated to discover essential truths of humanity such as the origin of religion or the nature of state society. This archaeology is the charter myth for pseudoarchaeology.

These stylistic callbacks to the Victorian era may signal bad methods and motives in the professional eye, but they also symbolize a lack of institutional constraints and a freedom from the gatekeepers of academia. Victorian science was to a significant extent predisciplinary, mixing approaches from various fields of study in a poorly regulated energetic anarchy (Clayton 2003:8). When lacking a paradigm within which to work, fact gathering will be nearly randomly undertaken by investigators unsure of the most productive steps to take or information to record. This leads to a complex and disorganized morass of information that does little to answer any real questions. At some point, one of these approaches will achieve some explanatory success and a new paradigm will form around this success, allowing other investigators to pursue more detailed and subtle data (Kuhn 1970:15–18). This process may be advantageous for human knowledge, but by definition it excludes all who do not agree with the values of the paradigm. This exclusion is typically enforced by the academic system of education and professional training.

Pseudoarchaeologists are not forced to work with Victorian material. The notion that pseudoarchaeologists would be directly dependent on outmoded theories, ideas, or evidence suggests that their research is primarily based on careful exploration and deployment of evidence. Experience with much of the "alternative" literature quickly cures one of this perspective. Actual research that contradicts older theories is routinely ignored, and known hoaxes or mistakes are everlasting in this world. Instead, anachronistic practices and notions are chosen as symbols of freedom from institutions that gatekeep the paradigm of scientific archaeology. Few pseudoarchaeologists have training in professional archaeology, though they may emphasize training in another field (e.g., Fell 1989:19–20) as a form of credibility. Much of the point of being an "alternative" archaeologist is to openly reject the standards, practices, and collected knowledge and ideas of professional archaeology (Holzer 1992:xxiv) or to claim that the profession of archaeology, or even science, rejects the alternative archaeologist.[1]

The more recent techniques and theory of scientific archaeology are generally spurned by the pseudoarchaeologist. To support hyperdiffusion, the pseudoarchaeologist turns to monumental architecture, artwork, and broad (typically spurious) linguistic comparisons, just like the Victorian investigator, over more recent and more appropriate techniques such as materials sourcing of artifacts (genetic evidence is sometimes used if it can be made to fit Victorian-style racial frames). Pseudoarchaeology is trapped in the creative tyranny of Victorian science because it is familiar and because its nonprofessional nature allows easy access by outsiders, echoing the days when one needed only a bucket of paint to add "Professor" to one's shingle. Archaeology has its own version of the "science fiction event horizon" (Harris 2008), the preservation in modern popular science fiction of outmoded scientific ideas in the form of tropes from the genre's "golden age." Not only is the "archaeological event horizon" damaging to human understanding of the past, but it can act as a reservoir for harmful ideologies and perspectives from a century ago, such as racial science, social Darwinism, gender inequality, and colonial ethnocentrism.

Comparative Anatomy of Steampunk Pseudoscience

This recognition of popular ideas of science being rooted in the Victorian era, and the concerns about the political ramifications of neo-Victorianism, has escaped into mainstream consciousness in discussion of the steampunk movement. The term is a modification of "cyberpunk," a science fiction genre of the late twentieth century that rejected the ideology of scientific and moral progress found in much of mainstream science fiction, instead addressing structural inequality, the information age, and radical transformations of the human body and consciousness (Sterling 1986). The term "steampunk" existed for about a decade prior to its watershed moment with the 1991 publication of *The Difference Engine*, an alternate history of a Victorian computer revolution by cyberpunk icons William Gibson and Bruce Sterling (Nevins 2008). This literary mark was eclipsed in the late 2000s (Carrott and Johnson 2013:8–10) by the explosion of the steampunk movement, a collection of makers, artists, writers, and fans who perform and live a Victorian-themed fantasy through clothing, music, artwork, games, DIY or Maker engineering projects, and other activities. Technology is a core symbol of this lived steampunk movement; its icons consist of brass gears, welding goggles, and anachronistic vehicles such as airships.

This technology is loud and clunky and, most important, visible. Countless statements and iterations of the ethos of steampunk have explicitly contrasted the movement against solid-state electronics such as smartphones (Donovan 2011:25). The smartphone is a generic device, a flat slate that can do (seemingly) anything, purposely erasing the wonder steampunks (and cyberpunks and hackers) have at knowing how a thing works and being able to modify and improve on technology (Carrott and Johnson 2013:325). The real or signified steampunk machine invites the user to understand and tinker (see Beisaw, this volume for a similar appeal of putting gadgets in the hands of ghost hunters in their unorthodox exploration of history). But the smartphone countermetaphor goes deeper. Steampunk is an expression of a larger unease with a lack of control over technology, or more particularly, a lack of ownership. A smartphone requires a network of some kind, and if it is to operate as designed, that network will be corporate. To modify one's phone for use with another operating system or network is ominously/liberatingly called "jailbreaking." On the most iconic smartphone, the iPhone, content is tightly controlled in a corporate store (Pellot 2014), the operating system is proprietary, and the physical components themselves cannot be tampered with. The "owners" in reality buy access to a machine they cannot modify, repair, or repurpose without company approval.

In the same way that steampunks imagine and build a physical critique of corporate consumerism using Victorian tropes of exploration and hands-on tinkering, pseudoscientists mine these same Victorian tropes of intellectual anarchy in their critique of or reaction to academic institutional science. Victorian tropes of exploration are common in discovery-based (Bader et al. 2010:12–13) pseudoscience, and some pseudoarchaeologists even cosplay (dressing as a fictional or historical character) the part of colonial explorers (see Pruitt, this volume). Pseudoarchaeology may have a particularly strong resemblance to the archaeological practices and ideas of the Victorians, but it is not alone in being a steampunk science-referencing activity. A comparison with some other forms of pseudoscience makes the anti-professional element clear.

Cryptozoology

Cryptozoology purports to be the study of previously unidentified animal species. At first glance, this would seem to differ little from zoology. New species are discovered by field and museum zoologists every year. Cryptozoologists cite these discoveries as justification for their search but often minimize or omit the fact that the discoverers do not identify as cryptozoologists and are often academically trained zoologists working in an ecological paradigm rather than organizing expeditions to seek out supposed examples of unusual and large creatures (Loxton and Prothero 2013:20–22). Cryptozoologists are the same enthusiastic amateurs, specialists in other fields, and nonacademic explorers found in pseudoarchaeology (Regal 2008:53–55), such as René Dahinden with his self-educated disdain for experts (Regal 2011:10). Blurry underwater sonar-triggered photos of the Loch Ness Monster were produced in the 1970s by Dr. Robert H. Rines, president of the Academy of Applied Science. This sounds impressive until one realizes that Rines was a patent lawyer, that his title of "Dr." derived from a degree presented in respect to a paper on starting high-technology companies in developing countries, and that the other members of the Academy of Applied Science were businessmen concerned with tax policy and entrepreneurship (Binns 1984:151). Some of the most prominent and credentialed cryptozoologists have been professional and lay biologists (and the occasional anthropologist and archaeologist [Regal 2011:35–53]) with no field training in zoology or biology who spend much of their cryptozoology "research" career not in the field or lab but on books and television presentations on cryptozoology and the paranormal (Loxton and Prothero 2013:11–12, 304–309). Cryptozoologists openly show their disdain and even hatred of professional scientists (Loxton and Prothero 2013:300–301; Regal 2011:3), including those who enthusiastically participated in cryptozoology (Regal 2008:56–57). Bernard Heuvelmans (2003:3), often considered the father of cryptozoology, railed against scientists as "high priests of this new religion . . . deemed capable of knowing everything and indeed were already thought to know most everything but for a few trivial details."

Just as pseudoarchaeologists study big monuments and big ideas vs. the potsherds and mundane issues of mainstream archaeological research, small or "mundane" species are not the main concern of cryptozoology. "Cryptids" such as hairy humanoids Bigfoot and Yeti, sea serpents and lake monsters (Loch Ness Monster, Ogopogo, and others), the bloodsucking chupacabra, the Mongolian Death Worm, or the dinosaur-like Mokele-mbembe are large, exotic, and/or often resemble mythical creatures of legend such as giants, wild men, dragons, or vampires. Though "unknown," most are framed in cryptozoology as remnants of long-extinct species (Loxton and Prothero 2013:17). Cryptozoologists have from the beginning openly defined the field with these aspects (extinct creatures, striking animals that lend themselves to mythification, and an emphasis on the unexpected) (Coleman and Clark 1999:15; Heuvelmans 2007:11–23) as something separate from mundane amateur field zoology.

Most cryptids are framed as the subject of indigenous legends typically collected in the Victorian heyday of comparative folklore, though such legends may be heavily modified or worse. Cryptozoology's complicated mix of sympathy, interest, and appropriation of indigenous culture (or non-indigenous construction of it) is also found in New Age circles and the dubious "Indian burial grounds" and other legends (Anson 1977:81) invoked in hauntings such as the "Amityville" hoax (Boyd and Thrush 2011:vii; Holzer 1991:177; Melton 2011), both of which echo a long history of Spiritualist reliance on "Indian guides" and genuine activism on behalf of indigenous rights during the nineteenth century (McGarry 2008:66–93). North American cannibal giant stories were appropriated in the 1920s and modified to create Sasquatch (Buhs 2009:51–53; Loxton and Prothero 2013:34–35) by a nonindigenous "Indian agent" teaching on the Chehalis Reservation in Canada. These legends of large unkempt people with settlements, language, and material culture do not resemble the later Western myth of Sasquatch, an unspeaking, fur-covered, giant ape resembling a bipedal gorilla and melding an indigenous pedigree with Victorian concerns over evolution (Regal 2011:24). More recently, indigenous perspectives have gained in strength over "traditional" cryptozoology, rejecting a strictly biological or ape-like characterization of the entities. In a parallel to some approaches to alternative archaeologies (Schadla-Hall 2004), Sasquatch as indigenous spiritual belief coexists more easily with science, including archaeology (Muckle 2012). The misuse, appropriation, or creation of non-Western legends is also found in pseudoarchaeology that heavily modifies ethnohistoric or epigraphic religious or mythic texts into historical accounts of "white visitors" or "ancient aliens." Even the Loch Ness Monster craze centered on Scotland was largely driven by English hoaxers and media as well as misused exotic and misunderstood Scottish supernatural legends (Loxton and Prothero 2013:122–125).

Cryptozoologists seek individual and presumably rare specimens that are physically impressive, mirroring the big-game colonial safari hunters who filled mansions and natural history museums with taxidermy of impressive beasts. Many frame their work as expeditionary,[2] traveling to exotic (formerly colonized) locations. Cryptozoology evokes the most popular images of field biology, often undertaken as much by hunters as by scientific researchers, from the era of European imperialism (Regal 2011:4–5). They cite previous discoveries of large or legendary creatures as justification for their search, virtually all from the era of European imperialism. The giant squid, equated with Scandinavian legends of the Kraken, was scientifically classified in 1857 (Eberhart 2002:282–284). Locally known animals were "discovered" by colonial Europeans: the mountain gorilla in 1902 (Coleman and Clark 1999:172–173); the panda between 1869 and the 1920s (Coleman and Clark 1999:92–93). The coelacanth, a "living fossil" previously only known from the fossil record, became an icon for cryptozoologists after living examples were identified in the Indian Ocean by a Westerner in 1938 (Coleman and Clark 1999:92–93), despite the fact that the discoverers were not cryptozoologists and the creature was not tied to legend.

Both pseudoarchaeology and cryptozoology deploy symbolism of an era when a preparadigmatic pursuit (antiquarianism, natural history) and "exploration" began to be replaced by institutional science and scholarship. The "event horizon" effect also helps explain cryptozoology's love affair with extinct species. Large fossil creatures, especially dinosaurs, captured the public imagination of the nineteenth century and became a major facet of the public understanding regarding biology and geology (Prickett 2005:74–80) as the new science of paleontology was forming. While professional biology was creating the underpinning of evolutionary theory in the mid-nineteenth century,[3] the more popular image of the science was the discovery of monstrous and bizarre exotic creatures in the fossil record (Freeman 2004:131–134) and in colonial wilderness unseen by white men. Recent historical examinations of cryptozoology suggest that this is not accidental. After Darwin, Victorians became obsessed with apes, replacing centuries of wild man and werewolf tales with ape tales and then ape-man tales (Bartholomew and Regal 2009). The Loch Ness Monster likely owes much of its origin and popularity to the release of the movie *King Kong* (1933) and other films and stories of dinosaurs found alive in Lost Worlds, typically located in exotic non-Western regions of the world (Loxton and Prothero 2013:129–134).

Other Pseudosciences

Similar dynamics occur in parapsychology/ghost hunting and UFO-ology (ufology). Technology has become a key symbol for ghost hunters, suspiciously growing in popularity after portable technology was on display in parapsychology movies in the 1980s (*Poltergeist* and *Ghostbusters*) but in many respects reflecting Victorian folk ideas about electricity (Clarke 2012:283; Hill 2010:35–38). The origins of the modern media-friendly ghost hunt can be traced to Harry Price in the 1930s (Clarke 2012:26–28). But significant elements of these activities persist from the nineteenth century, including mediums or psychic apparitions (Brown 2006:50; Clarke 2012:30–31; Hanks 2011; Hill 2010:38–39), pendulum dowsing, and Ouija talking boards (Beisaw, this volume; Brown 2006:54; Hanks 2011:199). "Spiritual research" and parapsychology emerged in this time period as an explicitly "scientific" rebuttal to Spiritualism, mediumship, and other forms of ghost and spirit mysticism (see Blum 2006, particularly pp. 75–83; Kripal 2010:49–50) and simultaneously a spiritual reaction to narrowly materialist science (Cooper 2005:147). Not coincidentally, this era also marks the emergence of psychology as a field of study, and the broader occult was significantly engaged with psychology (Kripal 2010:27). Both parapsychology and ghost hunting, which did at times intersect (Timms 2012), grew largely out of a British context. As in cryptozoology, those engaged in field research (ghost hunting) derided the elite laboratory researchers who were nonetheless engaged in psychic research (Timms 2012:91). The Society for Psychical Research supported parapsychology but detested mediums and ghost hunting, acting as an upper-middle-class gatekeeper that refused to accept more folkloric approaches to the numinous by working-class spiritualists (Clarke 2012:175–176). These more earthy ghost hunters appropriated the symbols of academia but emphasized action over scholarship and symbols of the loss of English identity to modernity, such as large stately manors like Borley Rectory (Clarke 2012:26–28; Timms 2012:92–95).

The UFO emerged at the dawn of the space age, straddling the transition of space travel from pulp fantasy to high-profile reality, and has ever since been tied to the immediate postwar era. A critique found within ufology is that it overemphasizes "best cases" taking place in the 1940s and early 1950s. In addition to the "event horizon" of preserving early elements of the UFO, these cases also resemble the pseudoarchaeological use of Victorian archaeology, including the resistance eyewitness and instrumentation reports collected decades ago have to skeptical reexamination today. Dominant Cold War themes that persist in ufology are paranoia, fixation on military conspiracies and bureaucracy, and messages of impending self-inflicted apocalypse (Denzler 2001:99–101; Peebles 1994:283–284).

Unlike pseudoarchaeology, cryptozoology, and parapsychology, ufology's "event horizon" is not Victorian because the science it draws imagery from (aerospace engineering) appeared in the mid-twentieth century. As with the Romantic characters of Victorian archaeology, colorful aerospace pioneers became ufological symbols of resistance to bureaucracy and institution. Clarence "Kelly" Johnson, designer of several famous "black project" aircraft, is cited as an important UFO eyewitness (Carpenter 2001; Moody 2012) though his belief in UFOs is debatable (Patton 1998:162). His creations were tested at Nevada's Area 51, a mecca for ufologists. Johnson's organizational skills led his "Skunkworks" facility to be famously underbudget and ahead of schedule in contrast with budget overruns, delays, and poor results from corporate management in the military-industrial complex (Cook 2001:143–144). Jack Parsons was a cofounder of the Jet Propulsion Laboratory and an important early figure in American aerospace. He was also an occultist involved with Aleister Crowley and L. Ron Hubbard, a freethinker, and an independent tinkerer who blew himself up in a home lab. Parsons has been incorporated into occult histories as having invited extradimensional UFOs into our reality as part of a magickal ritual (Brandon 1978:27; Redfern 2010:15–25). That American rocket pioneer Robert Goddard had a pre-

1947 lab in Roswell, New Mexico, is even cited by some ufologists (Redfern 2010:19–20). By contrast, corporate and government aerospace is accused of stealing technology from UFO crashes. Pseudoarchaeologists reject professionals as ignorant. Ufologists reject business and government as corrupt.

Roswell and UFO investigator Stanton Friedman proudly notes his work in nuclear physics in the 1960s before he became a full-time ufological speaker and author yet routinely disdains scientists and skeptics as "noisy negativists."[4] He attacks the Search for Extraterrestrial Intelligence (SETI) as "cultists" who ignore extraterrestrial "evidence" from UFO sightings and abductions (Friedman 2002; Friedman and Marden 2007:245–249). SETI efforts use radio telescopes and other tools of institutional astronomy (limited in access because of their cost) to search for extraterrestrial civilizations. Friedman's fixation on the early nuclear and space ages as inextricably linked to UFOs (he is a proponent of a common belief that atomic weapons explosions brought alien interest to Earth) strongly reflects the "event horizon" effect.

The Rejection and Revenge of Professional Science: Bigfoot DNA and Crystal Skulls

Alternative forms of inquiry resembling preparadigmatic practices are not an accidental byproduct but a desired rhetoric of open rejection of institutional science. Fagan (2006b:28–29) argues that early diggers like Heinrich Schliemann should not be considered pseudoarchaeologists, but the unregulated nature of these early investigations appeals to pseudoarchaeologists just as the barely formed earlier practices of zoology, psychology, and aerospace are emulated by other pseudoscientists who wear the symbols of science like a costume (Toumey 1996). Alternative theorists praise the amateur over professional education, such as Hooton's (1947:x–xi) impassioned praise of the amateur archaeologist Harold Gladwin. Neo-Nazi leader (Bernstein 2013:301) turned alternative archaeologist Frank Joseph (2002:5–9) praises the quest of a martyred schoolteacher to uncover a mini-Atlantis. Erich von Däniken trumpets his autodidactism as making him "completely free of all prejudices" (Roggersdorf 1970 [1968]). But they condemn mainstream archaeology for incorrect and distasteful conclusions (Holzer 1992:xxiv) and being afraid of new ideas (Gladwin 1947; Putnam 1887:120). They believe professional archaeologists are rewarded with funding if controversial ideas or data are ignored (Trento 1978:xx–xxi). This places archaeologists as new priests (compare with Heuvelmans's rage against critics of cryptozoology) for forces controlling the population (Kenyon 2005). Archaeologists are alleged to participate in a genocidal conspiracy of lies against Native Americans and other people (Clow 1992:xii–xiii; Holzer 1992:12–13) and to be hiding evidence of ancient catastrophes that could be vital for future human survival (Hancock 1995:468–479; Parsons 2005:67). Some "critics" have called for congressional hearings to investigate the profession of archaeology (Colavito 2014; Wolter 2014).

If the symbols of science can be easily co-opted, and the steampunk nostalgia for the creative energy of early scientific endeavors appeals more than the black box of scientific authority and institutions, professional researchers can rely on the analog for those beautiful and clearly functional machines: the actual practice of science. Two recent cases, one in cryptozoology the other in pseudoarchaeology, demonstrate the relationship between pseudoscience, amateur or nonprofessional science, and science. In both cases, pseudoscientific claims were seriously evaluated in an informal manner by advocates of science and then by professional scientists with institutional backing. In both cases, the new and important findings from professional analysis were minimized, misinterpreted, ignored, or attacked by pseudoscientists. Yet the practice and public presentation of actual scientific investigation impacted the media and the larger public.

The early twenty-first century saw a burst of academic interest in cryptozoology as several scientists, historians, journalists, and other investigators began serious examination of cryptids and the men who hunt them. Social and behavioral investigation found that monsters were not prehistoric survivals but the product of political disputes (Regal 2013), rumor panics and media influences (Radford 2011; Loxton and Prothero 2013:129–135), and changing gender and ecological politics (Buhs 2009:159–167, 234–237). These productive but primarily historical efforts were largely ignored within the cryptozoological community. The situation changed when biological scientists, specifically geneticists, entered the fray. Physical sciences, particularly genetics, have a powerful rhetorical effect in American culture and media as revealing truth without bias (Kruse 2010). New York University geneticist Todd Disotell (Holloway 2007) has cooperated with cryptozoologists in providing genetics expertise and laboratory facilities, but persistent findings of mundane species in supposed hairy humanoid cryptid samples have not pleased that community (Sasquatch Genome Project 2013). An alternative "analysis" led to bizarre quasi-paranormal results that were roundly criticized by professional geneticists for bad methodology and poor reporting, including publication in a single-issue journal owned by the study's primary author, and citation of satirical blog posts and comic books as legitimate scientific sources (Hill 2013). Oxford geneticist Brian Sykes responded with his own genetic project. His results were intriguing, including new information on bear population genetics (Sykes et al. 2014) and uncovering the likely historical truth behind a racially charged cryptid legend from nineteenth-century Russia (Channel 4 2013). These "mundane" results, even when backed by the rhetorical power of DNA, were ignored or derided by some cryptozoologists as irrelevant, incompetent, or conspiratorial (Phelan 2014; Woolheater 2014). Nevertheless the Sykes genetic work received significant press coverage, suggesting that scientific results had relegated the Yeti to the mythical.

The crystal skulls supposedly found in Mesoamerica provide a comparable case in archaeology. The British Museum skull had some credibility as a legitimate artifact based on similarities to Aztec art and because of the "primitive" appearance of the object. Explorer F. A. Mitchell-Hedges, an agent of major museums despite serious credibility problems (Brunhouse 1975:82–86; *New York Times* 1928, 1930, 1931b, 1931c), declared the existence of his mystical skull a few years before his death. His daughter Anna subsequently alleged to have found it at the Maya site of Lubaantun in Belize. The mysticism, Mitchell-Hedges's lack of credibility, and the nature of the sculpture led Mesoamericanists to ignore the skull despite its exhibition in a legitimate museum (Shirey 1972). The idea of a mystical crystal skull appears in pulp fiction at least as early as the 1944 story "The Crystal Skull" (Olsen 2006) and in 1949 in "the Mystery of the Magigals" (Gibson 1949; Olsen 2014) in *The Shadow* franchise. After *Indiana Jones and the Kingdom of the Crystal Skull* popularized the Mitchell-Hedges and British Museum skulls by name, a lawsuit was filed on behalf of authorities in the Belizean government against the Disney corporation over exploitation of Belizean cultural patrimony (7newsbelize 2012a, 2012b; Gardner 2012; Pappas 2012).

Beginning in the 1980s, noninstitutional investigators learned that Mitchell-Hedges had purchased his skull from a London art dealer and that it had already been examined by anthropologists, casting doubt on whether the sculpture had any Mesoamerican provenance (Morant 1936; Nickell 2007: 68–71). Professional examination of similar skulls led to the conclusion that they were likely carved with nineteenth-century powered tools by European (possibly German) craftsmen and subsequently sold by a turn-of-the-century French artifact dealer (Sax et al. 2008). Despite these findings, the skulls continue to be icons of paranormal belief. Nevertheless, popular media reported the evidence for mechanical sculpting, in part as a result of coverage of the research by the Archaeological Institute of America's popular magazine and website *Archaeology* (Walsh 2008).

Conclusions

Rhetoric and practice make it clear that alternative researchers, including pseudoarchaeologists, are by and large not interested in cooperating with professional science and are in many cases performing a stance defined by opposition to institutional science. The preference for preprofessional symbols of archaeology and other fields (safari and expedition style, racial theory, hyperdiffusion, jack-of-all-trades approaches, and other elements) punctuates the plentiful open proclamations against mainstream "dogma."

Both the cryptozoological DNA and archaeological crystal skull cases suggest potential models for how to engage with pseudoscientific claims and claimants, as well as the larger public. Popular interest and media attention initially drove social and historical investigation of these claims. The findings of these investigations were important and would play a role in later efforts but were ignored by the paranormal community and the larger public. Institutional scientists subsequently examined physical evidence of these claims. Scientists fired up their steam engines and got the pistons flying rather than simply declaring they already had disenchanted the world, solved all the mysteries, had all the answers.

While these findings were derided by alternative researchers, the mainstream media did pay attention and were largely sympathetic to scientific critiques of unsupported claims. In each case, scientists did not ignore or dismiss paranormal claims out of hand. They attacked such claims with full investigatory vigor as subjects of both physical and social science. Rather than just declaring from a position of authority, scientists undertook honest inquiry into such claims that led to their being treated as mythical or humorous in mainstream discourse. Outsiders may deploy the symbolic "brand" of archaeology more commonly and more effectively than professionals. But actual investigatory effort that produces an alternate story, backed by scientific method and authority, can feed and feed on popular interest in such "mysteries" and have a significant positive impact on public attitudes toward science and, in the case of archaeology, the human past.

Acknowledgments

I would like to thank David Anderson, April Beisaw, James Bielo, Jason Colavito, Stacy Dunn, Kenneth Feder, Sharon Hill, James McClannahan, and Homayun Sidky for their assistance in mentally exploring the lost world wilderness and lost civilizations of cryptozoology, pseudoarchaeology, and other alternatives to mainstream science and scholarship. A special thanks to Leonard Nimoy, for without *In Search of*. . . I may not have been driven to ask some of these questions.

Notes

1. A stance known as the Galileo effect, though any mythically doubted discoverer will do, as Sagan (1979:64) notes: "They laughed at Columbus, they

laughed at Fulton, they laughed at the Wright Brothers. But they also laughed at Bozo the Clown."

2. http://www.extreme-expeditions.net/, accessed June 23, 2013. Paying members of the Bigfoot Research Organization of *Finding Bigfoot* television fame can help search for Bigfoot during weekend "expeditions." http://www.bfro.net/, accessed October 10, 2015.

3. Creationists have embraced cryptozoology (Bielo, this volume), and some cryptozoological expeditions are funded and conducted by creationists hoping to disprove evolution. Antievolutionary sentiments are common in pseudoarchaeology (e.g., Lewis 2005).

4. Friedman's talking points can be found in many media appearances. I experienced these in a lecture he presented at the International UFO Museum and Research Center, Roswell, New Mexico, July 2002. A good example can be heard in an interview with *The Paracast* on August 3, 2014, http://www.theparacast.com/podcast/now-playing-august-3-2014-stanton-t-friedman/, accessed October 10, 2015.

I

Case Studies in Alternative Constructions of the Past: Methods, Ideologies, and Practitioners

2
The Lost White City of the Honduras
Discovered Again (and Again)

CHRISTOPHER BEGLEY

The legend of the Ciudad Blanca (White City), a lost city in the jungles of the Mosquito Coast of eastern Honduras, exists in many forms, from indigenous myths with a long history to recent iterations that seem to conflate a number of legends into a single story (Figure 2.1). None of these provide any criteria for identifying the city, and they vary greatly in details, such as what the White City contains, ranging from gold to endless supplies of food. The many variations heard in communities today represent the conflation of other lost city myths with local legends. None of this, however, has deterred (mainly) foreign adventurers from "finding" the lost city. In fact, they find it over and over again. From the colonial accounts of Cristobal de Pedraza (1544) to recent "discoveries" (Preston 2013, 2015), interest in the legend has not diminished. While some of the attention focuses on studying the metaphenomenon (Begley and Cox 2007; Stewart 2013), much of the rhetoric emphasizes the "discovery" of the city.

While many large archaeological sites exist in eastern Honduras (Begley 1999; Lara Pinto and Hasemann 1992), discussions of the archaeology of the region that invoke the White City as an organizing or explanatory concept attempt to leverage that concept in order to draw attention to themselves or to use it as a convenient shorthand to imbue the entire effort with grandeur and importance. This type of discourse invokes elements of an earlier archaeological discourse, especially the trope of "discovery," effectively severing the relationship between the contemporary residents of the region and the archaeology. Here I confront this kind of pseudoarchaeology and expose

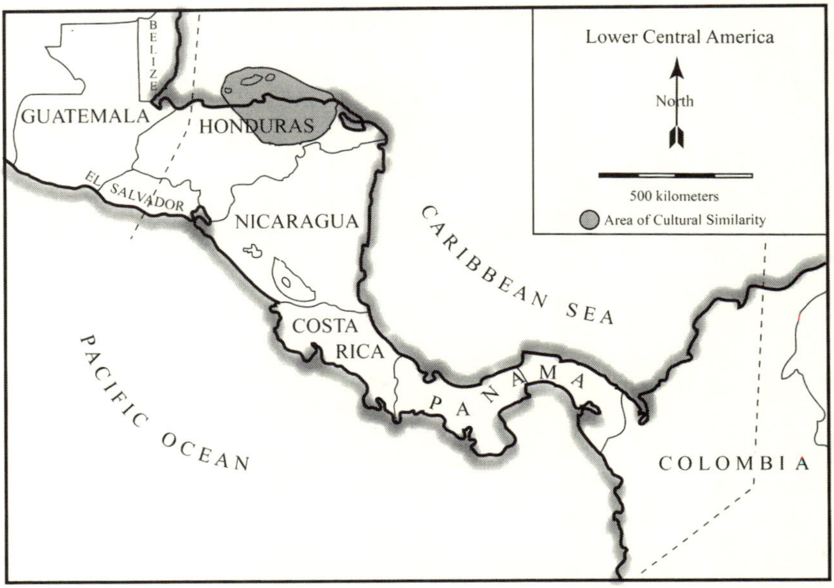

Figure 2.1. Central America, with Mosquito Coast shaded. Map by Christopher Begley.

the ways in which discourse of this sort creates both ethical and stewardship issues. This particular case study illuminates a clear example of this problem, and a pseudoarchaeological approach not only diminishes the contribution of local residents but also erodes our ability to understand and analyze both the Ciudad Blanca myth and the archaeology.

Archaeologists invoke the saying "it's not what you find, it's what you find out" to suggest that the archaeology is not about objects but rather an understanding of the past (Thomas 1989). However, the White City discourse perpetuates a disturbing and problematic element of archaeological discourse: the trope of discovery. This focus on finding, rather than finding out, has clear historical roots in an earlier discourse of exploration, wherein explorers representing colonial powers were often credited with "discoveries" already known to local residents (e.g., Carnochan 2006; Stone 1941). As was the case with the explorers of a previous era, differential access to expensive equipment (including remote sensing technology such as LiDAR) and to the media makes it difficult to challenge these claims. Not only does this differential access allow some to perpetuate the discoverer fantasy, it can obscure the critical role of local knowledge and previous research in understanding the past. The many purported discoveries of the White City perpetuate vestiges of a colonial discourse, camouflaging privilege and oppression within the seemingly neutral rhetoric of science, discovery, technology, and exploration.

The problematic nature of the discourse surrounding the White City phenomenon reflects the larger issue of appropriation of the past with which archaeologists struggle. Archaeologists, like other social scientists, are questioning the authority with which we investigate and present our objects of study. "Who owns the past?" is a standard, even hackneyed, question in archaeology now, focusing attention on the ways in which archaeologists have appropriated the past through practice, legislation, and proclamation. Archaeologists are acutely aware that they may be perceived as agents of hegemonic imperialism. While archaeologists make some attempt to limit their appropriation of the past and to minimize the perception of archaeologists as latter-day imperialists, there is a way in which this rhetoric retains a sense of entitlement, at least in the sense that archaeologists are framing and answering the question of who owns the past. Some variation of this discussion, of multivocality and ethics, emerged in postcolonial theory (e.g., Appiah 2006; Said 1979; Spivak 1995) and can be found in works by archaeologists such as Trigger (1984) and Hodder (2004, 2008).

During the course of my fieldwork in Honduras, it occurred to me that the issue of appropriation transcends questions of authority and even questions of the right to access the past. The problem we ultimately face is epistemological. How do we know what we know? What are the constraints on our knowledge? And how do we incorporate other ways of knowing, other understandings, into our work, which is cross-cultural in its focus and in its execution? Are other perspectives merely a way of enhancing our ways of knowing, or are they absolutely fundamental for a compelling understanding of the past? Does our discourse give voice to others or silence them?

Despite the common description of the Mosquitia region as "unexplored" (e.g., Preston 2013, 2015), archaeologists have worked in the area since the 1920s. Though my work represents the first long-term, extensive project in the region, notable work had been conducted there previously. I have conducted archaeological research in the Mosquito Coast of Honduras since 1991; prior to that, important work had been conducted by Strong (1934), Stone (1941), Healy (1984a, 1984b), and Lara Pinto and Hasemann (1988, 1992). The only new fieldwork in the Mosquito Coast recently has been a short trip by Preston (2015) to map some sites found with Lidar, although some museum collections have been reanalyzed (e.g., Dennett 2007). My research has addressed the strategies used by newly emerging elites to gain and maintain power, focusing on their use of powerful foreign symbols as a means of gaining legitimacy (Begley 1999, 2004). Since the adoption of these foreign symbols created some confusion about the identity of the ancient populations, I have written a good deal about the ethnic identity, or cultural affiliation, of the groups in the Mosquito Coast. Part of this process involved mapping the spread of settlements across space and time and attempting to understand the social and political landscape.

Contrary to the rhetoric surrounding the lost city legend, the archaeology of the Mosquitia is hardly unknown. My investigations in eastern Honduras include archaeological survey and excavation conducted between 1991 and 2011, both in eastern Honduras and the Bay Islands of Honduras. Regional settlement systems in eastern Honduras were investigated both systematically and nonsystematically, including total-coverage surveys of over 100 km^2 near Dulce Nombre de Culmi, Olancho. Nonsystematic surveys, primarily utilizing local informants, were conducted throughout the Paulaya, Plátano, and Wampú watersheds to the east, including large tributaries of the Wampú including the Pao, Aner, Ahuahuas, and Mahor. Around 150 sites were documented throughout eastern Honduras. Thirty sites were investigated with shovel probes, and nine of those sites saw small-scale excavations. The site of Difficulty Hill on the island of Roatan and the Talgua Village site, near Talgua Cave in the Olancho Valley, were excavated more extensively (Begley 1999). Two documentaries were produced on the region (Love 2000; Southwell 2001), two master's theses (Begley 1992; Dennett 2007), and one dissertation (Begley 1999).

The earliest settlements identified in eastern Honduras date to around C.E. 250–300, the beginning of Period IV-b (Healy 1984a). After this date, sites occur with great frequency, possibly representing an increase in population around this time. Even the earliest sites from the present project display evidence of significant complexity, dating between C.E. 250 and C.E. 600. A carbon-14 assay from the site of Altas de Subirana returned a date of 1510 B.P. +/- 130, associated with structures over 2 m high and over 50 m long (Begley 1999). From the earliest suggestion of complexity there is evidence of some degree of contact with Mesoamerica, seen most clearly in the formal, orthogonal site plans and in imported materials such as obsidian. This is unlike the contemporary sites to the south, in Nicaragua or Costa Rica (Hoopes 2005). This early interaction with northern groups appears to focus on elite paraphernalia and symbols, including jade, obsidian, and templates for public constructions.

A significant change appears to have taken place around C.E. 1000. Shortly after the Maya "collapse" and concomitant population declines or decentralization in central Honduras (Hirth 1989), the cultures of eastern Honduras (somewhat predictably) began showing fewer connections to the north and stylistically began to resemble their southern neighbors. This is most clearly visible in the ceramics. Period V ceramics, before C.E. 1000, included painted pottery, whereas Period VI ceramics are firmly in the incised-punctated tradition seen throughout the rest of Lower Central America. In other ways, however, eastern Honduran societies showed more Mesoamerican-like elements. Unlike most societies to the south, for instance, the eastern Honduran polities built enormous public constructions and appear either to have been organized in complex ways not seen elsewhere in Lower Central America (Hoopes 2005) or to have expressed it in a radically different manner.

It is unclear when societies in eastern Honduras reached their height. Healy (1984a) suggests an apogee in early Period VI, sometime after C.E. 1000. Data from my research suggest that settlements were more numerous and larger before C.E. 1000 than after, in at least some parts of eastern Honduras (Begley 1999). This variation within eastern Honduras may indicate that the region was not as homogenous as the material culture suggests.

There appears to have been a widespread demographic collapse or a radical decentralization of the population in western and central Honduras during Period VI, between C.E. 1000 and 1520 (Healy 1984a; Hirth 1989; Messenger 1991). However, eastern Honduran populations were stable during early Period VI (before C.E. 1300). Late Period VI occupations are scarcer, hardly represented in the archaeological record of eastern Honduras. It may be that late Period VI materials are difficult to distinguish from those of early Period VI, or it could be that a demographic shift happened during this period. This could have been a population decline or a dispersal of formerly nucleated populations into smaller sites with a greater chance of underrepresentation in the sample.

Judging from the artifactual assemblage, which yields little late Period VI material, many of the larger archaeological sites had been abandoned by the time the Spanish arrived. Early chroniclers, however, report large polities that declined radically during the sixteenth and seventeenth centuries (Samson 1997). No archaeological sites have yet been identified with these large polities described by the Spanish, although Healy (1984a:153) suggests that the site of Rio Claro in the Aguan Valley may be the village of Chapagua, the center of one of these.

The two important periods in the development of eastern Honduran societies were around C.E. 500–600 and C.E. 1000. The earlier period marks the date by which complexity had emerged in this area, while significant stylistic changes and a possible increase in population and the size of some regional centers occurred at the latter date. These may be related to events within Mesoamerica. The first date, C.E. 500–600, corresponds roughly to the beginning of serious political struggles in the Maya region (Martin and Grube 2008), the possibly related decline of Teotihuacan, and the catastrophic eruption of the Ilopango volcano (Sheets et al. 2012:264). The second date is about a century later than the Maya transformation or "collapse" and correlated demographic declines in central Honduras; it also marks the increase in long-distance trade at the beginning of Period VI (Andrews 1985; Chapman 1957). In both cases, the decline of powerful polities with extensive trade and communication networks is temporally correlated with an increase in sociopolitical complexity or population in eastern Honduras. Though it cannot be demonstrated that these events offered new opportunities for eastern Honduran elites or resulted in greater opportunities for trade and interaction by eastern Honduran groups, it seems unlikely that the correlation is completely spurious.

Many of the differences between Period V and VI, such as the increasing emphasis on incision as a decorative technique on ceramics, appear around C.E. 800. This may relate to the demographic collapse in the Maya area. Other related phenomena, such as the migrations of groups like the Pipil and Nicarao into El Salvador and Nicaragua at the end of Period V, probably affected the developments in eastern Honduras (Fowler 1989a, 1989b). The appearance of what could be feathered-serpent motifs on ceramics and rock art throughout the region may be related to these migrations. There is no archaeological evidence, however, for the migration of these or other foreign populations directly into eastern Honduras. Since no site occupied by Nahua-speakers at contact has been identified archaeologically, the material correlates that would mark the posited Nahua occupation of some parts of eastern Honduras at the time of contact remain unknown.

In the course of my investigations, I relied heavily on the local knowledge of residents of the area. This knowledge included the location of sites, the details of even the most remote areas, and, in some cases, an extraordinary ability by people like Pancho Bueso (of Sico, Olancho, Honduras) to synthesize data and envision the myriad connections and interactions that would have existed in the region. In the course of talking to dozens of residents of the area (and a few pseudoarchaeologists), one persistent question kept coming up: "Are you looking for the Ciudad Blanca, the lost White City?"

The White City legend is known to most Hondurans living in the eastern part of the country. I heard these legends in the course of working in the area and traveled throughout the Mosquitia in 2009 with author Christopher Stewart, gathering Ciudad Blanca stories from dozens of households and communities for the publication of his popular book *Jungleland* (Stewart 2013). The legend may have begun in 1544, with a letter sent from a priest, Friar Pedraza, to Spain, in which he mentions a sizable, wealthy civilization he observed in a large valley from a hilltop east of Trujillo, on the north coast of Honduras (Pedraza 1544). If this event happened, he would likely have been looking into the Aguan or Paulaya Valley, both part of an area of cultural similarity that encompasses most of the Mosquito Coast.

Two local indigenous groups, the Pech and the Tawahka, inhabit the forests of the Mosquito Coast and have legends about the lost city (Conzemius 1928, 1932; Herlihy 1997; Lara Pinto and Hasemann 1988; Rivas 1993; Samson 1997). The Pech are Macro-Chibchan speaking people with ties to groups in northern South America. The Tawahka are a Sumu group with ties to groups farther south, in Nicaragua. These groups now live far apart but were once neighbors (Davidson 1991; Samson 1997). The Pech refer to the White City as Wahia-Patatahua or Kao Kamasa, translated for me by my Pech informants as Place of the Ancestors and White City, respectively. I first heard a version of the Pech myth of the lost city during an extended trip into the rain forest in 1992. I had avoided talking about the legend with the Pech up to that point, in part because my goal was to gather data on the spread of the ancient civilization across the landscape and not on a single site but also because I did not want to sow seeds of suspicion that I might have been just another treasure hunter. After they brought up the subject, I admitted I had heard the stories, and I asked if they knew anything about it. They did, and they knew where it was. In fact, it was just upstream along the river where we were camped, on top of the mountain. I asked if we could go see it and was told I could not. "You can't see it if you don't speak Pech and know about the Pech, because this is where the gods fled after the Spanish came," one of the guides, Cipriano, explained. "If you go there and can't speak to them, they won't let you leave."

I heard many Tawahka accounts of the legend during the extended trip through the Mosquito Coast that I made with Christopher Stewart. The Tawahka stories are different from the Pech ones and are less consistent, and none of them places the White City in the same place as the Pech myths. Of the Tawahka stories I heard, most locate the lost city in the headwaters of a river that flows south into the Wampú River, which then flows southeast to the Patuca and east to the Caribbean. The Tawahka's river flows in the opposite direction of the river indicated by the Pech, which flows north to the Platano then northeast to the Caribbean.

The White City was never the focus of my research, but it was always compelling, and a few questions were always in the back of my mind. Why were the legends so pervasive? Why were they incorporated into the cosmology of the Pech and Tawahka? The Spanish legends, such as Pedraza's story, might be a sort of El Dorado legend, of which there are examples all over the Americas, but the indigenous myths were harder to dismiss as something imported from elsewhere. These stories seemed to be fundamental to an understanding of the past for both the Pech and Tawahka.

As part of my examination of the political organization of ancient eastern Honduran society, I surveyed large areas of the Mosquito Coast. I was able to piece together a partially complete picture of the settlement pattern in the Mosquito Coast from approximately A.D. 500–1500, the period during which most sites were occupied. Looking at the distribution of known sites across the landscape, I noted a single large site on each tributary of the main rivers like the Paulaya and Platano, usually located within a kilometer of the main river. A series of smaller sites were distributed throughout the floodplain of the tributary, with no sites along the floodplains of the major rivers, possibly because of flooding. I had not documented all of the sites, of course, or even all of the large sites, but I thought anything substantially larger would have affected the larger settlement pattern. That was only one bit of evidence I used, however. I also relied on information from many local residents, from all parts of the Mosquito Coast, who knew every river in the area. Year after year, local informants from all over the area would repeatedly refer to the same large sites I had already documented. It seemed that everyone had their own White City, and it was always one of these large sites. In fact, archaeologists have hypothesized that the legend was not based on a single site but was a composite legend that reflected the fact that large sites, large settlements, did exist in the rain forest. In other words, there were many Ciudades Blancas (Lara Pinto and Hasemann 1992). It is noteworthy that no documented site was identified by a Pech or Tawahka informant as the White City.

As part of my settlement pattern research, I began examining the distribution of indigenous groups in the Mosquito Coast at the time of contact and throughout the colonial period to see if the Pech consistently occupied the area under investigation. I examined analyses of census data by cultural geographers. Although there was no firm agreement, there was a general consensus that the Pech had occupied most of the northern half of the Mosquito Coast and that another group, possibly the Tawahka, occupied the southern part. Today, although the ranges are greatly constricted, the Pech live in the northern part of the Mosquito Coast with the Tawahka to the southeast (Conzemius 1932; Davidson 1991; Samson 1997).

During the course of my investigation into the distribution of indigenous settlement during the colonial period, I was told by many Pech that, as late as 1890, the Pech were living along the same tributary of the Rio Platano where they claim the White City is located. The area is abandoned today, now located in the center of the uninhabited rain forest. Not only was this river the site of the White City, it was also the last Pech settlement that was completely isolated in the rain forest; their other villages are along the frontier with the eastward expansion of nonindigenous Hondurans into the Mosquito Coast (Samson 1997).

The Tawahka had lost some of their traditional territory over the last century (Davidson 1991; Herlihy and Herlihy 1991) and, according to Tawahka informants from the communities of Krautara and Krausirpe, as recently as a hundred years ago had lived along the same tributary of the Wampu River in which they claim the White City is located. They have since moved farther downriver and this area is now uninhabited but facing encroachment by nonindigenous settlers. Like the particular tributary of the Rio Platano for the Pech, this river represented the last isolated settlements for the Tawahka. So both the Pech and the Tawahka identify the lost White City as being located up the rivers that represented the last isolated, independent settlements for each group. The indigenous White City legends, it seemed, reflected an idealized past. Among both groups, the legend speaks of ancestors or "grandfathers" keeping the site clean. Both describe the White City as a refuge for the indigenous gods. Both warn against nonindigenous people visiting the site.

It also seemed that the two indigenous myths referred to distinct places. After all, the Pech and Tawahka locate the White City in different river valleys, suggesting that it is impossible that it refers to a single place. I also was certain that no extraordinarily large site or primate center existed in the region, which, although remote, is routinely explored by Pech, Tawahka, and nonindigenous hunters and fishermen. The looting of even extremely remote sites, and the fact that things stashed in the forest for later retrieval (like canoes, food, or artifacts from archaeological sites) are routinely discovered and taken, suggested that little if any of this wilderness went unexplored for long.

In the late 1990s, after deciding to investigate some of these myths, I completed a thorough examination of maps of the region to explore the issue of the two river valleys and realized that these two rivers, although they flow in opposite directions, in different watersheds, have headwaters that emerge from the same section of the mountain range. If one were to walk up one river to its source, climb the mountain, and drop down the other side, one would be in the headwaters of the other. I wondered whether it would, in fact, be possible for a site to be considered in the headwaters of either river, depending on one's perspective.

Between the two rivers there is an unusually flat, intermontane valley. Peaks rise above the valley floor, which measures a kilometer or so wide by 3 or 4 km long. In essence, this valley forms a pass between the two river valleys. Although this looked like an unlikely place for a large, important site, I decided to visit this area.

In 1998, I finally explored the pass. It did contain archaeological sites, consisting of small mounds, some long mounds forming a plaza, but nothing very large. I will not provide details about these sites, including locations, because of the potential negative impact on sites from an association with the "Ciudad Blanca" label and because doing so is not particularly relevant to the discussion at hand. None of the nonindigenous locals, who often had their own opinions on which site was the White City, ever suggested this area. The only unusual feature of this site was the location of a series of archaeological sites up off the floodplain.

Later I reflected on this area. It was referred to in the indigenous myths but did not contain a particularly large site—certainly not a city. Then, however, I made my own discovery. I was reviewing the Pech and Tawahka myths and translated the Pech names for the White City that I had heard: Wahai Patatahua and Kao Kamasa (Conzemius 1928; Jesús Lanza and Escobar 1986). I discovered that these mean "Place of the Ancestors" and "White House," not "White City." My Pech informants had used the common Spanish moniker "Ciudad Blanca" to refer to this place when speaking to me in Spanish, although it was not an accurate translation of their terms for the site. When I had asked what those terms meant, my informants did not translate them literally but used the term that would be recognizable. Even in print, Kao Kamasa is mistranslated as White City (e.g., Jesús Lanza and Escobar 1986).

I had made a fundamental mistake. I had used the wrong criteria for establishing importance. I was looking for a large site, one that I could assign importance to in the anonymous manner that archaeologists often do when faced with limited data. I was looking for economic importance or another type of social importance that could be quantified and teased out of the past using measurements: the size of the site in hectares, the height of the mounds, and the massiveness of the construction. As a result of the use of the Spanish mistranslation, I had left unexplored my assumptions of the criteria for importance. Exploring the rain forests of the Mosquito Coast was not going to help me find something obscured by my own expectations.

Both the Pech and Tawahka are referring to this upland valley in many versions of their myths, but I was not able to determine if there was a particular site they had in mind, and most had never been to the area. No one reported having been to the site of the White House. I found several small sites in the headwaters of both rivers. Like the site in the pass, these other sites are not unusual in terms of scale. Unlike other sites, however, one (or maybe more) of these holds enormous cultural importance for these indigenous groups. Interestingly, all of these archaeological sites seem to date between C.E. 1000 and 1500, probably built by ancestors of the Pech but not the Tawahka, who probably correspond to a group located farther south, in the coastal plain, prehistorically and at the time of contact (Davidson 1991). The White House, or Place of the Ancestors, may have gained its importance for the Tawahka long after its construction.

The Pech myth that I heard is a postcontact phenomenon, referring to the coming of the Spanish and the retreat of indigenous gods to this remote place. It is possible, however, that the intruder changed over time and that the myth has existed long before contact, originally referring to a different intruding group. The place may even have changed. The current Place of the Ancestors, the White House, for both the Pech and Tawahka, is located in the last remote area in which the groups lived. But perhaps this changed over time. Also, it is possible that the site in the mountain pass has long formed a border between groups and that its importance is tied to that fact.

Removed from the particular historical situation, the power of this place is unrecognizable. Cipriano Carrasco was right when he said that I could not see the White City unless I spoke Pech and knew about them. In that knowledge lies the characteristics that define it.

In the midst of this experience, I considered the response of the archaeological community to the challenges of authority, representation, and multivocality (e.g., Hodder 2004, 2008; Stone 1941; Trigger 1984). Ultimately questions such as "who owns the past?" retain a veneer of arrogance. It is not our question to ask. My efforts at sharing my results, at not keeping the past for the academy, missed the real point. Not only do archaeologists not own the past, we cannot even find it, in cases like this, without other perspectives. In this case, we simply did not know what we were looking for and did not have the tools (the historical knowledge and understanding of the local perspective) to find it. The lost city was not lost in the jungle. It was lost in the oral histories of the Pech and Tawahka. And, most important, it was only lost to us.

3
Witches, Shamans, and Looters

Alternative Uses and Contemporary Ritual Reuse of Archaeological Remains in the North-Central Coast of Peru

STACY DUNN

Ancestor veneration, ritual sacrifice, and reverence for the dead are commonly portrayed as hallmarks of Peruvian culture (Benson and Cook 2001; Conrad and Demarest 1984; Ramos 2010). The pre-Hispanic dead "influenced politics, protected the living, symbolized the past, and legitimized claims over the land their descendants occupied, while the living honored the presence of the dead in numerous aspects of daily life" (Ramos 2010:5). The arid preservation in coastal Peru profoundly shaped attitudes toward human remains and death, focusing supernatural power in the desiccated flesh of ancestral mummies. Though these attitudes do persist to some degree, today multiple opposing patterns of using and abusing pre-Hispanic remains in Peru signal the radically different impacts of archaeology on the memory and manipulation of human and cultural remains of the past.

My work as an archaeologist in Peru has brought me into direct contact with a diversity of practices regarding the dead and archaeological sites. Emphasis on the "authentic" or "continuous" highlands has resulted in very little anthropological study of contemporary coastal society, especially outside of urbanization or immigration issues (Archibald 2011). The central coast, however, serves as an ideal location to examine the changing makeup of what constitutes cultural tradition and how it engages with archaeology as well as the popularized paranormal. This region consists of eight river valleys including a subregion known as the Norte Chico. Populations are concentrated in major cities at the valley mouths, with smaller towns scattered east-west on the terraces above the river and north-south at way stations along the Pan-American Highway. These communities exist among an abundance of well-preserved archaeological remains that represent the entire range of Andean prehistory; in the lower Huaura Valley alone (approximately 350 km^2), there are 555 identified sites, 121 with a cemetery component (Nelson and Ruiz Estrada 2004). The region is representative of Starn's description of Peru as "an intricate mosaic of cultural visions [that] has grown at the crossroads of tradition and transculturation from precolonial to contemporary times" (Starn et al. 2005:6–7). The ethnic composition of these towns varies widely, as do opinions toward ancestor veneration, *brujeria* (witchcraft), and archaeological sites.

I have experienced informal interactions at archaeological sites with locals, subsistence diggers, and even a self-proclaimed shaman. I suspect that most other Andean archaeologists have had similar experiences. Professional *huaqueros* (looters) scatter ancient bones on the surface of these sites in their search for artifacts to sell to a black market that is augmented by the value archaeological knowledge and study have placed on these items. Meanwhile, *brujos* (witches) obtain skulls from ancient cemeteries for nearby altars. These relics are used in ceremonies that incorporate both local and imported symbols from other Latin American or New Age religions as part of a larger entanglement of the archaeological past within a supernatural and paranormal world. Rather than search within these contemporary practices for some remnant of an "authentic and ancient" Peruvian belief or label these attitudes as the adaptation of indigenous belief systems to globalization, in this chapter I argue that they are excellent examples of the interaction among science, cultural identity, and religious practice, a combination somewhat distinct in Latin America but comparable with what is called pseudoarchaeology elsewhere.

A Diversity of the Living and the Dead: Issues of Terminology

There are a few consistent, frustrating patterns of discourse on authenticity, identity, and cultural continuity that affect our understanding of contemporary Andean attitudes, despite a growth in both the quantity and quality of ethnographic studies (e.g., Allen 2002; Taussig and Wachtel 1998). Most discourse emphasizes a divide between modern and traditional, urban and rural, and *ladino* and *indigena*. *Ladino* and *indigena* are some of the most commonly used and yet most problematic terms in Latin American studies (Adams 2005). *Ladinos* are defined as modern, globalized, Christian, Anglicized, light-skinned urbanites who successfully navigate government systems. In Peru, they are usually associated with coastal cities, especially the capital of Lima. They are contrasted in these studies with dark-skinned *indi-*

genas who persist in a traditional, rural, pagan, non-Spanish-speaking life-way in the highlands. In Peru, this concept was a direct result of the Indigenismo literary movement rather than a reflection of an objective reality (Archibald 2011:52–78).

Archaeological studies have contributed to this in the pursuit of finding remnants of ancient lifestyles in present groups and finding traces of present lifestyles in ancient groups (see Burkhart 1989:4–10 for a similar critique of Mexican prehistory), as found in the language that self-describes such work as discovering "insights into a culture that can trace its traditions back to the Inca empire" (Rowe and Cohen 2002:5). The rural-urban divide, with scholars heading into rural "traditional" areas to document an "authentic" culture, has a deep history in anthropological and folkloric studies, a legacy entangled with construction of nationalist identity (see Pruitt, this volume) and with the creation of alternative pasts to support nonmainstream ideology (see Anderson and Bielo, both in this volume). The romantic cliché of modern *ladinos* and traditional *indigenas* misrepresents the more complex reality of twenty-first-century Peru: a wide array of cultural viewpoints formed from a palimpsest of 5,000 years of continual occupation of the coast by a multitude of ethnic groups (Archibald 2011:113; Starn et al. 2005). There is a broad diversity of beliefs regarding the supernatural and its relation to ancient remains, and these divisions are not patterned according to ethnic identity or economic status. Rather, lived experience and interaction with archaeological sites have a greater impact on the supernatural beliefs of locals who live near archaeological sites and nonlocals who do not.

The treatment of human remains and archaeological sites makes it clear that current practices in this region are heavily influenced by archaeological research and broader mystification of the past. Treating these practices as categorically different from pseudoarchaeology, as a "survival of tradition," is not just in error; it gets to a key issue in how to address nonacademic views on the past. "Pseudoarchaeology" is not usually a term applied to actions of nonwhites, nonacademics, or those outside of the Western world (see Schadla-Hall 2004). "Alternative archaeology" is preferred for describing indigenous or subaltern attitudes toward the archaeological record when they differ from mainstream archaeology. This is done to soften the judgmental implications of the "pseudo" prefix and place nonscientific, culturally based hypotheses in terms of social empowerment of disenfranchised groups (Ross 2012; Simandiraki-Grimshaw and Stefanou 2012). Our categories of "academic archaeology," "religion," "cult archaeology," "pseudoscience," "alternative archaeologies," and so on are not only an attempt to create definitions but also part of our social maneuvering (Cook 2004). They are used to designate boundaries, identify allies, and create groups—as "expert," "mystic," or "crackpot." This debate is especially heated when considering whether "pseudoarchaeology" and "alternative archaeology" are interchangeable terms, a debate that shaped the development of this volume. Here we consider what judgment is being passed when one is forced to choose between these two terms and whether this is a valid distinction to make.

The debate over the word "pseudoarchaeology" is one of cultural sensitivity, akin to debate in medical anthropology over "unorthodox," "fringe," or "folk" medicines, now more commonly called "complementary and alternative medicine" (Loudon 2006; Ross 2012). Each of these terms comes with its own set of interpretive baggage, developed as the field of anthropology navigated ethical and political issues. Viewing all nonscientific treatments by non-Westerners toward their cultural heritage as different but still important ways that can better teach us about the past (an alternative archaeology) and distinguishing them as something separate from similarly styled practices by Westerners (as pseudoarchaeology) turn these labels into evaluations rather than descriptions. Opting for "alternative" passes different judgments on practices that otherwise have core definitional characteristics of pseudoarchaeology such as a lack of scientific method, an opposition to the archaeological establishment (often motivated by nationalist or religious concerns), and a tendency to present "common sense" themselves as simple answers to complex questions (Stiebing 1995). The "alternative" label lumps a number of disparate practices into one homogenous group (Simandiraki-Grimshaw and Stefanou 2012; see Ross 2012 for a nuanced discussion of the word "alternative"). In Latin America, the Romantic notion of an authentic Other has limited the differentiation of the pre-Hispanic (and aspects related to it in the present) from a larger medley of more recently created beliefs about the supernatural and the past in modern times. However, this creates an oversimplification of how the interaction between science and nonscience, cultural continuity and ethnicity, actually plays out on the ground. I borrow a role-based approach from Cook's research (2004:28–29) on volcano scientists, indigenous weather workers, and UFO investigators to examine the practices of the individual groups and how they intertwine with both archaeological research and the paranormal.

The Raw Material of the Ancient Dead

Ancestor veneration is a deep tradition in the Andes. That the Spanish campaign to Christianize the region faced greater difficulty in extirpating ancestor veneration over any other customs suggests this was an ancient practice (Conrad and Demarest 1984; Isbell 1997). The Late Intermediate Period (or LIP) (C.E. 1100–1400) and the associated Chancay culture before the fifteenth-century Inka conquest provide the best information on mortuary practices and concepts of death for the central coast. They also provide the majority of artifacts and human remains used by locals, *brujos*, and *huaqueros*.

Central coast burial practices involved mummification, aided by the removal of intestines and the placement of cotton bundles for absorption (Reiss and Stubel 1880–1886). Often naked with bound extremities, bodies were placed in flexed positions with crossed arms, red-painted faces, and copper in the mouth. The body was then wrapped in alternating layers of textiles, hides, leaves, or a net bag. The extreme arid preservation may have created a distinct attitude toward death in the Andes; rather than Hertz's (1960) classic juxtaposition of bodies viewed as either flesh or bone, a third category of "desiccated flesh" exists. The intent to preserve the corpse even to the point of replacing lost flesh with padding indicates that it is the dead yet preserved form that is important. The value of desiccated flesh and mummification is not at all found in modern *brujeria* or occult practices, underscoring the non-"traditional" nature of these practices.

Almost all burials included grave goods (ceramics, textiles, food items, metalwork) and bundles were grouped in underground chambers, likely demonstrating kinship relations (Lothrop and Mahler 1957; Nelson and Ruiz 2010). Mummy preparation was performed by those referred to as *sacerdotes* (priests) by chroniclers, whereas others interpret them as shamans (Silverblatt 1987). Regardless, it was through the creation of the mummy bundle that an individual could be transformed into an ancestor to be fed and consulted. As the Chancay expanded and established new sites, local long-term Huaura settlements were abandoned and reused as cemeteries by the Chancay to create a connection with local non-Chancay ancestors. Similarly with Inka conquest, the ancestor's body was key to production and reproduction of culture. Mummies of the nobility were prominent in the political, economic, and ceremonial life of the Inka, mirroring the importance of family ancestors in daily life (Isbell 1997). After the Spanish conquest, the dead were a strategic target for Spanish missionaries, as ancestor remains were actively sought out and burned in the campaigns against idolatry (Silverblatt 1987). The adoption of Christian concepts and an environment of persecution helped encourage the exotic "taboo" nature of indigenous beliefs, the ancient past, and archaeological sites themselves.

Locals: Neglect, Looting, Identity, and Magic

Despite efforts within Andean archaeology toward community engagement (Silverman 2002), the relationship between local communities and archaeologists in Peru is still often exploitative and influences attitudes regarding sites. People lacking basic human necessities—water, food, electricity—have concerns that seem to override any fear of retaliation, legal or supernatural, regarding interaction with these sites. For example, at the LIP site of Quipico, goat herders put up small lean-tos against the ancient adobe walls while the goats roam freely across the ruins. Other sites along the coast are used as garbage dumps and public toilets. The closer the sites are to dense populations, the more severe the degradation.

Other Peruvians do not see these sites as dead or abandoned. During Holy Week families go to both modern and ancient cemeteries, bringing food, flowers, and liquor to partake of and offer to the deceased (Bastien 1985; Buechler 1980). This common Latin American practice of ancestor veneration is best associated with Día de los Muertos, a holiday with roots in the European Christian All Saints' Day (Brandes 1997:287). Outings at Peruvian cemeteries involve casual digging of artifacts as well as activities indicating a more intense supernatural relationship with the past. Spiritual practitioners mediate with the dead and perform a mix of Christian and indigenous ceremonies to "draw artifacts out of the ground" (Atwood 2007:34). Digging in this context is not subsistence based but social: a back-lot hobby or family bonding time. After the intense international art market interest in Peruvian antiquities in the 1980s, some of this practice transformed into professional *huaqueria*. Yet a significant amount of casual digging still occurs. While I was visiting sites, one man invited me, several Peruvian archaeologists, and students on our project to view his large artifact collection (Figure 3.1). He had collected these items over the years from his fields and from nearby sites. He was a local, not an "outsider" from Lima; he was born in the valley and had moved part-time to the capital after his business proved successful. He had collected these items because it was *mi historia, mis antiguos*—his history, his ancestors. For some locals, this connection with the past is a point of pride: it is the tendency to collect things, the desire to show them to other people, and (at times) a sense of immortality/ancestral connection that drives many to acquire archaeological remains (Burcaw 1997:24–25).

This motivation is reminiscent of that found in other Norte Chico communities that are actively engaging with government and archaeological projects to improve regional stewardship for economic and cultural purposes. Information from these projects is being incorporated into local identity and religion. One example is the mythic story of Vichama (Teruel 2010 [1617]), which connects bodies and the fertility of the earth in a story of dismemberment and resurrections. Since the myth was featured in local museum publications, the local community has embraced it as emblematic of pre-Inka local beliefs. The historical reality, however, is that it is a mix of influences from different periods: the festivals are held at a LIP Chimu site to celebrate a myth told by a Spanish priest about Inka and Chancay deities with a

Figure 3.1. Pottery and other artifacts collected by local hacienda owner, Huaura Valley, Peru. Photograph by Stacy Dunn.

Western emphasis on bones as the locus for resurrection, set to modern panpipe music and featuring vendors selling an array of international spiritual paraphernalia. The entire production demonstrates the wide array of cultural viewpoints influenced by archaeological research and the paranormal.

Brujeria: Local Traditions, Foreign Practices, and Alternative Uses of the Past

In the complex religious world of coastal Peru there are a variety of non-ecclesiastical spiritual practices: *chamanismo* (shamanism), *curanderismo* (folk healing), *brujeria* (witchcraft), and *hechiceria* (sorcery). These terms, used academically and in everyday speech, originate outside Peru and are widespread throughout Latin America (Lewis 2003; Romberg 2003). Although anthropologists formally define them based on cross-cultural research (Tomoeda and Millones 1998), these words are more fluid and interchangeable for coastal Peruvians.

Shamans are spiritual practitioners who act in a positive way toward clients who hire them to diagnose and cure spiritually related illnesses. Coastal Peruvians view them as almost interchangeable with *curanderos*, except that a shaman is more likely to use items from the eastern slopes of the Andes.

This is likely an amalgam of Western concepts of the shaman tied to South American tropical forests, with a long history of association of the spiritual with plants, animals, and practices originating from the Amazon that can be seen throughout coastal Peru as far back as the Early Horizon (900 B.C.E.–C.E. 200) (Isbell 1997). *Curanderos* have a broader variety of supernatural sources to draw upon, including the ancestors. The north coast is known as the center of *curanderismo* (Tomoeda and Millones 1998; Velasquez 2001). Like Puerto Rican *brujos* who act as religious entrepreneurs (Romberg 2003), north-coast *curanderos* have a wide range of clients, both wealthy and poor. *Brujo* is usually a negative term, applied to those who use powers similar to those of the *curandero* but do so to cause harm to others (Tomoeda and Millones 1998). *Brujo* is also used in general to refer to all spiritual practitioners by those who dislike or disbelieve in the occult. In colonial times (Griffiths and Balinas 1998; Silverblatt 1987), the classic *brujo* was an apostate who had denounced God and made a formal contract with the Devil to obtain magical powers. *Hechiceros* cast spells to affect others, usually involving relationships. While not truly Satanic, they are also portrayed negatively for causing sickness that manifests in both physical symptoms and personal misfortunes (Joralemon and Sharon 1993).

In practice, this is not how all these practitioners actually behave; labels change depending on an informant's attitude toward occult or spiritual activities. They also differ based on the intent and power the practitioners draw upon, but even these lines are blurred; some *curanderos* attribute their powers to Satan (Joralemon and Sharon 1993). All are involved (to varying degrees) in complementary and alternative medicine (Ross 2012).[1] Three major themes emerge from the patterning of these spiritual practitioners. First, archaeological sites hold a significant degree of supernatural power. Second, a blend of multiple spiritual perspectives is important to both clients and practitioners alike. And third, only fleshless remains are to be used in rituals, a strong contrast from the pre-Hispanic LIP beliefs described earlier.

Modern-day spiritualist rituals occur within the archaeological site of Por Venir, located in the Norte Chico and occupied during the Preceramic Period (3000–1800 B.C.E.). Por Venir is a series of large stone platforms and mounds surrounding an open plaza-like space. Areas of the site were reused in later occupations for habitation and for two cemeteries subsequently heavily disturbed by looting. The site is surrounded by several small hills or ridges, which provide a clear view of the entire area to the river. Halfway up the side of the northernmost ridge is a small rocky alcove with a flat area in front of it (Figure 3.2); the alcove is aligned behind the largest Preceramic mound.

Today this is an active ritual area. The alcove is blackened with the soot

Figure 3.2. View of Preceramic mound and scatter from looting at Por Venir, Peru. Ritual alcove is located on hillside to the back right behind mound. Photograph by Stacy Dunn.

from the burning of many candles and small fires (Figure 3.3) and contains a stone circle used for seating or other purposes during rituals (Figure 3.4). At the base of the ridge on the edge of the cemetery is an altar formed from a pile of skulls. Scattered across the entire area is a large amount of debris from ritual activities: candles, candy, incense, empty two-liter bottles of liquor or soda, flowers, clothing items, photographs, wings from a dead bird (likely a corvid), coca leaves, "magic" tonic bottles, and scraps of printed incantations (Figure 3.5, Table 3.1). The tonics are mostly perfumed waters, some of which claim association with Siete Lagos de Huancabamba (the Seven Lakes of Huancabamba), a highlands pilgrimage site for *brujos*. This taps into the modern (primarily North American) academic emphasis on the Andean highlands as the source of cultural authenticity (Figure 3.6). Por Venir is not the only site in the region with evidence of *brujeria*. At the site of Lauri in the Huaura Valley, adjacent to a modern cemetery and frequently looted, I encountered the remnants of a *brujeria* ritual, similar to the items found at Por Venir, in the corner of an adobe structure.

For the most part, the potions and incantations are "good": rituals for finding love (although some are for breaking up couples), uniting people, improving health/averting sickness, protection from evil, and gaining money or success in business. One incantation directly calls upon the spirits of the

Figure 3.3. Close-up of right half of ritual alcove, with candlewax, scorch marks from burning, photographs, remnants of offerings, and skulls taken from the site below, Por Venir, Peru. Photograph by Stacy Dunn.

Figure 3.4. Stone circle/seating area adjacent to ritual alcove, with debris from ritual activity scattered around the area, Por Venir, Peru. Photograph by Stacy Dunn.

Figure 3.5. Blackbird wings and empty tonic bottle from ritual activities. The bottle is labeled "Agua de Kananga D'Leos," a perfumed water used by shamans to clear heavy energies, Por Venir, Peru. Photograph by Stacy Dunn.

site: "Ancestor, I call you, I invoke you; with your great power." For modern-day *brujos*, it is the ancestors that provide supernatural power, and most notably, these ancestors are represented by fleshless skulls and bones. Unlike the pre-Hispanic emphasis on desiccated flesh, the *brujos* select only bare, sun-bleached bones (mostly crania) despite the abundance of dried fleshed human remains. Rather than the precontact preference for mummies as the locus of power, this reflects symbolic values found elsewhere in non-Andean cultures and those outside of Latin America (Harris 1982; Hertz 1960) that it is the bones that have the power needed for ritual.

Christian deities are also invoked in many incantations: Díos Todo Poderoso (All-Powerful God), Maria Magdalena (Mary Magdalene), and Señor Jesucristo (Jesus Christ). This may be an attempt to legitimize *brujeria* practices by tying them to an "acceptable" religion. There can be a social stigma to hiring a *curandero*. In their interviews Joralemon and Sharon found that many locals, even those whom they knew had employed *curanderos* previously, would still claim a disconnection with such activities, reflecting the unsanctioned, underground nature of *brujeria* practices: "I would never go, but my neighbor . . ." (Joralemon and Sharon 1993:1). Although many of the ritual items can be purchased from stalls in the market or cramped storefronts, I have not yet seen any of the tonics or love spells openly for sale and the vendors I asked would not discuss where to purchase them.

Table 3.1. Inventory at the Por Venir Altar, 2004

Category	*Item*	*Estimated Count*	*Description*
Tonic bottles			
	Agua de Florida	15	perfumed water
	Agua de Kananga D'Leos	16	heavily perfumed water
	Sigueme-Sigueme	3	herb and perfume water to attract love
	Agua de 7 Contras	4	herb and perfume water from native plants and specially sourced from the Siete Lagos de Huacabamba to counter negative forces
	Agua de la Fortuna	2	herb and perfume water from the jungle and specially sourced from the 7 Lakes of Huancabamba to help in business/work and protecting money
Incantation papers		20–30	to invoke different things when burning specific candles: Vela para separar parejas (candle to separate couples); Vela Santa Muerte (candle for Saint Death); Pareja Amor-Atraccion (love-attraction for couples).
Human remains			
	human crania	15	mostly intact, none with flesh, some with signs of soot/burning
	human long bones	3	1 tibia, 1 fibula, 1 unidentified shaft
Animal remains			
	bird wings	3	not attached to rest of bird corpse, from a black medium-to-small bird (unidentified genus)
	dog bones	6	Fragments from crania, ribs, and long bones, all in same area

Continued on the next page

Table 3.1. *Continued*

Category	*Item*	*Estimated Count*	*Description*
Clothing			
	sock	3	1 is men's, black; the other two are white, gender indeterminate
	underwear	2	1 pair women's red lace bikini; the other is men's white briefs
	tops	3	1 sweater, 1 jersey, and 1 button-up shirt, gender indeterminate
To burn			
	box of cigarettes	1	empty, local brand
	boxes of fireworks	8	sparklers
	box of incense	1	honey scented
	wax drippings from candles	10–20	including red, orange, yellow, white, pink, and black candles
Food related			
	2-liter plastic bottles	20–30	from various brands of soda pop
	bottles	5	glass, from various soda pop and beer brands
	drinking glass	1	broken
	bowl	1	modern, china
	mandarin oranges	5	3 whole, 2 peels
	candy	10–15	wrapped (empty and full wrappers present), inexpensive hard candies only, fruit flavored
Containers			
	styrofoam trays	6	
	box	1	modern, wooden—labeled for money

	pottery	8	ancient, all partially broken (can still contain things, not just fragments)
	metal container	1	modern, heart shaped, containing coca leaves
Other items			
	newspaper clippings	5	love horoscopes and articles about a famous movie star's love life
	bags of coca leaves	3	each bag is approx. 1 liter in volume
	flowers	50+	yellow carnations, white daisies, and more unidentified types—some are burnt, all are scattered across site; some are fake, others are real and dried

Note: All bottles and boxes were found empty. Exact counts for many items are unknown because many fragments were scattered across the area and some were too weathered to identify.

Figure 3.6. Empty tonic bottle labeled "Agua de la Fortuna," a perfumed water used to bring luck to issues involving business, money, and studies. The side of the label states, as translated, that it contains "the best herbs and perfumes of the jungle and the Seven Lakes of Huancabamba, Peru," Por Venir, Peru. Photograph by Stacy Dunn.

In contrast to those who occupy the formal stalls, there are also street vendors who claim to be shamans from the eastern slopes of the Andes, similar to Kallawaya sorcerers traveling between the highlands of Bolivia and the valleys (Abercrombie 1998:34–35). They sell magic potions on the sidewalks and display bundles containing exotic Amazonian goods—snakeskins, dried fruits, jungle tree resins, preserved animal parts—that they advocate as homeopathic and herbalistic cures. Although some of their medical claims may come from CAM, the explicit identification by the practitioners themselves as homeopathy derives from a distinctly early modern European pseudoscience (Loudon 2006).

Both the street vendors and *curanderos* demonstrate a much broader conception of nonmainstream spirituality, one that incorporates occult and New Age beliefs, practices, and items from across Latin America and the wider world. Their displays and altars contain a mix of religious items from around the world: yin-yang symbols, mandalas, peace signs, marijuana leaves, Buddha figurines, sage bundles, a staff of the Guatemalan saint Maximón, and more (see Joralemon and Sharon 1993 for complete *curandero* altar inventories). A general pattern for *brujeria* throughout Latin America (Blea 1980; Romberg 2003) is a blended pan-spirituality, or a "spiritist bricolage"

(Knowlton 2012:247), that uses paraphernalia from various religious customs, the occult, and the modern New Age movement. The culturally distant nature of these items is another expression of what is more commonly called exoticism, the localization of supernatural power in items of the "Other" and the fetishization of ethnicity (Knowlton 2012), practices commonly associated with both colonialism and pseudoarchaeology elsewhere (Fennell 2007; Lewis 2003; Tilley 2005).

Even more directly tied to Western/Northern interaction and reconfiguration of Latin America, all of the *curanderos* profiled by Joralemon and Sharon (1993) either worked for an archaeological project or had artifacts from sites upon their altars (some obtained personally, some gifts from *huaqueros* they treated). Although not all participants in archaeological projects become so affected, for some the contact with the past gave them part of their power and training (Joralemon and Sharon 1993:18).

Notably, none of the *curandero* altars had human remains. Human remains are often a significant component of ancestor shrines cross-culturally (Davidson and Gitlitz 2002), in particular bones and ashes, so their absence on altars and shaman displays is distinctive. Instead, the use of human remains is exclusive to the on-site ritual areas, as in the case of Por Venir (Figure 3.7). Ancestral spirits are consulted and venerated in multiple locations (Davidson and Gitlitz 2002), but in coastal Peru they are the most appropriate and powerful at archaeological sites. This amplification of power is acknowledged by some *huaqueros* as well, who are concerned about entering the realm of the dead.

Huaqueros and Archaeology: Digging for Gain

The term *huaquero* derives from the Quechua word *huaca* for sacred spots (including natural features, contemporary constructions, and ancient ruins). *Huaquero* is used in much of Latin America to refer to professional, full-time looters of archaeological sites. Most can be considered subsistence diggers (Hollowell 2012 [2006]:202–206), but there is often a strong "treasure-hunter" drive that can motivate these diggers (Atwood 2006). *Huaqueros* on the central coast of Peru are generally outsiders coming from the north, since recent police enforcement has made it too risky to loot there (Atwood 2006), reasoning confirmed by a *huaquero* I met in the Huaura Valley.

Huaqueros focus on burials, knowing they contain valuable intact goods. Textiles are currently the most sought-after item, reflecting the current commercial market (Atwood 2006). Items that will not fetch a significant price, including well-preserved human remains, are scattered in the process (Figure 3.8). The callous disregard by *huaqueros* for human remains could not be

Figure 3.7. Human skulls, long bones, and pottery likely from the archaeological site, piled upon a stone altar with recently burnt papers, candles, and a modern heart-shaped metal tin filled with coca leaves, Por Venir, Peru. Photograph by Stacy Dunn.

clearer (Figure 3.9), but some *huaqueros* harbor concerns. To some, these sites are still places of supernatural power and *huacas* are living forces who must be appeased; the equation of archaeological sites with the paranormal is at least as common as it is in North America or Europe (Stiebing 1995). These practices are overlain atop ancient remains but less as a continuing tradition from the pre-Hispanic Andean past than as an expression of general Latin American occultism and folk practices (such as with known imported Hispanic beliefs like the evil eye [Cosminsky 1976:172]). A classic example of this is the phenomenon of "treasure lights," balls of flame that appear above archaeological ruins at a preappointed time and signal where to dig for treasure. These lights and similar phenomena are reported in Central America and Peru (Gaddis 1994:58–59; Gann 1926) and are a popular topic on modern Latin American treasure-hunter message boards.[2] Their origin, however, is in European traditions (Feilberg 1895:298); a modern variant in-

Figure 3.8. Scatter of artifacts (textiles, pottery, lithics) and human remains left on the surface by looters at the cemetery at Luriyama, Peru. Photograph by Stacy Dunn.

Figure 3.9. Human remains left on surface from looting activity at Luriyama, Peru. Note the scalp and flesh previously attached to the bones were ripped off by the looters when removing the textiles from the mummy bundle; fragments of these textiles are scattered around and some still adhere to the flesh. Photograph by Stacy Dunn.

volves using specific camera models to catch these lights (Dunn 2009). For looters in coastal Peru, treasure lights are not the only indicators of valuable archaeological items. *Huaqueros* chew coca leaves not only to warm and energize themselves but also as a supernatural indicator to determine whether they are about to find something valuable; the leaves taste sweet when the *huaca* "is about to give you something" (Atwood 2006:37).

These mystical practices are comparable to the repurposing of ancient architecture and artwork by those making claims of ancient alien visitors, hyperdiffusions, and other alternative uses of the archaeological record. Coastal Peruvian (and, more broadly, Latin American) repurposing of the past is not framed as directly in a scientific, archaeological manner, and it is carried out more on a daily grassroots level than on television or in books. But it is at least as pervasive and popular in terms of how the past is viewed in Latin America, where even the middle-class bookstores in Peru stock large sections on mysticism, usually next to or mixed in with the archaeology sections.

Some *huaqueros* fear curses, though experience may assuage such concerns (Atwood 2006, 2007). The fear of being cursed by an archaeological site is now inseparable from the popular image of archaeology. This stems from mid-1800s fiction writing and was popularized after the excavation of Tutankhamen's tomb in 1922. Today there is an abundance of pseudoscientific explanations for the curse (Day 2006:46–53, 153). In Peru, *curanderos* tend to be hired by workers who contract *aire de huaca*, an illness caused by the air from archaeological ruins (Joralemon and Sharon 1993:36). Like the classic Egyptian mummy's curse, the Andean version does not differentiate between archaeologists and thieves. Both *huaqueros* and archaeological workers also seek out *curanderos* to alleviate *huaca*-related curses. In return, the *curanderos* often receive gifts, small artifacts looted from the sites, as signs of gratitude (Joralemon and Sharon 1993). The indiscriminate nature of these afflictions highlights the unclear divide that sometimes exists between *huaqueros* and archaeological workers. Both are professionals who earn money from foreigners by digging things up at ancient sites, and depending on when these excavations have occurred in the history of archaeological interest in the Andes, the only difference is that one is illegal and the other is government sanctioned. While there may be a very real, physical component to this sickness, such as mold or dust, both groups visited a *curandero* rather than a medical doctor for treatment because of the perceived spiritual aspect of their condition.

Broken artifacts rejected by *huaqueros* are collected by locals who sell them on the street to tourists or incorporate them into new creations. Tiny scraps of textiles are resewn with modern materials into small dolls reminiscent of classic Chancay figurines. These are sold in markets to tourists or merchants who then resell them in their stores in other countries; I have encountered these dolls in Antigua, Guatemala, and Oxford, Ohio, reflecting the ties of these sites to the global economy. Ceramic fragments are ground up to serve as temper for replicas and forgeries. A Norte Chico craftsman told me that by putting the ancient pottery into the new ones, he felt it made these items "more real, more ancient, and more sacred." Again, we see the inconsistent connection between archaeology and the spiritual; it is the connection with the past that imbues some items, but not others, with meaning and power in the same manner that the sites themselves do for the *brujos*.

Pseudoarchaeology and Other Supernaturalist Approaches to the Past

Rather than the common portrayal of a unified "native" worldview, modern Peru displays a diversity of attitudes toward the ancient dead and the uses different groups—locals, *brujos*, *huaqueros*—have for archaeological sites and the remains they encounter there. Many of these individuals have a viewpoint that is consistent cross-culturally: that the dead continue to exist and have influence on the affairs of the living (Davidson and Gitlitz 2002). If they did not believe that the ancestors could affect events, they would not appeal to them. The "Other" is an important distinction here. Not only does it serve as a source of supernatural power for spiritualists, but it also shapes attitudes toward those who interact with archaeological sites. *Huaqueros*, *brujos*, and archaeologists are all perceived on the central coast as outsiders (regardless of reality), coming from the north and associated with a wider global world and greater access to wealth. All are dangerous in some aspect—*huaqueros* for the guns they carry, archaeologists for the governmental legal backing they have, and *brujos* for their ability to curse—and they all act in the spiritually charged locus of an archaeological site. There has even been a backlash against the use of archaeological sites, like the tongue-in-cheek arrangement seen at the site of Por Venir, Norte Chico: human long bones were used to spell out "Leave the dead in peace" (Figure 3.10).

Brujeria and *curanderismo* are not entirely transnational; they do include both broader Latin American and globalized ideas of alternative spirituality and the occult as well as indigenous Andean conceptions of the dead. At the same time, the compartmentalization of *brujeria* to indigenous continuous traditions, or even as "semipure" colonial syncretic constructions, is clearly inaccurate. *Brujeria*, *hechiceria*, and *curanderismo* practices have different local expressions but are broadly recognizable across much of Latin America, including the problematic collision of indigenous realities with colonial fan-

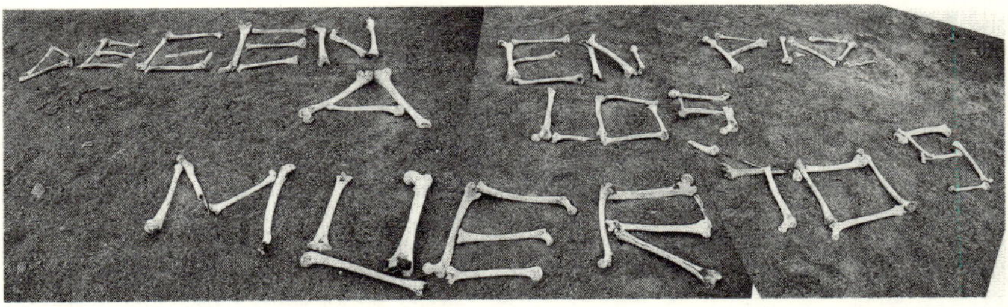

Figure 3.10. Panoramic photo of message laid out in human limb bones on the surface at Por Venir, Peru, stating, "Degen en paz a los muertos" ("Leave the dead in peace"). Photograph by Stacy Dunn.

tasies of the indigenous. Latin American folk spirituality uses a post-1492 framework that is still alive and readily modifying a bricolage that incorporates paranormal notions. This mirrors Barkun's (2003:26–29) discussion of stigmatized knowledge, of occult and conspiracy theory worldviews that bundle together concepts that might share only one element: that they are alternatives to mainstream knowledge. The appropriation of the pre-Hispanic (informed by archaeological research), the complex question of indigeneity in the face of neocolonial oppression and New Age fantasies of the primitive (Tilley 2005), and the complex nature of separating different strands of secret knowledge (Fennel 2007) all cloud the issue.

While some of this involves issues of power and colonialism, the greater issue is that of whether we are addressing abuses of the science of archaeology or abuses of the past. Elsewhere in this volume, Anderson addresses the notion that the alternative archaeology of oppressed people (Schadla-Hall 2004) is less deserving of criticism than pseudoarchaeology. The *brujos* of Peru are not arguing from a scientific paradigm, nor is it likely they would as scientific research remains the domain of the urban government and foreign archaeologists (Archibald 2011). Yet the belief framework discussed here and found in various expressions throughout Latin America directly impacts the physical and intellectual past in Latin America in a more profound way than do ancient aliens, Atlantis, or Black Olmecs. Rather than using pseudoscience as a rigid category, perhaps studies of pseudoarchaeology could benefit from a more precise role-based model like that provided by Cook (2004:297–299) of orthoscience (those aligned with the dominant orientation), heteroscience (those opposed to the dominant orientation), and extrascience (those involved in the arena but not necessarily oriented one way or another).

Regional expressions of *curanderos*, the emphasis on fleshless remains in *brujeria* practice, and the attitudes toward archaeological sites exhibited by locals and *huaqueros* alike are not simply indigenous belief systems adapted by a globalized nation. They are the active regional and historical constructs, reflecting a broader process of the mystification of the past and placed squarely within the domain of paranormalism and pseudoarchaeology in Latin America.

Notes

1. I use these terms according to the self-ascription of the informant, and if that is unavailable, then by what activities are being done.

2. http://www.buscadores-tesoros.com/search?search_keywords=luces&typerecherche=interne&show_results=topics, accessed October 10, 2015.

4
Black Olmecs and White Egyptians

A Parable for Professional Archaeological Responses to Pseudoarchaeology

DAVID S. ANDERSON

One of the most complex problems surrounding pseudoarchaeology is how professional archaeologists should respond to alternative claims about the human past. While it is perhaps true that the proverbial "true believer" will never be swayed by the refutations or denials offered by archaeologists, the contributors to this volume strongly believe that some form of response should be offered. We are thus left with asking how we should respond and in what context a response is appropriate. Tim Schadla-Hall (2004:269) has suggested that archaeologists must "distinguish qualitatively between different kinds of alternative archaeology, rather than treating it as if it were all the same." The importance of context for both understanding and responding to pseudoarchaeology is addressed in several chapters in this volume. However, in this chapter I argue that the qualitative distinction set up by Schadla-Hall ultimately creates an ambiguity that hampers our ability as archaeologists to promote the results of our research.

Schadla-Hall proposes that alternative views of the past can be divided into two categories. His first category includes pseudoarchaeological claims such as ancient alien contact or the plethora of lost continents allegedly littering the bottoms of our oceans. He argues that these claims "should be strongly challenged on grounds of their implicit or even explicit ideology or blatant commercial distortion" (2004:269), an assertion with which we can easily agree. His second category, however, is more problematic. In this category, Schadla-Hall includes oral traditions and histories of indigenous groups from around the world. While one might wish to argue that pseudoarchaeology and indigenous histories should not be placed side by side, we can approach them both from the perspective that they present human histories that may not be supported by archaeological data. In regard to this second category, Schadla-Hall suggests that these "alternative views should be acknowledged and celebrated as elements in the diverse ways in which people experience the past" (2004:269).

Modern archaeology, in comparison to its colonial roots, has made great progress in improving its relationship with descendant communities whose ancestors had been excavated and placed on display in museums for many centuries without their consent (e.g., Colwell-Chanthaphonh et al. 2010; Gallivan and Moretti-Langholtz 2007; Robles García 2010; Watkins 2012). More progress is necessary, but most archaeologists today agree with Schadla-Hall's assertion that "we should respect the views and interpretations of indigenous peoples" (2004:268). However, the boundary between Schadla-Hall's two categories of alternative claims is not as definitive as we might wish, and archaeologists should speak out against all distortions of the archaeological record, regardless of their authorship.

A Parable of Racial Interpretations of the Archaeological Record

In the archaeological literature about prehistoric cultures, the concept of race is rarely mentioned. Instead, when talking about these populations, archaeologists focus on concepts such as individual agency, social and political organization, and ultimately culture and ethnicity. These concepts, however, are academic in their origin or interpretation. The general public does not share the same approaches to understanding people in the present or the past. This dichotomy between academic discourse and public interest can be seen clearly with the concept of race. Conceptions of race have been considered outmoded in anthropology for several decades and have been replaced by the more precise concept of ethnicity and critical examinations of the cultural bases for biologically informed racial systems. Many excellent academic arguments support this transition (American Anthropological Association 1998; Boas 1928; Lieberman et al. 2003), but in the world outside of academic discourse, the biological basis of race is still a very real concept that has important effects on people's daily lives. Thus it is natural for the general public to have an interest in the role played by race in ancient cultures. As modern archaeologists typically do not engage in attempts to identify the race of ancient peoples, many pseudoarchaeological claims have attempted to fill in the gap, particularly in the form of linking contemporary racial groups with the ancient past.

In this chapter, different interpretations of the racial makeup of populations found in ancient Egypt and Mesoamerica are examined. Despite their disparate geography and chronology, these examples present a set of simultaneously interrelated and contrasting claims that allow us to highlight the problems inherent in both pseudoarchaeology and archaeological attempts to respond to pseudoarchaeology. The examples are approached chronologically, starting with early archaeological interpretations that openly included discussion of race, and then move to modern pseudoarchaeological claims that have resurrected the early archaeological interpretations despite decades of research that have superseded them.

Early Archaeological Scholarship

During the 1850s, José María Melgar y Serrano encountered what he thought was the bottom of an overturned iron cauldron on the grounds of his hacienda, Hueyapan, in Veracruz, Mexico. Melgar y Serrano ordered his workers to dig up the cauldron so that it could be put back to use, but to his surprise (and presumably the surprise of the excavators) the cauldron turned out to be a giant stone head carved from a single piece of basalt. Melgar y Serrano (1869, 1871) published his findings several years later where he named the sculpture the "Colossal Head of Hueyapan," and he stated, "That which most impressed me was the Ethiopic type which it represents; I reflected that indubitably there had been negroes in this land" (Pool 2007:35). Melgar y Serrano's racial interpretation of the statue was based on its facial characteristics, which can be described as having a broad nose and thick lips. Today the discovery of the colossal head of Hueyapan is recognized as a notable moment in the history of archaeology. This statue represents the first known material remains of the Olmec, one of Mesoamerica's earliest and most impressive complex cultures. Today we know of hundreds of sites associated with Olmec culture, and a grand total of 17 colossal heads have been discovered at four different sites (Figure 4.1) (Pool 2007).

As more was learned about Olmec culture, Melgar y Serrano's interpretation of the monument as African was quickly dropped. Instead, many scholars noted the strong stylistic similarities between the colossal heads, other Olmec sculptures, and the iconography of later Mesoamerican cultures. These similarities were so impressive that some scholars began to argue that the Olmec must be the "Mother" of all later Mesoamerican cultures (Caso 1965; Coe 1965; Covarrubias 1942, 1957). Significant disagreement exists today over the idea of the Olmec as a "Mother culture" (Flannery and Marcus 2000; Grove 1981; Hansen 2005), yet the point remains that when compared with the Mesoamerican cultural context, Olmec sculptures are not strange or unusual but form part of a well-known continuum of stylistic norms. As such,

Figure 4.1. Olmec Colossal Head 10 from San Lorenzo, Veracruz, Mexico. Photograph by David S. Anderson.

any claim that the sculptures may be associated with a non-native racial, or ethnic, group becomes highly problematic.

A few decades after Melgar y Serrano's discovery in Mexico, the archaeologist Sir Flinders Petrie was beginning his extraordinary career studying the origins and development of ancient Egyptian culture. Among his many groundbreaking discoveries, Petrie (1896) was the first archaeologist to recover materials dating to the Predynastic and Early Dynastic periods, predating the well-known Old Kingdom pyramid age. Petrie's intensive analysis of these Predynastic materials led to the development of the seriation techniques that became a foundational tool of archaeologists working around the globe (Petrie 1901; Petrie and Quibell 1896). For the next four decades Petrie worked at numerous sites throughout Egypt and became a highly influential figure in Egyptology (see Wilkinson 1999). As his career progressed, Petrie's writings turned to a synthetic approach in an attempt to present a complete understanding of ancient Egypt, including his 1939 work, *The Making of Egypt*. In this book, he proposed the idea of a "dynastic race" that had invaded Egypt from the Near East, bringing with it the concepts of state and civilization that resulted in the origins of Pharaonic Egypt: "It is clear what an enormous advance was quickly made by the incoming of the dynastic race. The confusion and poverty of the decadent [indigenous] Gerzean culture, failing in every respect, is succeeded by an outburst within a few centuries on an entirely higher plane. This new civilisation completely wiped out many old ideas, such as the use of the slate palette, and it brought in writing" (Petrie 1939:102). While Petrie's research was grounded in a detailed understanding of the archaeological record, his interpretation was primarily an argument from a diffusionist perspective. Notions of diffusionism were popular explanations for cultural change among archaeologists during the first half of the twentieth century (Trigger 1996:chapter 5). By the standards of his day, Petrie was noting that complex political organization appeared to have developed first in the ancient Near East and thus must have diffused to Egypt by the arrival of a new group of people. Petrie's interpretation of a "dynastic race" was widely accepted for many decades to come, partly because of his influential career (Derry 1956; Edwards 1964).

Petrie's interpretation was far more thoroughly researched and received broader professional support than did Melgar y Serrano's simplistic interpretation of a solitary sculpture; nonetheless, his claim of an immigrant dynastic race is no longer supported by modern Egyptologists. Knowledge of the Predynastic period has increased exponentially over the past 60 years. As early as 1949, Emile Massoulard was able to propose that archaeological data supported an indigenous development of Egyptian sociopolitical complexity, and by 1979 Michael Hoffman published a detailed account of the Predynastic period in Egypt and its gradual development into the Early Dynastic period. Modern accounts of the origins and development of Early Dynastic Egypt relegate Petrie's "dynastic race" to a notable moment in the history of the discipline rather than an interpretation still worthy of consideration (Kemp 2006:47; Wilkinson 1999:15).

The use of race by both Melgar y Serrano and Petrie in their interpretations is generally representative of attitudes about race and archaeology in the late nineteenth and early twentieth centuries. Synthetic treatments of human history written by Western authors during the early twentieth century were often extremely Eurocentric (e.g., Churchward 1921; Massey 1907; Smith 1923), placing Europe and its inhabitants at the peak of complexity and development among human societies. Quite frequently, any impressive achievements outside of Europe, most notably the cultural developments in Egypt, were assimilated into the Eurocentric narrative.

While we can look back at some of these early scholars and critique their ethnocentrism, their work generally does not fall into the category of pseudoarchaeology (see Card and Anderson, this volume). These authors were working within, and constrained by, contemporaneous schools of thought that heavily influenced their interpretations of a limited set of archaeological data. Today their work has been largely superseded by contemporary scholarship. As the discipline of archaeology continued to develop, professional archaeologists improved the rigor of both their investigations and interpretations, including a more nuanced and critical engagement with race and ethnicity (Trigger 1996; Willey and Sabloff 1993). The changes within professional archaeology and anthropology, however, did not remove the interest in race from public attitude toward the past. No matter the professional anthropological opinion on the validity of race as a concept, race is a defining feature of the modern world and has a massive impact on people's daily lives.

Afrocentric Reinterpretations

Afrocentrism is a movement dedicated to reclaiming the achievements of people of African descent from the centuries of Western hegemony and oppression (Asante 1996; Moses 1998; Woodson 1933). This movement has been particularly prominent in the United States where there is an intense and well-documented history of racial oppression, discrimination, and repression of history toward people of African descent (Gates 2011). In this way, Afrocentrism represents an attempt to correct the long-term effects of these social ills and empower new generations of African Americans.

Unfortunately, some Afrocentric reinterpretations of the archaeological record have stepped past undoing the damage of a history of repression and into a field of ill-founded pseudoarchaeological claims. Some of the most well-known and influential examples from this genre are the publications of Ivan van Sertima (1976, 1985, 1987a, 1987b, 1988, 1995, 1998). Van Sertima has long been an advocate for ideas surrounding the achievements of what he terms "Negroid" Africans in the human past. In his most successful book, *They Came before Columbus: The African Presence in Ancient America*,[1] Van Sertima (1976) takes Melgar y Serrano at his word that Olmec colossal heads represent clear examples of black-skinned Africans in the New World, and he goes on to advocate that many more works of Mesoamerican art depict pre-Hispanic contact between Africa and the Americas. If we look at all of Van Sertima's evidence as a whole, he has proposed that there was substantial, influential, and ongoing contact between these two regions from as early as 800 B.C.E. to as late as the era of European contact, when Van Sertima claims that Columbus and other Spanish explorers heard rumors of black-skinned foreigners. Van Sertima also makes extraordinary claims regarding the geographic extent of this contact, stating that there is evidence for African contact as far south as Peru and as far north as New Mexico, including significant contacts in Mexico, the Caribbean, and Brazil. This chronological and geographical extent alone suggests the improbability of Van Sertima's claims. If such widespread contact occurred over such a long period of time, the archaeological record would be replete with evidence, other than monumental artwork, left behind by these individuals. In an attempt to explain the lack of such an archaeological record, Van Sertima (1976:31) invokes a conspiracy, stating that the evidence for artistic depictions of Africans in New World monuments is so readily apparent that "investigators have been forced to ignore their embarrassing existence." However, the Olmec colossal heads that form the centerpiece of Van Sertima's alleged evidence have been proudly displayed in Mexican museums for many decades (Museo Nacional de Antropolgía 1956), which is generally not the manner in which cover-ups are carried out.

Many archaeologists have critiqued Van Sertima's work, including most prominently Bernard Ortiz de Montellano (Feder 2010; Haslip-Viera et al. 1997; Ortiz de Montellano 1995; Ortiz de Montellano et al. 1997). From the perspective of the archaeological record, the claims made by Van Sertima represent gross exaggerations, misinterpretations, and even willful misrepresentations of data. For example, Van Sertima (1976:34) claims that African skeletons were found in the Pecos River Valley of New Mexico and Texas by the physical anthropologist Earnest A. Hooton. As evidence he quotes a passage from Hooton's book *Apes, Men, and Morons* (1937) where Hooton states that "the Pecos skulls resemble most closely crania of Negro groups coming from those parts of Africa where Negroes commonly have perceptible infusion of Hamitic blood" (as quoted in Van Sertima 1976:34). We could level legitimate critiques toward Hooton's research and the racial identification of his skeletal material, but these issues are overshadowed by Van Sertima's dishonest representation of Hooten's work, which included removing significant material from the quoted source. Hooton actually wrote, "The Pecos '*Pseudo-Negroids*' resemble most closely crania of Negro groups coming from those parts of Africa where 'Negroes' commonly have some perceptible infusion of *White*, Hamitic blood" (Hooton 1937:183, emphasis added to portions missing from Van Sertima's quotation). Through his use of the term "Pseudo-Negroid" Hooton was suggesting the crania resembled but were distinct from "authentic Negro crania." Also of interest is the fact that Hooton identified other skull types at the same Pecos site as belonging to additional racial categories, including "Pseudo-Australoid," "Long-faced European," and "Pseudo-Alpine" (in reference to people of the European Alps). While Van Sertima makes use of Hooton's data to suggest African presence in the pre-Hispanic Americas, he makes no mention of a possible Australian or European presence. This deliberate distortion of data is an excellent example of the bias found throughout Van Sertima's work.

Despite the title *They Came before Columbus*, much of the book actually focuses on reinterpretations of the archaeological record of Egypt rather than that of the Americas. Van Sertima and many other authors have become champions of the claim of a "Black Egypt" (Ankh Amen 2001; Bauval 2011; Bernal 1991a, 1991b; Diop 1974; Van Sertima 1976, 1995). This claim is a direct response to the Eurocentric diffusionist human histories created by European authors in the early twentieth century, which appropriated ancient Egypt as a Western or European phenomenon (Churchward 1921; Massey 1907; Smith 1923) rather than as an African, or even Egyptian, phenomenon. Van Sertima and his colleagues present themselves as righting this wrong and returning African civilization to its rightful racial origins. These authors argue that the ancient Egyptian state owed its success to "Negroid" or black Africans from Nubia and regions farther south rather than to a local Egyptian population. The racially oriented nature of these claims is made clear by simple geography. The claim that Egypt is an African culture is well substantiated by virtually any accurate atlas. Van Sertima and his colleagues, however, are particularly interested in the influence of dark-skinned Africans on the culture of ancient Egypt. The popularity of "Black Egypt" claims is well-documented, not only by the number of books published and lectures given in favor thereof but also by the experiences of Egyptologist Ann Macy Roth. Roth taught Egyptology at Howard University, a predominantly African American university within the United States, and wrote an excellent article entitled "Building Bridges to Afrocentrism: A Letter to my Egyptological Colleagues" (1995). Roth frequently found herself responding to questions and claims regarding the racial classification of Egyptians, noting that the idea of a Black Egypt was viewed as a source of historical pride among contemporary African American university students. As a result of her experiences she advocates for more nuanced responses to Black Egypt claims rather than simple dismissals.

As with other forms of pseudoarchaeology, the evidence proposed by Black Egypt supporters is a scattered and willful selection of limited points of data that ignore the larger context. For example, Van Sertima (1976:120–121) claims that "the Sphinx was a portrait statue of the black Pharaoh Khafre" and that "the greatest of all the pyramids was built during the reign of the African Khufu." No evidence to support the racial nature of these claims is given; instead the reader is referred to another Afrocentric source, *Destruction of Black Civilization* by Chancellor Williams (1987). The argument that the Sphinx represents a dark-skinned African is ultimately the same one made regarding the Olmec statues. The claim of a racial identification is simply asserted as self-evident (Figure 4.2). Van Sertima (1976:121) further

Figure 4.2. The Great Sphinx, Giza, Egypt. Photograph by David A. Anderson.

suggests that mainstream archaeology is part of a conspiracy in which "inscriptions are defaced, noses are chiseled down, photographs are taken from misleading angles or through misleading filters, [and] nomenclatures meant to confuse are pasted over the archaeology and documentary evidence."

A Eurocentric Reinterpretation of the Afrocentric Reinterpretations

Writ large, the Afrocentrist movement has had notable success within the United States with the overall population gaining greater awareness of African American culture. This success, however, has sparked reactions from certain individuals broadly affiliated with Eurocentric or "white pride" movements. From the perspective of archaeology and pseudoarchaeology, this reaction is best captured by Arthur Kemp's claims of a "white Egypt." The white Egypt argument claims archaeological evidence proves that ancient Egypt was founded and ruled by Caucasians (Kemp 2012).

Kemp argues that he is attempting to correct the reinterpretations being spread by Afrocentrists. In his books *March of the Titans: The Complete History of the White Race* and *The Children of Ra: Artistic, Historical, and*

Genetic Evidence for Ancient White Egypt, he revives Petrie's "dynastic race" interpretation, specifically claiming in the latter work that Petrie had suggested that "evidence indicated that the first proper civilization in Egypt had been the result of an invasion of a founding Caucasian race (what he called the 'Dynastic Race'), from the north, and specifically from Mesopotamia" (Kemp 2012:2). While Petrie (1939) did refer to an invading race from the Near East (broadly speaking incorporating Mesopotamia), he did not refer to them as Caucasian, or even white for that matter. Much like Van Sertima took the more than 100-year-old interpretation of Melgar y Serrano as fact, Kemp embraces his own modified version of Petrie's interpretation despite nearly a century of Egyptological research that has since disproved Petrie's concept of a "dynastic race."

In terms of evidence for a white Egypt, Kemp falls back on a limited set of carefully selected data. To prove that Egyptians came from Europe, or at least not from Africa, he argues that the use of bull horns as decoration at both Çatal Hüyük in Turkey and at a single tomb at the site of Saqqara in Egypt is evidence to support Petrie's allegation that the Egyptian pharaohs had come from outside of Africa (Kemp 2012:13). We have known for decades, however, that the famous bull shrines of Çatal Hüyük predate the tomb at Saqqara by several thousand years (Emery 1954; Mellart 1967). Such a drastic difference in chronology, and the simplistic analogy based on two sites using bull horns as decorations, would not stand up as sufficient evidence for contact among modern archaeologists, or even among the archaeologists of Petrie's era. Kemp goes on to present additional evidence in the form of several mummies that he interprets as white, as well as many artistic depictions of Egyptians that he also suggests prove that the ancient Egyptians were white.

Overall, Kemp is forceful in his opinions about how the race of individuals affects the tides of human history. In the conclusion to *The Children of Ra* he suggests that ancient Egypt represents a clear example of what happens to a society that allows racial mixing, stating that "ancient Egypt is possibly one of the clearest-cut cases of the iron law of nature which says that if a society which has produced a particular civilization stays intact as a racially homogenous unit, then that civilization remains active. If, however, the society within any particular area changes its racial makeup—through invasion, immigration, or decline in numbers—then the civilization which that society has produced will disappear with them, to be replaced by a new civilization reflecting the new inhabitants of that territory. The lesson of Egypt is plain to see, and all white nations of the world would do well to learn from this ancient example" (2012:72–73). Modern anthropological research on ethnicity and cultural interactions can in no way support Kemp's warning.

A Comparison of Claims

Although both Van Sertima and Kemp present diametrically opposed interpretations, they make use of extremely similar methods. In seeking to prove the influence of "Negroid" Africans Van Sertima frequently falls back on selecting individual examples from the artistic record of the New World and ancient Egypt. Rather than provide a comprehensive interpretation of the representation of facial characteristics of people in pre-Hispanic American cultures, he finds particular examples that depict what he believes must be black Africans. Kemp goes through the same process in his examination of ancient Egyptian art. He finds examples that he feels best represent his point that ancient Egyptians had light-colored skin. Kemp does point to examples depicting black Africans in Egyptian art but fails to present a comprehensive view of race in ancient Egypt. Both men also turn to the biological record. As seen, Van Sertima makes very poorly substantiated claims for the existence of African skeletons in pre-Hispanic contexts. Kemp makes similarly simplistic claims about Egyptian mummies, stating that their race is self-evident while giving little to no discussion of the effects of mummification on the body or the effects of thousands of years of decay. Furthermore, both men fall back on extremely outdated scholarship and ignore interpretations of these data by contemporary archaeologists. Kemp seeks to revivify Petrie's "dynastic race" interpretation, with the added layer of identifying that race as Caucasian, and Van Sertima blindly accepts Melgar y Serrano's racial identifications as well as highly questionable accounts from early European explorers in the New World.

A final similarity between these two authors comes from their method of publication. As their ideas have been more or less universally condemned by the academic audience and thus academic publishers, both Van Sertima and Kemp have resorted to creating their own publishing houses. While *They Came before Columbus* was published by Random House, most of Van Sertima's subsequent publications (1985, 1987a, 1987b, 1988, 1995, 1998) were published by the *Journal of African Civilizations*. This journal, which is more of a book series, was founded by Van Sertima (Journal of African Civilizations 2013), and it appears that every book they have published was written or edited by Van Sertima.[2] Kemp's books have been published by a company called Ostara Publications. The company's website does not list Kemp as the founder or owner, but it does state that the company was founded for the purpose of publishing Kemp's book *March of the Titans* (Ostara Publications 2013). Ostara Publications has gone on to publish books by other authors, but there is a notable Eurocentric theme to these publications, as well as to the merchandise for sale on their website.

The Moral of Our Parable

To discuss the moral of this parable in terms of archaeology and pseudo-archaeology, we need to return to the concepts of indigenous views of the past raised by the work of Schadla-Hall (2004). In the case of Van Sertima's claims about the Americas, an excellent response is found in the article "Robbing Native American Cultures: Van Sertima's Afrocentricity and the Olmecs" (Haslip-Viera et al. 1997). Haslip-Viera et al. clearly demonstrate that Van Sertima's claims are undermining the cultural heritage of indigenous groups within the Americas. When we move to Egypt, however, we encounter a different problem. Both Van Sertima and Kemp are making specific claims about the racial identity of the indigenous population of Egypt—or more specifically, they are making claims about the racial makeup of the ruling class in ancient Egypt. Regardless, both authors present themselves as advocates for the modern-day descendant communities of the racial group responsible for the achievements of ancient Egyptian culture. In a very real sense, they are presenting their claims as if they were the descendants of an indigenous population that they believe has been misrepresented by modern-day archaeologists.

Schadla-Hall (2004) proposes that archaeologists should not only respect claims made by indigenous groups but celebrate their alternative views of the past. The question then arises, should we embrace and celebrate the claims made by Van Sertima and Kemp since both authors believe they are writing about their own ancestors? Most archaeologists are likely to answer no because in this case we believe that both authors are making flawed arguments based on misinterpretations of the archaeological record and thus they do not represent the true descendants of Pharaonic Egypt. But by this very argument we are superseding the claims of a modern ethnic group with archaeological data. That is to say, we are telling a group of people that their beliefs about their own past are in error, precisely what Schadla-Hall is advocating we should not do.

Thus we see the problems inherent in Schadla-Hall's two-part categorization. Indigenous views of the past should certainly be respected, but when those views are in direct conflict with the archaeological record we need to explore where the roots of that conflict lie. If the conflict lies in a distortion of the archaeological record, then archaeologists should be obliged to confront that distortion. At the same time, archaeologists should have a well-informed awareness of the limits of archaeological data. There are only so many conclusions that we can draw about past cultures with absolute certainty, and those conclusions hardly make up the full and rich diversity of a living culture. Thus, when working with descendant communities, we should be particularly aware that we do not know everything about a culture's ancestors, and we should respect their own traditions as sources of information for how people view themselves and their own past.

When archaeological data conflict with views of the past we should not simply avoid presenting those contradictions. Instead we should present them for precisely what they are: one source of information about the past. We have an ethical responsibility to report our data and make our best effort at an objective interpretation of those data while at the same time recognizing that our interpretation is just that: an interpretation subject to our personal biases. In the examples presented in this chapter, archaeological data clearly demonstrate that the claims for Africans in the Americas, as well as the claims for either a black or white Egypt, are patently incorrect. When someone misrepresents and distorts the archaeological record, we have a responsibility to respond. Schadla-Hall's dichotomy of pseudoarchaeology distorts our responsibility rather than strengthening it. When pseudoarchaeological claims ignore the well-established archaeological knowledge base, they should be challenged and debunked by archaeologists.

Acknowledgments

I wish to thank the many people who helped shape and improve this chapter. The discussion of Egyptian materials was greatly improved by commentaries from Leslie Anne Warden (however, any perceived slights against Sir Flinders Petrie are the fault of the author and not Dr. Warden). Commentaries from my coeditor, Jeb J. Card, as well as Kenneth L. Feder were of immense assistance in focusing the desired message of this work. Finally, commentaries from two anonymous peer reviewers were of particular help in clarifying the finer points of the chapter. Many aspects of this chapter may be viewed as contentious, and I welcome correspondence with anyone who thinks that his perspective has been misrepresented.

Notes

1. Total sales figures for books are not officially tracked by any objective body, but in 2013 *They Came before Columbus* was listed on Amazon.com among the top-10 best sellers in the categories of African History Books, World Expeditions & Discoveries, and African American Studies.

2. The web page for the *Journal of African Civilizations* does not include a comprehensive list of publications. All books listed on the journal's web page as well as all books listed as associated with the journal on Amazon.com in 2013 were either written or edited by Ivan van Sertima.

5
Creationist History-Making

Producing a Heterodox Past

JAMES S. BIELO

Kentucky's Dragons

It was late November 2012, and I sat in a creationist design studio in northern Kentucky. In his cubicle, Travis, the youngest of the creative team's four core members, searched online to find a perfect one-liner for the new Dragon Legends exhibit. He chose three lines from an 1892 translation of the Old English epic poem *Beowulf*: "First they beheld there a creature more wondrous, The worm on the field, in front of them lying, The foeman before them: the fire-spewing dragon."

The team works for the creationist[1] ministry Answers in Genesis (AiG) and are the creative talent behind the $30 million Creation Museum that opened in 2007. They are now working on another ambitious project, Ark Encounter: a proposed $150 million biblical theme park, to be set on 800 acres of Kentucky rolling hills, 40 miles south of Cincinnati. The centerpiece of the park will be an all-timber replication of Noah's ark, built to creationist specification from the text of Genesis 6–9. The completed ark will use three and a half million board feet of timber, contain more than 100,000 square feet of themed exhibit space, and stand 75 feet wide, 50 feet tall, and about 510 feet long.

From October 2011 to June 2014 I conducted ethnographic fieldwork with Ark Encounter's design team, examining the making of a creationist theme park as an act of cultural production.[2] By following the process of production, "the making of," distinctive insight is gained about cultural content, aspiration, and identity compared to analyses limited to completed products or acts of consumption (e.g., Engelke 2013).

Fund-raising for the Ark Encounter proceeded much more slowly than the ministry initially predicted. The original opening date of summer 2014 has been delayed several times and is currently advertised as summer 2016. As of late 2012, they had raised a little less than $10 million of the $24.5 million needed to begin construction. While waiting for Ark Encounter funding to materialize, the team worked on a variety of smaller projects. Enter the dragons.

Since the Creation Museum's opening, AiG's alliterative theological shorthand—"the 7 C's of History—Creation, Corruption, Catastrophe, Confusion, Christ, Cross, Consummation"—has been the featured exhibit in the museum's front portico. The portico is a narrow, curving walkway, approximately 93 paces, that guides visitors to the Main Hall. Travis explained that the ministry wanted a new exhibit for the Memorial Day opening of the summer 2013 tourist season. The team wanted to "up the cool factor" yet still teach creationist content.

For Dragon Legends, the "big idea" is to establish "the plausibility of man and dinosaur coexisting" by linking their literal reading of Genesis 1 with dragon stories from around the world and across different historical periods. Travis was careful, as was the entire team, to distinguish dragon "legends" from the inerrancy of sacred scripture. This is why the pitch for exhibit approval led with *Beowulf* and not a biblical text: the historical veracity of the epic poem is ambiguous, whereas the Bible is believed to provide an exact historical record. As I elaborate later, the epistemological status of "legends" significantly shaped the team's artistry. On one hand, Dragon Legends teaches differently from other Creation Museum installations. It speaks in a suggestive register rather than declarative certainty. On the other hand, legends allow for "artistic freedom" in a way that their representations of scientific inquiry do not (e.g., visual depictions of why natural features like the Grand Canyon are the product of the Noachian Deluge). In this way, Dragon Legends invited creative agency. As we discussed his selection from *Beowulf*, Travis enthusiastically reflected on his interest in Middle Age war regalia, particularly helmets. Flipping through one of many caches of artwork files stored on his computer, he showed me different helmets with unique designs on each panel. Breezily, Travis noted the aesthetic variations between "early" and "late Roman influences."

History-Making

This fieldwork scene captures several themes discussed in this chapter. How do creationist artists understand and represent the past? How do they make decisions and claims about legitimate, ambiguous, and contested historical evidence? How do they use material culture to help create historical narratives? To address these questions is to address the cultural work of creationist history-making.

The use of the term "history-making" here can be defined as the field of dialogue and action that produces claims about the past and frames those claims with symbolic, cosmological, and moral significance. History-making expresses the more fundamental issue of temporality, that is, cultural models for the nature of time and its passing (Bialecki 2009). Given the theological emphasis on eternal salvation and, for many Christians, the expectation of a messianic return, Christianity is often described as a religion of the future. While this is not untrue for creationists, they are largely distinguishable by their discourse about the past: the biblical authority of Genesis, the age of the earth, antievolutionism, humans and dinosaurs coexisting, a global flood, a providential boat, and eight survivors.

History-making respects the crucial distinction between *the past* and *history*, a distinction insisted upon by scholars across disciplines. Postprocessual archaeologists established that claims about the past are made through interpretation, representation, and consumption rather than any direct, unmediated, or uncontested reporting about the past (Shanks and Tilley 2007). The philosopher and literary critic Walter Benjamin wrote, "The true picture of the past flits by. The past can be seized only as an image which flashes up at the instant when it can be recognized and is never seen again" (1968 [1955]: 255). The museum historian Mike Wallace writes much the same: "There is no such thing as 'the past.' All history is a production—a deliberate selection, ordering, and evaluation of past events, experiences, and processes" (1996:24). In their ethnography of Colonial Williamsburg, Richard Handler and Eric Gable stress the discursive production of history: "'The past' exists only as we narrate it today. The past is above all the stories, not objects" (1997:224). This, then, presents a fundamental tension: the past is gone yet always with us through constant remembering, forgetting, and rediscovering.

The past, though quite real, is forever and densely mediated by this production of histories. As a cultural process, history-making is a social and ideological accomplishment that is achieved through material means and infrastructure. In turn, the anthropology and ethnography of history-making confront important questions: How are different relationships to the past cultivated? What strategies and resources are marshaled to perform history-making? And what is up for grabs in competing acts of history-making?

One of the primary goals of this volume is to develop better ways of thinking about how nonprofessional historians and scientists perform the work of history-making (see Beisaw, this volume). The AiG creative team reminds us with little subtlety that the past is ideologically contested and that even the most scientifically established historical claims can be actively challenged. As the historian Raphael Samuel writes: "History is not the prerogative of the historian, nor even, as postmodernism contends, a historian's 'invention.' It is, rather, a social form of knowledge; the work, in any given instance, of a thousand different hands" (1994:8). Moreover, those thousand hands are not working in concert, which means the present hosts multiple historical narratives vying for cultural authority. Anthropologically, our remit is to understand whose hands are doing what and to seek a full ethnographic account of all history-making projects, including those of creationists. To aim for any less is to shrug off our most profound scholarly responsibility.

When it comes to mainstream archaeologists' history-making antagonists, creationists play a leading role (Harrold and Eve 1995).[3] This is partly due to creationists' persistent presence in the public sphere: introducing pro-creationism bills to state legislatures, revising textbook standards to undermine evolutionary theory, and supporting multimillion dollar projects like the Creation Museum. The antagonism is also due to the fact that mainstream and alternative archaeologies "both fulfill a similar demand of providing the present with larger historical perspectives and narratives" (Holtorf 2005:547).[4] More broadly, creationists and scientists are convinced of the universal legitimacy of their respective projects; both desire to "create a totalizing understanding of the world . . . one that is valid for all cultures and nations at all times" (Coleman and Carlin 2004:6). This totalizing drive derives in part from the shared assumption that knowledge about the past matters dearly for life in the present. Like secular natural history museums, the Creation Museum is grounded in the notion that "understanding our origins will tell us important information about who we are today" (Asma 2011:162). These shared desires and assumptions underscore the contested nature and authoritative stakes of history-making.

In a fundamental way, creationism is incommensurable with mainstream archaeology. This becomes immediately visible through four commitments of creationist history-making:

1. To borrow the preferred biblical language of creationists, the human race is a special creation made in God's image. This forecloses any possibility that modern humans evolved from any kind of primate ancestor. Human evolution is, of course, a definitive research interest in prehistoric archaeology and is one of archaeology's pivotal "meta-stories" (Holtorf 2010:384).
2. The earth is between 6,000 and 10,000 years old. This dating derives from a method of calculating chronology in the Torah, first enumerated by the Irish bishop James Ussher in 1650. In step with other sci-

entists, mainstream archaeologists estimate the age of the earth to be approximately 4.5 billion years old and date the earliest human technology to 2.5 million years ago based on finds from Goma, Ethiopia.

3. A universal flood, detailed in Genesis 6–9, was a real historical event with geological and biological implications. Geologically, the Noachian Deluge is the basis of "flood geology," which is said to explain an array of natural formations (e.g., Arizona's Grand Canyon) and archaeological finds (e.g., fossil distribution). Mainstream archaeology summarily rejects the historical validity of any universal flood. Biologically, because Noah and his family were the only human survivors of the biblical deluge, all of the world's past and present peoples are descendants of Noah's three sons and their wives. Mainstream archaeology explains human biological variation through discoveries of human skeletal remains and genetic modeling.
4. These three commitments are ultimately about authority. Why do creationists accept these claims and treat them as nonnegotiable? It is because they are committed to a literalist textual ideology that interprets biblical stories as real history and elevates scripture as true over and against any other knowledge source (Bielo 2009). For archaeologists, there is no direct textual equivalent. Authority is diffused among ways of reckoning with materialist facts: scientific methodology, dating techniques, the comparative archaeological record, and explanatory theoretical models (see Card, this volume).

In short, creationism and mainstream archaeology are at historical, methodological, epistemological, and ideological loggerheads. This impasse highlights a pivotal aspect of history-making: "It is not the past as such which attracts interest and gains social significance but rather important issues that an engagement with the past brings up" (Holtorf 2010:384). Mark Noll, a historian of American evangelicalism, argues likewise: "As was the case in the first half of the 19th century so also now in the third decade of the 20th: much more was at stake for American evangelicals in the cosmological meaning of science, much less in the actual doing of science" (1999:112).

Rather than simply reject creationist claims about the past as absurd, the necessary anthropological stance is to view creationists as social actors contending for cultural authority. Pierre Bourdieu's sociology provides a framework for understanding this contention. In struggles for symbolic power (such as the power to define what legitimate history or science is), Bourdieu outlines three positions: doxa, orthodox, and heterodox (1977 [1972]:159). Doxic conditions are those in which a dominant position persists unchallenged, where no alternative possibility is advocated by minority or marginal actors. This has not been the case for America's creation-evolution dialogue for a long time. Before Darwin's *On the Origin of Species* in 1859, Charles Lyell's 1833 book *Principles of Geology* and the Scottish theologian Thomas Chalmer's 1815 popularization of gap creationism were upsetting the young earth apple cart.

Creation-evolution is a case of heterodox-orthodox struggle. Science, evolutionary theory, and mainstream archaeology occupy the orthodox stance in American public life; they harness more symbolic capital by being invested with more authority in more influential sites. Secular skeptics might be quick to disagree, perhaps citing national polling results from Gallup and Pew as evidence. But Bourdieu's framework is not about counting heads; it is about access to power, the production of legitimized knowledge, and the exercise of symbolic capital (think federal and state funding; feature stories in *National Geographic*, *Scientific American*, *Nature*, and *Science*; National Public Radio reports; displays at world-renowned museums such as the Smithsonian in Washington, D.C., and the Field Museum in Chicago; and what earns a science course "A" at state and Ivy League universities). Indeed, the reason that creationists appeal to science so frequently is because of science's "high social status" (Lewis and Andersson 2012:121).

Creationism occupies the heterodox stance: a socially real intrusion on the "universe of possible discourse" (Bourdieu 1977 [1972]:169). Ministries like AiG simultaneously work to establish their own legitimacy while disrupting the accepted legitimacy of evolutionary theory and mainstream archaeology. Cultural productions like the Creation Museum and the Ark Encounter are very visible and very expensive strategies in this contention for authority. For creationists the Creation Museum and the Ark Encounter are safe havens for consuming their kind of history-making, protected spheres of shared heterodoxy and alternatives to scientific orthodoxy. Travis articulated this very clearly in our first interview. When I asked him about his artistic influences for creating representations of the past, he answered: "The secular world owns probably 99 percent of all the material out there. So, you have to like reinterpret most of it. And you've got all these years you have to, in a sense, compact into 6,000 years because that's, you know, my biblical worldview."

AiG seeks to educate, and they hope enlarge, that creationist 1 percent. The Creation Museum and the Ark Encounter are sites where reinterpretation, secular-to-creationist translation, reading between the lines, and other heterodox acts become unnecessary. This is why, on any given visit to the museum, you are likely to see cars in the parking lot with bumper stickers announcing: "We're Taking Dinosaurs Back!" Dragon Legends is yet another tactic in the strategy of taking dinosaurs back. To understand this, we must begin not with the cultural productions but with the cultural producers.

Creative Creationists

AiG was founded in 1994 by three former employees of the Institute for Creation Research.[5] When I interviewed one of AiG's cofounders, he described their desire to start "a populist ministry" that would complement the more "technical" approach and persona of the Institute for Creation Research. What is the cultural content, and gain, of populism as a presentation of self? A populist ministry would aim to reach as wide a portion of the public as possible. This includes making core creationist commitments and anti-evolution arguments as accessible as possible to nonprofessionals in science. AiG's populist striving is also mirrored in their choice of location for the Creation Museum. Why northern Kentucky? The ministry website explains that "almost two-thirds of America's population lives within 650 miles."

Along with these pragmatic and strategic ends, populism has a historical resonance. William Jennings Bryan, famous for his prosecuting role in the 1925 Scopes Trial, advocated gap creationism because of his religious beliefs but also because he was a dogged defender of democratic principles (Larson 1997). (According to this populist logic, if a local school board wants to ban the teaching of evolution in public schools, and the local tax-paying population agrees, then "who the hell are non-locals to say otherwise, even if they are 'experts'?")[6] From its beginnings, then, AiG has targeted the broadest public possible, not the elite echelons of professional science (see Harding 2000; Numbers 1992; Toumey 1994).

AiG's populism is most evident in the ministry's biggest achievement to date, the Creation Museum. The museum opened in 2007 after six years of construction and nearly 30 years of planning. In a 2010 article, the anthropologist Ella Butler provides a close reading of museum content and a productive theoretical framing. She argues that the museum functions by combining a secular-derived science studies critique (à la Bruno Latour) with conspiracy theory. For the former, "scientific practice is always influenced by the starting assumptions of its practitioners," which prompts the widely accessible conclusion that creationism ("creation science" in the ministry's terms) and science ("secular evolutionists" in the ministry's terms) merely begin with diverging ideological commitments ("human reason" vs. "God's Word") (2010:231). For the latter, "like the conspiracy theorist, the creationist is here positioned as a kind of knowing subject who is enabled to see the truth behind the [evolutionist] façade" (ibid.:237). Butler's argument helps show how the Creation Museum produces heterodox history. Alongside equipping the already converted with resources for teaching and evangelism, the museum seeks to "destabilize scientific claims to objectivity" and, by extension, the authority of science and mainstream archaeology (ibid.: 231). All this is performed through the populist registers of cinematic film, multisensory displays, interactive media, replicas, animatronic figures, and a narrative-driven presentation of material culture.

A distinctive contribution of my fieldwork is the privileged access to the producers of these populist registers and their process of production. By devoting close ethnographic attention to the making of (instead of completed products or acts of) consumption, we gain unique insight about the material and ideological process of creationist history-making. Who, then, are the four creative team members who led the museum's design, Dragon Legends, and now Ark Encounter?

Patrick is the creative director. Now in his 60s, he joined AiG in 2001 after working as a theme park designer in Tokyo for several years. Patrick's impressive résumé also includes working on the 1984 Summer Olympics, the 1986 Statue of Liberty refurbishing, and Universal Studio's *Jaws* and *King Kong* attractions. Jon was the first artist hired when plans for the museum got underway. Before AiG, he illustrated for a Christian educational book company and a non-Christian studio firm that contracted art production with entertainment corporations like Milton Bradley and Fisher Price. Jon also taught art at a Christian college, which had the useful ethnographic effect of his being adept at explaining art to me while working. Kristen has a master's degree in theater design from the California Institute of the Arts, the private university founded by Walt Disney in 1961. Patrick hired her in 2005 to design buildings and sets for the museum. And there is Travis. Now 27, he started working for AiG at age 18, after completing his homeschool education in Michigan.

Each member plays a distinct role on the team, a complementary dynamic they repeatedly laud. Along with managing the team's responsibilities and the "vision" of each project, Patrick writes scripts for individual attractions and displays. Jon is the lead illustrator, producing "concept art" at various stages that bridges the team's initial brainstorming and final versions. Kristen is the spatial design expert. Travis specializes in sculpture, costume design, and historical context. Their talents complement one another, but the team also describes a productive friction that occurs because of their differing acumen. Jon, Kristen, and Travis have all described (usually with a smile and a funny anecdote) how Travis's realist fidelities confront the more fantasy-inflected imaginative strivings of Jon and Kristen.

As artists, as designers, as creatives, the team conceives their task as special. They must produce creationist content that is equal parts educational and enjoyable. From early in my fieldwork, one word emerged as vital to this task: "immersion." Whatever the project, their goal is to create an immersive environment where visitors can "experience" a teaching message. The version of immersion the team abides by is less about sensory overload and more about establishing conditions in which visitors actively participate in a multisensory experience (cf. Beisaw, this volume). Kristen articulated this well during an interview, when I asked her to describe her role in the creative process: "My role on the team is, I, if you know what an imagineer is at Disney. That's what we do. . . . We dream up, conceptualize an experience where we're trying to either one, tell the story, or two, teach something. Where we're concerned, we are wanting people to understand the Word of God in a simple and fun way so that it's not overwhelming or it's not something that they sort of turn away from because they can't understand it. Do you know what I mean? So, here, we're trying to create fun atmospheres. You start with an idea, a concept, a script, and then you sort of flesh it out." Creationist imagineers: this is the disposition the team brings to their work of cultural production. Their history-making is grounded in blurred boundaries: among entertainment and piety, awe and education, fun and faithfulness, immersion and antievolutionism.

Given their résumés and project budgets, AiG's design team is an especially ambitious and professionalized species of evangelistic entertainers, but their genus is not unprecedented. The entanglement of play and piety is not unique to creationists or twenty-first-century America (Messenger 1999). Religious actors have employed the cultural resources of entertainment throughout U.S. history (Moore 1994). One of the first sites to do this was New York's Chautauqua Institution in the 1870s, in particular their immersive uses of a scaled topographic model of biblical Palestine (Rowan 2004:258). Other examples abound in contemporary America—from hell houses (Pelligrini 2007) to faith-based family tourism in the Ozarks (Ketchell 2007) to Arkansas's Great Passion Play (Long 2003) to Orlando's Wycliffe Discovery Center (Shani et al. 2007)—and elsewhere in the world, from Israel's Nazareth Village to Brazil's Temple of Solomon and Jerusalem re-created in Argentina (Ron and Feldman 2009).

One of the nearest contemporary parallels to the history-making work of AiG is the Holy Land Experience (HLE) in Orlando (Rowan 2004). A prime example is the John Wycliffe display in HLE's "Scriptorium" (a guided tour of biblical textual transmission).[7] In a small, dimly lit room, an animatronic figure of Wycliffe sits translating scripture at a desk. An audio-recording played through overhead speakers explains the fourteenth-century illegality of translating the Bible into any vernacular language. The overhead soundtrack abruptly shifts into a generic British accent, Wycliffe describing "my dangerous task." Projected shadows on the wall and rustling sounds re-create the experience of authorities busting into Wycliffe's home. "Leave now through the fireplace," the accented voice urges, and a hidden door opens to move to the next display. As you leave a different accented voice asks demandingly, "You there, what have you got?" Like the work of the AiG design team, HLE's presentation of Wycliffe relies on immersive entertainment to accomplish religious teaching.

Dragon Legends

The Creation Museum unveiled its newest addition over Memorial Day weekend 2013. The website promo for Dragon Legends uses this teaser:

> Regale yourself with delightful artwork and other beautiful adornments as you stroll beneath extraordinary Chinese dragons in the museum's portico. Learn about fabulous encounters with these incredible beasts from China to Africa, Europe to the Americas, and Australia to the Middle East. Discover what ancient historians have written about these creatures, and examine armaments that may have been used by valiant dragon slayers. Why are there so many *Dragon Legends* from cultures around the globe? Why do descriptions of these magnificent animals often sound similar to what we call dinosaurs? How could our ancestors carve, paint, or write about these creatures if they have truly been extinct for millions of years? Evolutionists struggle to explain the intriguing evidence that people lived at the same time as dinosaurs. God's Word indicates that dinosaurs and man were created on the same day, so biblical creationists are not surprised to uncover clues that ancient man had indeed seen these beasts.

The critique of evolution is both subtle ("our ancestors") and overt ("evolutionists struggle"), and the creationist blending of entertainment ("delightful artwork," "fabulous encounters"), scientific ("explain the intriguing evidence," "uncover clues"), and religious ("God's Word," "biblical creationists") registers is diligent.

How do creationists "explain the intriguing evidence"? Why do dragon legends "demonstrate the plausibility" of humans and dinosaurs coexisting? Their argument goes as follows. Specific dragon legends have varying degrees of truth, but all were inspired by real events. At some point in the past, humans interacted with animals resembling the dragons of lore, which then became more fantastical over time and through storytelling. The most likely candidates for that interaction are the animals we now call dinosaurs.

AiG follows three moves in tracing the biblical evidence. It begins, inevitably for creationists, in Genesis 1 and 2, when all animals, land and sea, were created alongside humans. The literalist reading is that every animal we have any fossil evidence for must have coexisted with humans, including dinosaurs. From here, they go to the Book of Job chapters 40–41. As God reprimands Job, chastising him for forgetting the vast gulf that separates human fallibility and divine glory, God describes two beasts. First: "Look at Behemoth, which I made along with you and which feeds on grass like an ox. What strength it has in its loins, what power in the muscles of its belly! Its tail sways like a cedar; the sinews of its thighs are close-knit. Its bones are tubes of bronze, its limbs like rods of iron" (Job 40:15–18, NIV).

Then there is "Leviathan": "Its snorting throws out flashes of light; its eyes are like the rays of dawn. Flames stream from its mouth; sparks of fire shoot out. Smoke pours from its nostrils as from a boiling pot over burning reeds. Its breath sets coals ablaze, and flames dart from its mouth" (Job 41:18–21, NIV). The literalist reading is that Behemoth and Leviathan were both what we now call dinosaurs. These were the creatures that humans saw, told stories about, and eventually became the stuff of elaborate legends.

Dragon Legends is the team's imagineered version of this argument, conjuring a mosaic past through eight display cases (41 x 27 x 17 inches). The first four cases address the existence of dragon tales across historical space and time, artistic depictions of dragons (e.g., "Native American pictographs"), and eyewitness accounts (John of Damascus, Marco Polo, Athanasius Kircher, and Herodotus) (Figures 5.1 and 5.2). The other four cases profile dragon slayer legends: Romans, St. George, Beowulf (Figure 5.3), and frontier cowboys in the American West.[8] Each case mixes material culture replicas, crafted by Travis, with explanatory text and images. Art panels illustrated by Jon flank the sides of each case. The eight displays run the length of the museum portico, each separated by about 30 feet. The team designed the exhibit so that visitors could choose to studiously examine all eight cases, leisurely inspect them, or quickly glance at only a select few.

I sat with Travis as he finalized the preliminary exhibit budget of $86,000 for approval. Intending a lighthearted moment, I asked if duties like making budgets were a low light compared to his more creative work. No. He does not mind budgeting because it "helps [him] stay grounded" and not "dream too big." This was a refrain throughout my fieldwork; knowing exact financial realities are necessary for determining the design work that is feasible. In creationist history-making, much like evolutionary museums, creativity sparks within the bounds of practicality.

An interview with Jon early in the design process helped me understand how the team negotiates historical accuracy and creative license in their

Figure 5.1. Moche pottery replicas "with dinosaur-like creatures painted on them," from one of two "Dragon Legends around the World" displays in the Creation Museum. Photograph by James S. Bielo.

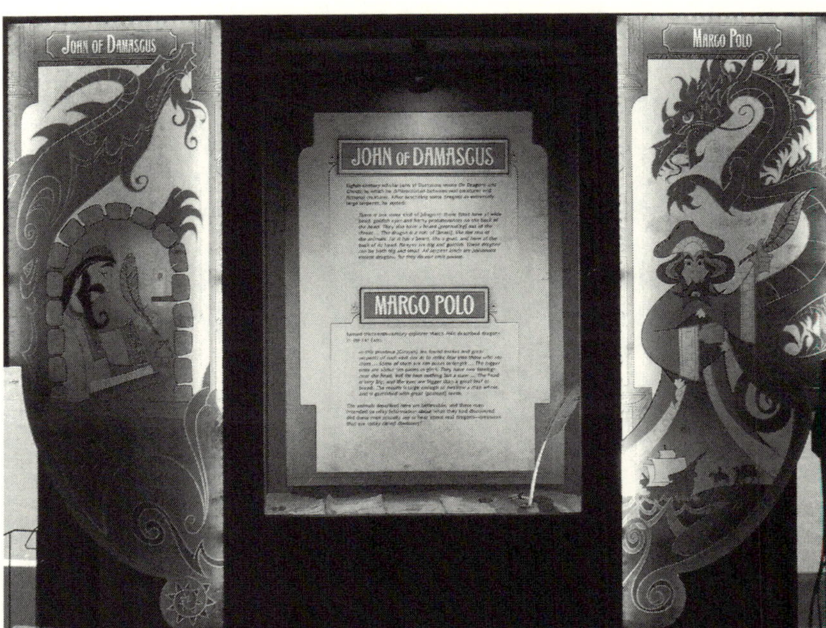

Figure 5.2. Marco Polo, one of four "eyewitnesses" displayed in the Creation Museum. Photograph by James S. Bielo.

Figure 5.3. Beowulf, one of four "Dragon Slayer" displays at the Creation Museum. Photograph by James S. Bielo.

art. We talked in his office cubicle while he worked on prototypes for panel designs. He was quick to specify the truth-value of what they were doing: "We're not showing any reality and we're not saying [legends] are proof [of dinosaurs]. It's more, we're asking, 'Could it be?'" This rhetorical device of "just askin'" is a revealing strategy, as it is found in other forms of pseudo-archaeology and it works in tandem with the ministry's broader strategy to disrupt scientific authority. Jon continued: "[Dragon Legends] is a more playful, fun thing; just a fun, expressive way to tell stories." He contrasted this with their work on Ark Encounter, which he described as "hyperrealism," offering far fewer opportunities to "go stylized." But realism still matters for Dragon Legends. Eyewitness accounts, as empirical evidence, are vital to the creationist argument. To bolster this element, Jon chose to depict all

Figure 5.4. Close-up of the Kircher display, one representation of quill in hand indexicality, at the Creation Museum. Photograph by James S. Bielo.

four eyewitnesses with quill in hand (Figure 5.4). Writing and its materiality function indexically, suggesting an unmediated link between "legend" and the recording of an actual past. Jon continued: the team's first idea was to approach Dragon Legends with "a more classic" style, which he demonstrated by showing me an image on his computer (Figure 5.5). They decided against this approach because it made discerning "what's real and what's not" more difficult. Visitors would have to spend too much time parsing truth from fiction. Again, the team wanted Dragon Legends to be more suggestive, "play-

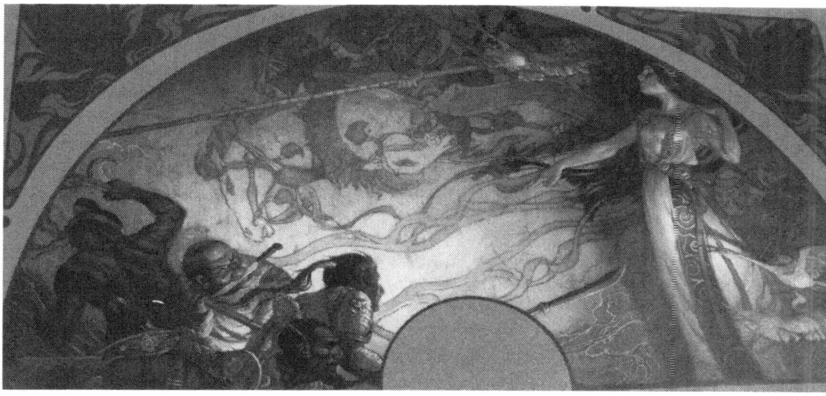

Figure 5.5. Example of the Creation Museum design team's initial intertextual inspiration, which they eventually discarded. Photograph by James S. Bielo.

ful," and "stylized" than "hyperreal." As an alternative they chose a style "akin to *The Secret of the Kells*," an animated feature film released in 2009 (Figure 5.6). The film is an adventure story set in eighth-century Ireland. It fictionalizes the making of *The Book of Kells*, a lavishly illustrated copy of the four Gospels (c. 800). *The Book of Kells* is a significant artifact in the national history of Ireland, the Christian biblical tradition, and the Anglo-Celtic Insular art movement of the Migration Period (Dodwell 1993:85). This intertextual moment is instructive for understanding the team's creative process and their work of history-making. For artistic inspiration they chose to model their depictions of eyewitnesses and legends on contemporary film animation. This is a common strategy for the team. In interviews, Jon and Kristen both named animation companies and individual artists as important influences. Around the office, art books from popular films (e.g., *Jurassic Park*, *Star Wars*, *The Lord of the Rings*) are constantly on the move between bookshelves and cubicle desks. In this case, it is not just any animated film. It is a film that portrays a time period resonant with portions of Dragon Legends and a film that portrays the making of biblical artistry. Naming *Secret of the Kells* as the center of creative gravity is one way the team casts themselves as the latest in a venerable Christian tradition that combines art, faith, storytelling, and representations of the past.

Travis's production of replicas is also instructive. In late January 2013, I spent most of the morning sitting with Travis in his cubicle as he searched potential materials for the St. George dragon slayer display. His searching process was patterned. He began by typing a search term into Google Images, then read the Wikipedia page of the search item. Sometimes he pro-

Figure 5.6. Example of *The Secret of the Kells* artwork at the Creation Museum. Photograph by James S. Bielo.

ceeded to several other Internet sources or his shelf full of history books (most published by Answers in Genesis, but there are also university and popular press titles). Other times he used only Wikipedia. In one instance, he puzzled for several minutes over which cross symbol would most likely have adorned St. George's shield. He searched "Chi Rho," assessed the Wikipedia entry, and determined this was probably not the right cross. He also compared different helmets. The displays do not have enough room for full armor, but Travis was certain that "a helmet will give a good character to the period." Eventually he concluded that he would need to sculpt the helmet by hand because all the affordable replicas are wrong by at least two centuries (Figure 5.7).

Travis also fashioned the cowboy hat and gloves for the American West display. He explained that a good replica hat is between $300 and $500, but a basic hat that he can craft to look worn and weathered was only $30. Given

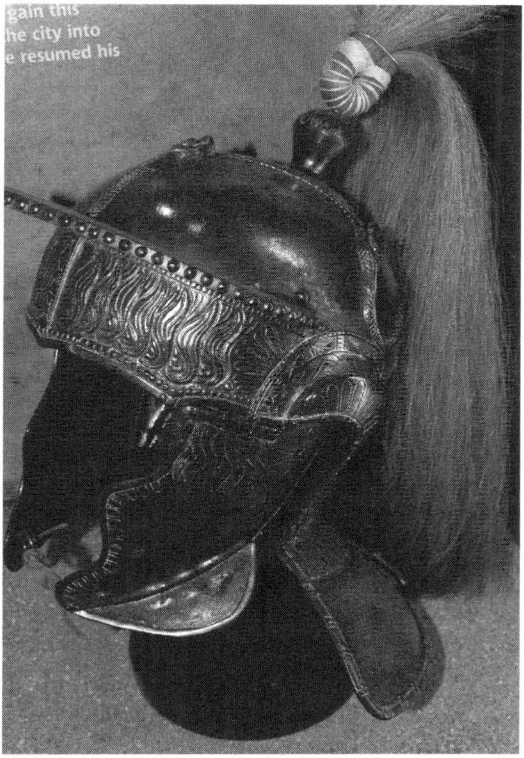

Figure 5.7. Close-up of the displayed replica of St. George's helmet at the Creation Museum. Photograph by James S. Bielo.

Travis's heavy reliance on Internet sources, I asked how he "vets the credibility of different websites." His response contained six points: the best source for researching Dragon Legends is a rare book that costs $600, but that exceeds the project's budget; he never uses dates from sites that sell replicas because there is too much danger of misinformation; he is cautious when there is a lack of specificity in period marking (e.g., when "Roman" is not qualified); he does not prioritize .edu sites; he does prioritize reenactor sites; and, last, he "can usually smell out the fishy stuff . . . you know it when you see it."

Consider three observations about Travis's creative process. First, as with generating the budget, practicality structures creativity. Full-body armor would have a more immersive effect, but the space allows for only a few selected items. Again, affordability impacts artistic choices. Second, Travis's preference for reenactor sites over .edu sites is revealing. The vast majority of .edu sites will likely be from an evolutionary standpoint, which forces him back to his heterodox tactic of reinterpreting the 99 percent. Reenactor sites are more unpredictable in their standpoint, but more important than this for Travis is that he believes reenactors are extremely careful historians. Trustworthiness derives from immersive pickiness.[9] Third, Travis's intuitive-driven closing is not happenstance. A common habit when all four team members discuss their artistry (even Jon, who has been most adept at this because of his teaching experience) is to highlight a basic ineffability about the artistic process. Not every creative move requires a how-to formula. Some things are just "cool," "interesting," or "fun" and some are just not. Some historical replicas just smell fishy, some just do not. Like religious experience and the miraculous more generally, artistry cannot always be distilled into a ready explanation.

Conclusion: The Court of Public Entertainment

In this chapter we have explored the creative process of a team of creationist imagineers. While the ethnographic material is specifically about the making of Dragon Legends, it also reveals some fundamental dynamics of creationist history-making. Like all acts of history-making, creationist productions enter into a contested cultural field, dialogically engaged with competing producers of history. For creationists, they are engaged with mainstream archaeological and evolutionary claims about the past, all of which are ideologically antagonistic to their own claims. With respect to the cultural authority that is at stake, creationists occupy a heterodox stance. Just as their foundational claims about the past are rejected by mainstream science, historical productions like Dragon Legends seek to delegitimize the authoritative position of science in American public life.

Having established that history-making is about vying for cultural authority, we can conclude by reflecting on the nature of the power being targeted by the Creation Museum and Ark Encounter. These sites are an attempt to complement the creationist movement's initial strategy of targeting public school science education. This strategy began in force with a 1973 Tennessee state law requiring "equal time" for evolutionary and creationist teachings. Certainly, public education is a site of power. Andrew Ross, writing about school board struggles in the incipient Disney town of Celebration, argued: "In the absence of a national religion or shared cultural traditions, the public school has long been held up as the unique source of American national unity. It has ended up serving too many agendas as a result" (1997:38). This powerful valence of American public education helps explain why creationist attempts to introduce antievolution and/or procreationist material into K–12 curriculum are so vehemently contested.

However, power in modern American society is diffuse and variable. The civic institutions of government and education are not the only sites where hearts and minds are won. The creative team's history-making draws us into the power that is up for grabs in the cultural field of entertainment. The anthropologist Peter Stromberg suggests that this field is "arguably the most influential ideological system on the planet" (2009:3). Our shared appetite for fun not only unites the public, it becomes the means of competing for the attention and loyalty of publics: "As Darwin argued for the survival of the fittest, we now have survival of the most entertaining" (ibid.:8).

The entanglement of history-making with entertainment is well-documented in studies of heritage marketing (Baram and Rowan 2004). Whereas mid- to late twentieth-century archaeologists investigated the ideological uses of material culture by states to fuel nationalist causes, the focus is now broadening to states and corporations competing for heritage-derived profit: "Commercialization seems to be the next frontier of challenges for archaeologists and others concerned about accurate and meaningful presentations of the past" (ibid.:9). Archaeo-tourist sites increasingly borrow, as if by gravitational force, strategies of teaching and representation from the likes of Disney (Lovata 2007). This assemblage of heritage, material culture, and entertainment fosters a global dynamic: history-making sites "are interested in constructing authentic relationships with a particular retelling of the past, and that past assists them in the construction or reaffirmation in a sense of identity" (Rowan 2004:263).

Science and history museum professionals are also well aware of this new Darwinian contest of public entertainment. Their production staffs confront many of the same questions as the AiG design team, as they work to integrate art, entertainment, and authoritative knowledge in their history-making displays. For example, Stephen Asma's book *Stuffed Animals and Pickled Heads* takes us behind the scenes of Chicago's Field Museum. Asma was particularly interested in how exhibit designers managed the dual imperatives of fun and learning: "Many [curators, designers, and developers] were very concerned that the cost of some of this increase in entertainment might be a decrease in scientific content" (2001:15). This sentiment echoes the prescient anxiety Stephen Jay Gould voiced about the dangers of edutainment: theme parks "are, in many ways, the antithesis of museums. If each institution respects the other's essence and place, this opposition poses no problem. But, theme parks represent the realm of commerce, museums the educational world—and the first, by its power and immensity, must trump the second in any direct encounter" (quoted in Asma 2001:35). Whereas a secular logic seeks to keep the categories of "museum" and "theme park" separate and distinct, AiG employs both (Creation Museum and Ark Encounter) in their work of history-making. What secular critics fear, or implement with trepidation, creationist imagineers do with gusto.

In the ongoing orthodox-heterodox struggle between evolutionary science and creationism, we are left with several pressing questions. Can productions like Dragon Legends immerse and entertain in ways that trump secular museums? In contrast to the hotly contested field of public school curricula, where symbolic capital derives from scientific legitimacy, can creationism score a victory in the court of public entertainment, where creative capital speaks in an artistic register? When it comes to history-making, is creationism more fun than evolution?

Acknowledgments

Special thanks to Simon Coleman, Steve Watkins, Omri Elisha, Jeff Guhin, and Joe Webster, all of whom provided helpful feedback on an earlier draft of this chapter. Jeb Card has provided instructive feedback on this chapter and enthusiastic, critical support throughout the project. Also, I thank two anonymous reviewers for their revealing readings of an earlier draft. My deepest debt is to the Ark Encounter design team, who generously enabled my fieldwork and patiently endured my constant questions.

Notes

1. The term "creationist" is used here to capture the young earth creationism promoted by AiG. This is a stylistic choice and should not be taken as glossing over the many variations of historical and contemporary creationism (Scott 1997).

2. The methodological details of this fieldwork were unconventional in several ways. I was not granted complete open access to the team's creative labor. I had to arrange each fieldwork visit weeks ahead of time with the team. Throughout the 43 months of fieldwork, planned visits were rescheduled by the team on numerous occasions, often with little advance notice. Ultimately I logged approximately 125 hours at the design studio. During this time, my primary forms of data collection were observing and interviewing the artists while they worked at their cubicles and recording team meetings. When possible, I would audio-record my informal interviewing with the artists at their desks. Because the offices were filled with concept art and other material culture items, I relied heavily on fieldwork photography (with a cache of more than 750 JPEG images). I also audio-recorded semistructured interviews with each team member. The Ark Encounter website has been an additional data source, in particular the project blog that provides selective updates on the team's progress and theological arguments in support of the ark project. I supplemented this fieldwork with observations at the Creation Museum on numerous visits, observations at other

AiG events (e.g., the much-publicized Ken Ham and Bill Nye debate in February 2014), and observations at other evangelical museum and entertainment sites (e.g., the Holy Land Experience in Orlando, Florida; the Living Bible Museum in Mansfield, Ohio; and the Billy Graham Center Museum in Wheaton, Illinois).

3. I use the qualifier "mainstream" not to invite any complicity with creationist aims but to mark the fact that creationists also organize and conduct archaeological excavations.

4. The framing terminology here is an important point of contention. Holtorf (2005) prefers "alternative archaeologies," while archaeological critics of Holtorf prefer "pseudoarchaeology" (Fagan and Feder 2005). This chapter's analysis is more sympathetic with the broader epistemological commitments of Holtorf.

5. The Institute for Creation Research was founded in 1972 in San Diego and was among the first institutionalizations of the modern creationist movement. The location of San Diego is revealing because Southern California was an important site for the development of the modern evangelical movement (Dochuk 2010).

6. Note how this form of populism is not limited to matters of scientific authority. For example, similar arguments were, and are, made about granting and denying civil rights.

7. The following is based on a February 2014 fieldwork trip to the Holy Land Experience.

8. See Card, this volume on cryptozoology's relationship to making alternative pasts.

9. Matters of social class are important here as well. While Travis's affinity for reenactor sites over and against .edu sites is explicitly about immersion, it is also a reproduction of his position in the American class structure. I thank Jeb Card for reminding me of this observation.

6
Creating Pyramids

Participation, Performance, and Pseudoarchaeology in Bosnia-Herzegovina

TERA C. PRUITT

In a time when media routinely offer books and documentaries about Atlantis or television series like *Ancient Aliens*, we are forced to question the value and worth of imagined history. What happens when invented history brings in real money? When it seems more exciting than real history? When invented stories supplant history with *knowing* support of the public? What does it all mean?

In April 2005, a man wearing a khaki vest and a wide-brimmed fedora stood in front of television cameras. Behind him was a mountain range with a prominent, strikingly triangular mountain. He cleared his throat to drum up suspense, opened his arms, looked poignantly toward the sky, and announced a great discovery: the largest and most ancient pyramids *in the world* had just been unearthed in a place no ever suspected. This man was not Indiana Jones, not Zahi Hawass—no, this was a new television personality: Semir Osmanagić, a Bosnian American businessman and alternative historian from Texas. His pyramids? Apparently there are five of them located in a small town named Visoko, Bosnia-Herzegovina, only 20 miles northwest of Sarajevo.

Back in 2004, if you Googled the name "Semir Osmanagić," your search would yield a smattering of facts about a fairly ordinary man. Osmanagić was born in Bosnia but left for Houston, Texas, before the Yugoslav civil war tore his country apart. In Houston, he demonstrated significant managerial and business skill by founding a metal construction business and growing it to over 100 employees (Foer 2007). By 2004 he was interested in "alternative" or "fringe" archaeology: archaeological claims promoted outside of traditional science. These theories sit "on the fringe" of science, usually advanced as "alternative" ideas created by amateur archaeological sleuths who dislike theories backed by most archaeologists. Osmanagić's early work is illustrative.

For over 15 years, Osmanagić has "studied" pyramids. He has traveled the world, looked at pyramids, felt their stones, thought up original hypotheses, and published papers to advance his theories—all fringe ideas deeply rooted in hyperdiffusionism, pop-culture mysticism, and esoterica in the tradition of Erich von Däniken. For example, in *The World of the Maya*, Osmanagić argues that the Maya were descended from aliens from the Pleiades, that they "inherited knowledge from their ancestors at Atlantis and Lemuria," and that "pyramids erected on these energy potent locations enabled the Maya to be closer to the heavens and to other levels of consciousness" (2005:70). Rather than dying a quiet death from a lack of evidence, his theories were turned into a PhD thesis on unconventional theories on the Maya, which he defended successfully in 2009 at the University of Sarajevo (Osmanagić 2009). He was awarded a doctorate at the peak of his fame in Bosnia—fame he achieved through his promotion of the Bosnian pyramids.

To understand the Bosnian pyramids, you have to mentally parachute into the Visočica River valley where you will find a sleepy countryside, a small town, a lazy river, and, most important, a number of pointy, pyramidal-shaped mountains dotting the landscape. According to Osmanagić, five of these mountains are actually *man-made* pyramids, technological feats of a Paleolithic Bosnian supercivilization (BosnianPyramids.org 2006; ICBP 2008). The three largest pyramids purportedly form a perfect triangle, and the four sides of the largest hill (which Osmanagić has renamed Pyramid of the Sun) align to the four cardinal points of the compass. According to his hypothesis, an intricate underground tunnel network connects these pyramids, and their walls supposedly reveal the world's earliest writing, which resembles ancient Nordic runes. Osmanagić also associates two other sites with Visoko: a hypothetical "rock quarry" site in the nearby village of Gornja Vratnica and a river ravine near the city of Zenica, which is filled with ancient "mysterious stone balls" (Osmanagić 2007a, 2007b).

In April 2005, Osmanagić launched an impressive media campaign to raise public awareness of the pyramids. His project quickly gained local and national attention and support, as well as broader support from members of the international alternative history community (Coppens 2006). People trekked to the site, locals volunteered to excavate, media buzzed with the tale of pyramids, countries like Germany offered the use of their military equipment to help excavation, and—importantly—tourist money began to trickle, then flood into the region (Foer 2007; Woodard 2007).

Meanwhile, Osmanagić established a new organization called Archaeological Park: Bosnian Pyramid of the Sun Foundation, a business and administration center supporting research and tourism. By 2008, the foundation supported a team of 35–80, depending on the season, mostly amateurs with an interest in history (ICBP 2008). The foundation's ultimate goal is to get the pyramids listed as a UNESCO world heritage site (Bosnian Pyramid of the Sun Foundation 2009).

Today the team runs fully invasive and extensive excavations in Gornja Vratnica, at Visočica Hill (Pyramid of the Sun) and Plješevica Hill (Pyramid of the Moon). They consistently report new discoveries such as ancient concrete, mysterious artifacts, and other pyramid proofs. Osmanagić and the foundation publish voraciously: anything from scientific reports aimed at a lay audience to tourist brochures that boost business in the region. These contain everything from excited announcements of new evidence to bitter insults toward those who criticize them (Bosnian Pyramid of the Sun Foundation 2009; ICBP 2008). Osmanagić also runs a worldwide lecture circuit, which has included talks at Bosnian embassies (Osmanagić 2007a) and fringe archaeology conferences. He has hosted two sizable international scientific conferences (ICBP 2008) and has made frequent appearances in local schools and on television (ABC 2006).

On the surface, this might seem impressive, except nothing about the Bosnian pyramids is factually true. Most archaeologists agree that Osmanagić's theories are not supported by any evidentiary material found at the site (Bohannon 2006; Rose 2006a). All artifacts found can be explained by other theories; for example, a "pyramid chisel" is likely an Iron Age nail, an orderly "pyramid floor" is probably a fossilized riverbed. The team employed only one reputable archaeologist (who began working on the project thinking his employer was legitimate and then quickly resigned); he says that he found no credible evidence for pyramids during his short time excavating in Visoko. In an interview, he explained: "Nearly everything was fantasy during my time there. Only the burnt stones from the Moon pyramid were real and older than the war . . . about 10% of what was in there was real. The rest was fossils or 'pretty stones'. There was some Neolithic and medieval pottery, a flintlock, an iron knife (presumably medieval) some animals and glass, and 10–20 animal bones, along with some bone fragments" (qtd. in Pruitt 2011:195). More complete accounts of the exact pseudoscience involved at the Bosnian pyramids site can be found in other publications (Pruitt 2011), but suffice it to say that the international archaeological community has been outraged. They particularly criticize the haphazard and destructive methods the team has used. For example, Osmanagić's group has damaged genuine medieval and Iron Age archaeological remains in Visoko during their search for proof of ancient pyramids, causing international outcry (Rose 2006a).

In response to the outcry, the Bosnian Pyramid project has tried to "outsource authority" in order to create a project that *looks* legitimate, even if its science stands on shaky ground. For example, Osmanagić has hired accredited archaeologists to excavate for short periods (Pruitt 2011:195), has sent samples off to accredited radiocarbon laboratories like Oxford and Kiev to be tested (Pruitt 2011:218–229), and has hired accredited professionals to attend conferences so that he could say a large number of Egyptologists and other PhDs attend his lectures (ICBP 2008; Pruitt 2011:171). However, these experts merely "attend" or "show up"; meanwhile, Osmanagić performs pseudoarchaeology based on inaccurate assumptions about the source material, drawing illogical interpretations from the results. By referencing a connection to credible scientific sources and discourses, the Bosnian Pyramid project has outsourced its own accountability and authority; it has used a sprinkling of "scientific" data based in fact but has ultimately taken such data out of context to yield outlandish interpretations. This translation creates a complex web of performance, authority, and accountability. Far from being unique, the Bosnian Pyramid project offers a window into a common activity in many pseudoarchaeological projects, which often rely on outsourcing authority by hiring out and showcasing accredited experts who supposedly support their interpretation (see also the introduction to this volume).

After studying the Bosnian pyramids for nine years (see Pruitt 2011:61–65 for ethnographic methodology), I understand the site as a particularly good example of pseudoarchaeology. As a "classic" case of pseudoarchaeology, the project "invokes the aura of scholarship without being scholarly in fact and blurs the distinction between real scholarship and 'alternative' output" (Jordan 2001:288–289). Unlike simpler cases of pseudoarchaeology,[1] where an alternative archaeological theory may be simply that—alternative and marginal—here the alternative vision of the past has become a preferred account of history for much, if not most, of the Bosnian public. This is something of a *carnival*, à la Mikhail Bakhtin (Jung 1998), where a subaltern vision of science has upstaged archaeology to become the dominant view of the past for the public. Despite vocal objections by archaeologists, this amateur project continues to thrive with continued support from the Bosnian public, media, and government.

Politics and Money

To say that the pyramid phenomenon in postwar Bosnia was an overwhelming success in the mid-2000s would be an understatement. It brought important positive economic changes to the postwar town of Visoko (Foer 2007). Bosnia experienced a great deal of suffering from its civil war in the mid-1990s, and the country has since been divided ethnically and politically, leaving its citizens insecure and its government politically disjointed: "Fears, hatreds, memories, grief for the dead, nostalgia for the lost native places and homes, shattered dreams, insecurity, disappointment, pessimism are continuing to haunt everybody" (Zhelyazkova 2004:17).

In this context, the pyramid project has offered the country a unifying premise; it provides a positive symbol for postwar Bosnian nationalism, promotes an ideology of all-inclusive peacefulness for all ethnoreligious backgrounds, and identifies a time when the region must have been extraordinary because its people built great things. The story of pyramids in Bosnia incorporates the hope of positive international attention after a devastating civil war, as well as the idealistic narrative of a united prehistoric "Bosnian Golden Age."

More practically, much of the enthusiasm behind the pyramid project is related to the tourism money it brings to the region. Thanks to the pyramids, Visoko has already changed dramatically from its dilapidated postwar condition. Before pyramids were announced, the town received around 10,000 visitors a year and had high unemployment rates; afterward, authorities reported that many visitors in a single day and better employment conditions. Tourists brought a flood of new money to the town (Foer 2007). Many politicians realized that the foundation's excavations were controversial and potentially damaging to cultural heritage in the region, yet they continued to approve of the project because of its tourism potential. Asked whether the project should be shut down, former president Haris Silajdzic said, "Let them dig and we'll see what they find. Besides, it's good for business" (qtd. in Harding 2007:44). In 2006, Christian Schwarz-Schilling, a spokesman for the foreign Federation representative in charge of Bosnian Affairs, voiced support for the project, calling it "the world's first victimless pyramid scheme" (Foer 2007).

These ideas have had a profound, if potentially unsustainable, impact on the country as a whole (Pruitt 2011:156–216). The excavations raise questions about sustainability, money, and ethics. As archaeologists, what should our role be in such a situation, especially when we are mostly cultural outsiders facing weighty economic and social forces (see Kohl 2004:299)?

Furthermore, we must ask whether sites of pseudoarchaeology like the Bosnian pyramids can function almost like "subsistence looting" (Yates and Brodie 2012), where members of the public are only surviving each day by making a living off of dubious archaeological activity. If a country allows the destruction of its own archaeological heritage and happily replaces genuine archaeology with a fictional, preferred past—a past that makes more money and gives its citizens a better life—could that fictional archaeology be worth more to its citizens than the original archaeological resource?

Pseudoarchaeology and Performance

When confronted with such a pervasive case of pseudoarchaeology, we must first ask, where does this authority come from? How can pseudoarchaeology be so compelling and contagious? The Bosnian pyramids case involves multiple levels of complex sociopolitical negotiations, representations, and social arenas of support or dissent. Since the sociopolitical and economic issues behind this case study have been thoroughly covered elsewhere (Pruitt 2009, 2011; Woodard 2007), I address the Bosnian pyramids from a more nuanced but no less important angle: that of performance, representation, and theatrics. The performative side of pseudoarchaeology is one of the most important ways alternative claims about the past are developed and spread. In recent years, a great deal of research has addressed why these ideas take hold (e.g., for political reasons, for personal gain, to satisfy a community economic need, etc.), but less has been said in any detail about how pseudoarchaeology actually operates—and in particular, how it performs.

The Role of Media

The media have been the single most important reason that information about the pyramid project has spread so rapidly, allowing a support base to grow. Media interactions between Osmanagić's team and the general public, politicians, and academics have created a complex web of performance, contribution, theatricality, and distribution. Within a national climate of postwar depression and institutional instability, and with the support of lax reporting from media that welcomed an exciting story, the Bosnian pyramids became an overnight success in Bosnia.

Print media coverage of the pyramid scheme began in the fall of 2005, when Bosnia's highest-circulation newspaper, *Dnevni Avaz*, ran a story on Osmanagić's theories. The BBC translated the story and ran with it; then several other international news outlets, such as *USA Today* and *National Geographic*, followed suit (BBC 2006; Cerkez-Robinson 2005; de Pastino 2006). Mark Rose, of the Archaeological Institute of America, wrote in 2006, "The story has swept the media, from the Associated Press and the BBC, from papers and websites in the U.S. to those in India and Australia" (2006a).

Most early reports expressed support for the project. According to Rose, "every major media outlet that initially covered this story got it wrong. It's clearly crackpot stuff, but apparently nobody bothered to check the story" (qtd. in Woodard 2007). As news outlets did begin to check the story, more skeptical reports were released; however, local Bosnian newspapers "don't have science desks. . . . Bosnian archaeologists dismiss the majority of local

Figure 6.1. Locations discussed in chapter 6. Courtesy of Jeb J. Card.

journalists as ill-educated. Hence April's *Avaz* headlines like 'The Pyramid Will Be Visible by the End of the Year'" (Kampschror 2006:27).

Television was perhaps the most influential in spreading supportive information to a wide audience. Woodard reports, "Federation television, the largest Sarajevo-based network, provided extensive coverage, and soon thousands of people were visiting Visoko every day" (2007). Local media stations arranged for "face-offs" between Osmanagić and mainstream archaeologists, and Osmanagić often appeared more fresh and exciting than museum professionals. Internationally, foreign television stations like ABC offered excited programs that "travel[ed] to Bosnia to follow this modern day Indiana Jones" (ABC 2006). To capitalize on his growing fame, Osmanagić traveled around the world to showcase pyramids with Bosnian TV in places like Easter Island, Peru, England, and Jordan, which resulted in a 12-episode documentary that boosted his profile. In the meantime, private groups released independent, professional documentaries about the Bosnian pyramids (Huttinger 2006). Local newspapers relished the attention from foreign press, exaggerating foreign interest: "All local television news shows trumpeted the presence of CNN, AP, Reuters, and the BBC—without mentioning that most outlets covered it as a cute human interest story" (Rose 2006b). With international media attention fueling the local media, excitement and positive press spread the story like fire. Almost overnight, Osmanagić became the mastermind and poster boy of a national sensation (Figure 6.1).

While the project gained momentum primarily through traditional media, scientific opposition was marshaled mainly on the Internet. Rose writes that "one might have thought that the Ice Age Bosnian pyramid story would collapse like a bad soufflé, but no. Mainstream media has become somewhat more critical of stories emanating from Visoko, but much of the real work in dissecting the claims has appeared on blogs and message boards, such as The Hall of Ma'at" (2006b). Websites like In the Hall of Ma'at maintain a general list of articles and forum discussions that dispute alternative history stories for the general public. Katherine Reece, the site developer, says, "I wanted to help those people who were searching for the truth about history to have an easily accessible 'mainstream' counter to these 'alternative' claims" (2006:103). Discussions about the Bosnian pyramids have appeared frequently on her site forum, involving heated and emotional debate about the project's pseudoscience (Reece 2015). Other sites like Irna are blogging websites that frequently release news, information, and arguments against the pyramid project (Irna 2009), highlighting the Internet as the medium of choice for those who oppose the pyramid project.

Inventing Authority, Performing Pyramids

When faced with the question about why the public believes the pseudoarchaeology they see on TV, it is useful to think of the Bosnian pyramids through the blurring of what scholar Barbara Kirschenblatt-Gimblett terms "actualities" and "virtualities" (1995:375). She addresses heritage situations, such as museum reconstructions, when something "virtual" becomes "actual"—when an imagined or reconstructed thing becomes "hyperreal" as it replaces truth in its own right. The "hyperreal" characterizes a viewer's inability to distinguish between the "actual" and the "virtual." For example, if a person sees a television broadcast of a man walking on the moon, then he has only seen a "virtual" image of an "actual" moonwalk. He thinks of the man's walk on the moon as "truth" (and of course it is), but the viewer's reality and understanding actually come from a mélange of facts and information shaped and filtered by the media; thus, his reality is "hyperreal." This is something that the scholar Jean Baudrillard (1988) calls a *simulacrum*, something virtual that becomes truth or replaces truth in its own right.

Media communication (using language, images, and a combination of performance and participation) acts as a medium in which Osmanagić and others collectively create a simulacrum of pyramids for their viewers. Unlike the moonwalk example, however, the Bosnian pyramids case is based more on imagination than fact. This is best explained with an example: a 2006 broadcast about the Bosnian pyramids by the television network ABC Houston. This transcript exemplifies the way the project sustains itself through popular culture, scientific performance, public participation, and national pride, and maintains a simulacrum:

> [*Image appears on-screen: a logo of a pyramid with the text "Houston's Indiana Jones"*]
>
> DESK ANCHOR: Travel to Bosnia to follow this modern day Indiana Jones and his search for Bosnia's great valley of pyramids!
> [*Footage of Osmanagić walking on a hillside, wearing a khaki shirt and an Indiana-Jones hat*] . . .
>
> ANCHOR: You don't know Semir Osmanagić, but to the people of Bosnia, he is a national hero. [*Cut to a scene with school children clapping*]. Congratulated, applauded, and loved wherever he goes. [*Cut to more children presenting Osmanagić a pyramid-shaped cake*]. This is a land which has been torn by war and civil conflict, but resurrected in a way by one man. . . . Indeed, his story, if true, could change the history of the world. . . .
>
> OSMANAGIĆ: All you need to do is disregard the trees, the greenery, the soil, and you will see the object, clearly in your mind. . . .
>
> ANCHOR: Semir used satellite, thermal, and topography analysis on tens of thousands of hills in his search for pyramids. . . . If a person could look back and just visualize this place as you see it, eight thousand, ten thousand years ago, they would see a massive stone city.
>
> OSMANAGIĆ: What they would see would be the most magnificent city ever built on the face of the planet. (ABC 2006)

In this broadcast, Osmanagić and his supportive media have performed a virtual pyramid site onto the landscape in Visoko: the story invites viewers to "disregard" the site as it stands today and supplant it with the ideas Osmanagić has created, asking them to "visualize" a "magnificent city." This evocation of simulacra—images not only of the pyramids but of the supposedly scientific archaeological project that found those pyramids—occurs in four distinct ways, discussed in the following sections.

Self-Representation: Icons and Personalities

First and foremost, Osmanagić represents himself as a romantic adventurer (see Holtorf 2007:64–65). He builds on Indiana Jones iconography: the rough explorer who knows that "anyone is capable of discovery and the non-professional may participate in the grand adventure" (Ascher 1960:402). Osmanagić fully endorses this image, always wearing khaki clothing, looking rugged, and rarely appearing in public without his wide-brimmed fedora. He describes his work with adjectives like "dangerous," "brave," and "mysterious." His tone is dramatic, suggesting "secrets," "mysteries," or "treasures" of the past. In the ABC Houston episode discussed, for example, he is a "living Indiana Jones, [who] travels the world, exploring mysteries" (2006).

Osmanagić offsets this image with two contradictory self-representations: those of the hardworking academic and pop-culture celebrity. He asserts that his time is dedicated "to the intensive research of certain enigmas of the past" involving cultures such as the Maya, Assay, and pre-Illyric cultures in Bosnia, and he has "read 40–50 books a year" (BosnianPyramids.org 2006). But Osmanagić has also been initiated into the artsy, "just plain cool" side of popular culture: the pyramid excavations have been launched with concerts of popular rock groups, fashion shows, and pyramid-themed art installations. He has even appeared in a music video (Hodzic 2007).

Osmanagić also represents himself as a hero-crusader, on a quest for truth, trying to save "little Bosnia." The ABC Houston show, for example, explicitly calls him a "national hero" who will "resurrect" a war-torn country (2006). A humble public servant image is not far behind (see Hamilakis 1999:66–68; Holtorf 2007:91). In one interview, Osmanagić recognizes that he is in the spotlight of his project but says "affirmation of the project on the world wide scene and of course the contact with the media, are all a part of this process. However, I will slowly move away from the center of the attention as more people get involved in various activities" (BosnianPyramids.org 2006). He portrays himself as a dedicated, self-effacing servant: "I was aware in this initial period there would be critics who will publicly or privately, speak out, insult and challenge this vision. That is why I did not want to put anyone else forward, but instead I answered to all provocations with the culture of dialogue and scientific arguments" (BosnianPyramids.org 2006).

With these conflicting personalities, it might seem surprising that Osmanagić has achieved such a successful media image. But he has, for two reasons: the first is that these images are stereotypes, pulled from a collective understanding of what an archaeologist is (from pop-cultural icons like Indiana Jones to academic notions of public servitude and intensive research). The second reason that these multiple personalities work together to create a whole image is because Osmanagić has established one solitary opposite force: the villain. Osmanagić juxtaposes himself against one antagonist, giving his character and project a sense of worth and weight.

Narration of Villain

Garrett Fagan writes of pseudoarchaeology that "there is another powerful storytelling feature in this genre, one usually lacking in good archaeological television: a villain. For many pseudoarchaeology shows, the villain is archaeology itself" (Fagan 2003). Osmanagić has successfully established archaeologists as the villains in his story.

Osmanagić has consistently kept up a performance of a classic hero fighting against the bad guys, saying that "every new idea has oponents [*sic*] in the beginning. The bigger the idea, more aggressive the oponents [*sic*]. But, it does not influence my goals and determination for an inch" (Pruitt 2011:265). Osmanagić and his team disparage professional archaeology as incompetent and lax, exploiting the weakness of a postwar heritage system in Bosnia that has unstable or nonexistent institutions and funding (Kampschror 2006:27; Zhelyazkova 2004:12). He has accused Bosnian archaeologists of "long-time carelessness" and has cited foreign scholars as "clueless about the real situation and state of Bosnian Cultural Heritage" (BosnianPyramids.org 2006).

Osmanagić and his foundation have represented academics as insulting, fearful groups who conspire to attack his higher truth. He directly politicizes and polarizes his academic opponents: "Convinced about their conservative views, [they] promptly attacked the hypothesis and tried to debunk its author. Some of them, showed a typical bosnian [*sic*] propensity, by launching labels and insults from behind the scenes" (Osmanagić 2006). He demeans scientists as afraid, jealous, and small-minded: "Are they afraid about the material evidence that will make collapse [*sic*] their world views?" (Osmanagić 2006); "the trades like geology and archaeology will be the last to accept [the pyramids], because it's a revolution" (qtd. in Foer 2007).

Logos and Branding

Osmanagić and his foundation also use the authority of branding (cf. Holtorf 2007). They do this in several ways, from the promotion of cultural assumptions about foreign academia to the use of brand names and signage. They use media, which by nature "enable marketers to project brands into national consciousness" (Muniz and O'Guinn 2001:413). Osmanagić often mentions that he has been living and working in Houston, Texas. According to some

Bosnians, living and working abroad (especially in powerful Western countries) can be considered an attractive and authoritative feat in its own right (Hadžabdić 2007). Osmanagić also builds his self-image on prevalent pop-cultural icons. His "sort of modern-day Indiana Jones" image is his own personal brand (ABC 2006). Headlines refer to him as "Bosnia's Indiana Jones," "Houston's Indiana Jones," or "Indiana Jones of the Balkans" (ABC 2006; Hawton 2006). This provides drama and gives Osmanagić a look of amateur authority and makes him easily recognizable in media contexts.

As well as branding himself, Osmanagić also seizes every opportunity to promote other people with official political labels or degrees behind their name. Along with encouraging national political sponsorship (Bohannon 2006), Osmanagić and his foundation court professors and students who give an impression of authoritative, scientific presence (Schoch 2007)—an "outsourcing of authority," as mentioned in the first section of this chapter.

Osmanagić's penchant for logos and branding appears most clearly in his foundation's shiny, official-looking logo, which directly echoes the Bosnian national flag. He also attempted to trademark the names of his pyramids and his Bosnian Pyramid of the Sun Foundation (2009). In the town of Visoko, official government signs point toward the pyramids, and an array of formal, authoritative signage marks the site. This obsession with branding creates the feeling of establishment and authority—a point that also emerges in the way Osmanagić represents the site as "scientific."

Scientific Representation

Finally, Osmanagić constructs an *appearance* of methodology by mimicking genuine scientific documentation and the rhythm of scientific language. He moves seamlessly from denigrating elite academics to promoting his own team of elite experts, who carry out intensive and detailed scientific analyses. Osmanagić and his team have carefully manipulated images, language, and camera angles so that their methods appear scientific.

For example, Osmanagić has always argued that he has conducted serious academic work dedicated "to the intensive research of certain enigmas of the past" involving cultures such as the Maya, the Assay, and the pre-Illyric cultures in Bosnia (BosnianPyramids.org 2006). He stresses that his research is an extensive, controlled scientific experiment. In 2007, he released a document called "Scientific Evidence about the Existence of Bosnian Pyramids," which states, "The Archaeological Park Foundation believes that only a multi-disciplinary approach, with serious scientific argumentation on internationally recognized level will yield a successful realization of the Bosnian Pyramid project. The team, therefore, includes not only archaeologists, but also geologists (mineralologists/petrologists, hydrologists, and sedimentologists), geophysicists, paleontologists, speleologists, anthropologists, mining engineers as well as anthropologists. Each one of these experts brings a new element of problem understanding and integrates their qualifications and expertise into the project with a great enthusiasm and collegiality" (Osmanagić 2007b:1). Such language intentionally connects the pyramid project to mainstream scientific work and methodologies. However, these statements are rarely supported with undisputed evidence. They never explain why the project has geologists speaking authoritatively about archaeological remains or why Egyptologists are recruited to speak about the Bosnian Paleolithic.

Osmanagić's "Scientific Evidence" document contains scientific-sounding section titles: "Apparent thermal inertia measurements" and "Geodetic topographic contour analyses." His data, however, are vague generalizations: "geospatial anomalies" exist (Osmanagić 2007b:2); "the sides of [the] Bosnian Pyramid of Sun are exactly aligned with the cardinal sides of the world (north–south, east–west), which is one of the characteristics often noted with the existing pyramids" (Osmanagić 2007b:3). Each data entry has a corresponding image, which at first glance appear to be technical and evidentiary; however, upon inspection, these figures are quickly found to be meaningless, merely topographic maps with red lines drawn haphazardly over them.

The "Scientific Evidence" document illustrates that *what* Osmanagić says is less important than *how* he presents it. This "scientific" format relies heavily on the trust and power vested in scientific presentation standards, a tactic used as much by orthodox science as by alternative or fringe groups (Hodder 1989; Pruitt 2011). Here, the project's documents mimic the language patterns of genuine scientific documents, formatted in a formal, official style. But they do not employ actual evidentiary support or academic argument to back their claims. This gives the project's work a feeling of weight and worth by alluding to established authoritative scientific traditions, establishing authority by performing the imagery of science.

Inventing History

Holtorf and Schadla-Hall (1999:230) write that "it has become a truism that every generation has the past it desires or deserves." This statement also proves true in a narrower sense with the Bosnian Pyramid, where a nation is inventing the past it desires and feels it deserves. Through his faux excavations and scientific-appearing documents, Osmanagić is inventing and constructing the image and physicality of an archaeological park. Through the participation of an eager, avid public on the other end of the media projection, the invented pyramids are actively sustained in a greater public understanding.

For reasons both ideological and economic, the public accepts and actively encourages the notion of pyramids through their continued vocal support and active public discourse about the site. They physically visit the site. They consume products like souvenirs, news, media, and other documents related to the site, and they volunteer in the foundation's ongoing excavations (Pruitt 2009). Through their agency and participation, the public is contributing to the construction and continuation of pyramid pseudoarchaeology at Visoko. This is a process of performative inventing—Osmanagić and his team are inventing a site by performing the roles of amateur archaeologists, but their supportive public also keeps the site alive through their continued participation in and interaction with the project.

Part of performative inventing involves the way Osmanagić and his supporters use "performative language"—the process of saying things that makes things happen—or, specifically in the case of the pyramids, making things exist when they were nonexistent before. In the book *How to Do Things with Words* (1962), J. L. Austin distinguishes between "statements," which are utterances that simply describe something, and "performative language," which is made up of neither true nor false statements but utterances that perform certain kinds of action. When you utter performative language, and the circumstances are appropriate, the language does not describe something but rather *does* something (for instance, saying "I name this ship the *Queen Elizabeth*" in the appropriate circumstances will perform the action as it is said). Although Austin was certainly discussing a narrower class of utterances, the general idea applies to the performances occurring at Visoko. By repeatedly saying that there are pyramids in what appear to be authoritative circumstances, Osmanagić is creating pyramids. By saying on ABC Houston television, for example, that "if a person could look back and just visualize this place as you see it, eight thousand, ten thousand years ago, they would see a massive stone city" (2006), he is uttering performative language. He is not describing the actual remains of this city because they do not exist. Instead, he is inviting his audience to participate with him in visualizing an imaginary city of ancient Bosnia, and the authoritative presence of the media helps make his narrative "actual."

This act of creation is not limited merely to narrative. When visitors approach the Pyramid of the Moon, they find large-scale excavations of monumental steps leading up the mountain. Joshua Foer, who visited the site, exclaims: "Suddenly it dawns on me—and I'm shocked that it has taken me so long to figure this out—that Osmanagić is *carving* pyramids out of these pyramid-shaped hills" (2007, emphasis added). Osmanagić's team is actually chipping away at the mountainside with their trowels until it physically resembles pyramid steps.

This project is also sustained through participatory inventing. As previous studies have illuminated in much more depth (Pruitt 2009; Rose 2006a; Woodard 2007), the pyramid scheme is deeply ingrained in national and ethnic Bosnian history. A variety of interest groups have attached different values and meanings to the site. Eric Hobsbawm writes: "'Invented traditions' have significant social and political functions, and would neither come into existence nor establish themselves if they could not acquire them . . . the most successful examples of manipulation are those which exploit practices which clearly meet a felt—not necessarily a clearly understood—need among particular bodies of people" (1983:307). Such a need for pyramids clearly exhibits itself at Visoko. Osmanagić's pyramid site satisfies specific sociopolitical needs. It offers a world-class monument that outstands and outsizes every other major national monument in the world, right there in "little Bosnia," opening up profound economic and ideological opportunities for a postwar country.

Participation from a supportive audience allows his ideas to gain momentum and security. Osmanagić presents his simulacrum, his "virtual" story that overlays the "actual" truth—but it is only through an observer's acceptance and participation in this vision that the site comes to fruition. In the past, the impact of the media on the spread of information and public consumption was thought to occur in a linear progression: message production, transmission, and reception, with one entity creating and transmitting a message that another entity passively received. This notion has been challenged in the past decade, and media have been "examined not so much as definers of 'reality,' but as dynamic sites of struggle over representation, and complex spaces in which subjectivities are constructed and identities are contested" (Spitulnik 1993:296).

This sense of dynamic message construction and participation has also arisen in museum literature. For example, in a discussion of museum exhibitions, Baxandall rehashes the common paradigm in the museum world where three active agents are involved in exhibitions: the maker of the artifact, the exhibitor, and the viewer (1991:36–37). A museum exhibition has meaning through the dynamic participation of all three agents. The situation in Visoko can be seen as an interplay of analogous agents: Osmanagić and his foundation (the producer/makers), the media (transmitter/exhibitor), and the public (viewers/audience). The participatory role of the media and, especially, the public is what has helped invent the project and keep it alive. This active, participatory inventing is exemplified by a local business owner's statement to a visiting journalist: "If they don't find the pyramid, we're going to make it during the night. But we're not even thinking about that. There *are* pyramids and there *will be* pyramids" (Foer 2007, emphasis in original). This is exactly what the participating public, media, and Osmanagić are doing: constructing pyramids through their participation.

Conclusion

The obvious thing for an archaeologist to do when confronted with the Bosnian pyramids is to decry, "This is pseudoscience!" However, our inquiry should be pursued further. The pyramid project presents its public audience with a choice: believe a mundane truth or participate in an extraordinary story of national exceptionalism. Most academics will choose the cold truth, but choosing otherwise does not signify pure ignorance. The Bosnian public wants these pyramids. They have an economic and emotional stake in keeping the story alive. How does the sterile truth of an unremarkable hill with an unremarkable past make their daily lives better?

We are left with more questions than answers. As archaeologists, should it be our job to "put a stop" to this? Perhaps so, as our mission is to tell the true story of the past. However, I wonder whether we can do this without alienating a public that seems to be finding meaning—and money—in pseudoarchaeology. As others have noted, "interpreters and archaeologists may find it difficult to communicate and agree on what the public 'should' appreciate, and what that public is likely to retain" (Baram and Rowan 2004:19). Despite the difficulty, this is arguably one of our central duties: to understand what interests the public and why it interests them, and to communicate to ourselves and the public what we think is appreciable or why we believe a site is misleading or troubling.

The real lesson of the Bosnian pyramids is that archaeologists need to pay attention not just to the what of pseudoscience but to the why and the how. Our active engagement with the details of how a site is constructed and operates may give us more direction and may help us answer some of the more tricky questions about archaeological stewardship.

Notes

1. I use "pseudoarchaeology" and "alternative archaeology" interchangeably as they are intricately connected.

II

How Archaeologists Should or Should Not Engage with Pseudoarchaeology

7
The Central Australian Face

A Study of Archaeological Responses to a Pseudoarchaeological Claim

DENIS GOJAK

On February 18, 2010, an email was sent from Australia to 120 media outlets and academic archaeologists around the world. It announced the discovery of a gigantic terrain feature in central Australia. Clicking the hyperlink embedded in the email opened a digital map showing an unblinking oval face, clearly distinct from the rugged landscape around it. The sender of the email believed that it was artificially created, although he did not say by whom, or what, and said that he intended to visit and explore the remote site. He was not asking for help or confirmation. It was an announcement of his claim as discoverer. No other information was provided in the email.

This type of contact will be familiar to many archaeologists. Out of the blue an email, or letter, or phone call arrives asking about some old or unusual object. Soon enough it becomes apparent that the object is nothing out of the ordinary, but when the inquirer is told that, he sees it differently: "It can't be just a lump of stone! Look, it fits my hand perfectly." "A cousin's sure he's seen the same things in museums or on a cable show." Soon enough he dismisses the freely offered archaeological opinion initially asked for and seems to become even more convinced that his first inclinations were correct, and the experts be damned. In many instances it seems as though he was not asking for an opinion at all—he just wanted confirmation of this. Because you are supposedly an "expert," then either you are not really that good or you are just possibly up to something.

Most public interactions do not have this frustrating end, but a small, significant portion do, and they are all memorable and usually bewildering at the time. Belief in the face of evidence and expert opinion to the contrary is not that unusual in society as analysis of any major social or economic debate will show (e.g., Knight 2013 on climate change; Pigliucci 2002 on evolution). The ability to contest expert or authoritative positions is a fundamental precept of democracy, but usually it does not end in the ugliness as when dealing with pseudoarchaeological claims. The key thing that distinguishes these interactions from genuine public inquiries, which may also involve a misidentified lump of rock, is the unwillingness of the discoverer to change his mind when a more parsimonious explanation is offered. At the same time as there is a rejection of the advice there is also an (almost magical) transfer of onus of proof from the finder to the expert. As the finder is usually the only audience, this becomes a matter of the expert becoming more exasperated as he attempts to convince the no-longer-listening inquirer. It is no surprise, then, that after a few of these incidents archaeologists feel they are wasting their time and seek to actively avoid such encounters. But will this strategy work?

When I was young, Erich von Däniken's *Chariots of the Gods?* (1969) was launched in its first English-language edition to a great reception. As someone even then interested in ancient archaeology it was a fascinating and magical introduction to a range of mysteries around the world and inspired me to read what I later came to know as the classics of our profession. However, as I read more, growing more critical in my thinking, I became skeptical about Von Däniken and eventually reached the point where none of his claims had more traction than the factual alternative. I always wondered whether his success was because of the story. The alien input to Earth's early human history certainly seemed cool to this 10-year-old; it hit the zeitgeist of the late 1960s, its questioning of authority and orthodoxy allied to a well-oiled publicity machine, already trialed in Germany and now aiming for the vastly bigger English-language market, seemed compelling at the time and unchallenged (Krassa 1978). Later, as an archaeologist, I wondered whether its message resonated so well was because I heard almost no countercommentaries from archaeologists. In fact there were, but they were pretty low key and very reactive (Rathje 1978; Story 1976; Thiering and Castle 1972; White 1974).

Something similar took place with the theories of Immanuel Velikovsky, Von Däniken's precursor in terms of sensationalist maverick ideas contrary to the establishment, which ultimately involved rewriting planetary physics and the chronology of ancient literate civilization. His books were a popular sensation, best sellers that captured the public imagination but had academics seething. Although Velikovsky claimed to rewrite ancient history to provide a consistent alternate account that required wholesale revision of chronologies of many cultures, the debate was largely taken up by the astronomical community, with archaeologists and historians almost invisible in the response (Bauer 1984; Gordin 2012).

Despite a considerable literature examining pseudoarchaeological claims from both archaeological and advocate perspectives, little attention has been given to how such claims emerge from the initial observation and develop an audience. There is no commentary that seeks to identify the factors that result in many sinking without trace, while a select few like the claims of Von Däniken gain major popularity. Within other disciplines there are now a number of careful examinations of the emergence of particular pseudo-scientific claims. Both Gordin (2012), examining the work of Immanuel Velikovsky, and Wertheim, who looked at advocates in unorthodox physics (2011), focus not only on the proponents, and whatever background they have and their inspiration, but also the reception that they received from professional and disciplinary audiences and the public, as well as how effective this dialogue was in tempering their claims' reception.

Could a more concerted, better-promoted response from archaeologists have challenged Velikovsky and Von Däniken so that their particular take on the human past did not gain traction? Would it have been a vacuum into which other equally appealing pseudoarchaeological ideas could have been embedded, or would academic archaeology have flourished, extending the glory days of a narrowly defined, academy-based, largely masculine and WASPish culture into the 1970s and beyond? Unfortunately we cannot crystal ball such answers. However, we can begin to explore the dynamics of the dialogue between archaeology as a discipline and pseudoarchaeology as a construct. Some elements of this dialogue can be carried out differently, so that archaeology's message is both better targeted and better heard.

No systematic information has been collected on how archaeologists manage the initial approaches made by members of the public and whether this influences the eventual outcome of the inquiry, particularly whether it results in acceptance of expert opinion or its rejection. What is apparent is that the Internet's impact on communication between the public and professionals is growing.

There is no information from within archaeology about how public inquiries that could be either straightforward or contentious are managed, and particularly whether it makes a difference in how recipients respond to those claims. The Central Australian Face email provides an opportunity to track such a claim from its beginning and to follow the path of its announcement and the reaction to it from the academic community and news media in detail. This allows an examination of how specific claims were addressed by those contacted and maps the process by which such a claim may develop into something pseudoarchaeological. The often hostile dialogue between archaeologists and pseudoarchaeologists is normally only documented in retrospect and therefore lacks the immediacy and awareness of contextualization of individual responses and reactions to the claims that may shape the later relationship between the parties.

At a professional level there is no consensus about how archaeology should respond or whether there is greater benefit in challenging claims or ignoring them. In fact there is still a discussion worth having about whether the collective actions of archaeology constitute the archaeological response. Although this is a much larger question, the evidence presented in this chapter suggests that the two are and should remain conceptually different. Therefore this discussion is explicitly about archaeologists and leaves to others the question of collective responses across the profession.

If only part of the discipline responds and the rest ignores such claims, which prevails? A detailed analysis of how the Central Australian Face claim unfolded identifies how part of the Australian professional community reacted and the way that this influenced the progress of the claim. This analysis also shows that there are both preconceptions and misconceptions that shape how archaeologists will react to such claims. Awareness of this is important if the broader profession is to adequately deal with the public, regardless of what it is asking. Ultimately the profession has to be able to understand and manage public interactions sufficiently to maximize positive outcomes and minimize negative or unhelpful results.

The remainder of this chapter assesses the Central Australian Face email and its validity and how it relates to other claims made for artificial terrain features, and then it examines how the email was handled by the recipients. The academic responses are examined in detail and provide new information on the management of pseudoarchaeological claims within a professional context. The final part of the chapter asks whether archaeologists' responses are effective in managing pseudoarchaeological claims and how archaeology as a discipline may position itself to better manage this aspect of public advocacy. Although targeted by the mass email, the media are largely absent from this discussion. They did not bite at the email, and barely at the follow-up survey.

The Initial Claim

The Central Australian Face email was sent out on February 18, 2010, at 4:14 p.m. Australian Eastern Summer Time by Phillip Mitchell (a pseudonym) to 120 recipients. Under the subject line "New discovery—Archaeological—Australia" there is a brief message, reproduced here:

> Dear Sir/Madam,
>
> Below you will see a link to a satellite image which clearly shows a large artificial landmark in Northern Territory Australia—
> http://maps.bonzle.com/c/a?a=p&x=129.304305798085&y=-25.9097658110046&w=5000&h=5000&i=554&j=554&p=11736&pp=11736&fc=1&wnb=78326727#map
>
> This is my discovery. I was hoping to get permission from the Central Land Council to gain access to the site. I believe that this site could have significance to human history and should be researched and protected.
>
> Phillip Mitchell

Apart from the hyperlink, there was no additional information or any further emails relating to the claim.

Analysis of the Message

The Image

Opening the link revealed a segment of a map based around a terrain model on the Bonzle.com travel information site, with the title "Map of Kalitjukara." The only named geographical feature visible was Mount Samuel. At its center was an elliptical smooth-featured feature, distinct from the broken country around it, oriented with its long axis running north–south. The direction of light from the top right of the frame creates shadows—or, more correctly, digital processing creates the illusion of three-dimensionality, which gives the overall appearance of a face: two eyes, the peak of a nose, and a slightly lopsided mouth.

The exact location was easily found by zooming out the map until other named landmarks appeared. The face feature is located in the southwestern corner of Australia's Northern Territory, about 25 km from Surveyor General's Corner (the Northern Territory–South Australia–Western Australia border junction), at latitude 25° 54' 29.59" S longitude 129° 18' 17.57" E. It is situated on land controlled by the Central Land Council, an Aboriginal corporation, as was correctly noted by Mitchell. The nearest settlement is the small town of Kaltukatjara, formerly Docker River, about 65 km north. Uluru Resort is about 200 km northeast. Once identified, the same location was easily relocated on Google Maps, a process that took me less than five minutes from first opening the email.

The knoll is a substantial feature, measuring approximately 750 m east–west by 950 m north–south and is clearly distinct from higher ground to the north, east, and south and level plain to the west. It is also partly framed by two drainage lines. The map itself is not a satellite image but a modeled surface derived from digital terrain information using shadowing to indicate three-dimensional topography. The website host, Bonzle.com, is an Australian-based outdoor travel website featuring maps, photographs, and place information. Bonzle creates its "Digital Atlas of Australia" using licensed Geoscience Australia digital data, based on 1:250,000 national map coverage (Digital Atlas Pty Ltd 2010).

Comparing what is shown on Bonzle with the same location in Google Maps presents a completely different appearance. The face is no longer a discrete knoll but part of a large elevated area extending eastward beyond the presumed margin of the face. While in closer detail a series of uneven dips and bumps can be seen, none forms the sharp shadowed facial features seen in the Bonzle image. An aerial view shows a rocky knoll with steep rock outcrops on the southern margin and deeply incised drainage lines on the north and west. Apart from these features the remainder of the knoll is naturally shaped with no indication of terrain modification, roads, mining, or other cultural activity. The contour lines make it clear that, rather than being a symmetrical mound with the highest point along the midline, the face rises steadily toward the east so that the vertical difference between the western and eastern eyes, which should be level, is about 30 m.

Geologically the knoll is near the western end of the Mann Range and is likely part of the Pre-Cambrian Musgrave-Mann Metamorphic formation, rising above Quaternary alluvium on its southern and western margins (Forman 1972). It lies within the traditional territory of the Pitjantjatjara-speaking Anangu people of Central Australia. Because of its remoteness this area was not visited by Europeans until Giles's 1872 expedition. Sporadic prospecting and exploration parties made their way through this area, searching for gold from the late nineteenth century onward. Following the lonely death of prospector Harold Lassetter, and the publicizing of his claim that he had found a vast gold reef, as many as 50 private prospecting parties also came into the area during the 1930s alone (Smith 2005:fns 141, 234, quoting Terry and Gara, respectively). One of the few Europeans known to have made multiple trips was Michael Terry, who traversed this area by camel and motor vehicle in the late 1920s and 1930s as an expedition leader and guide for such prospecting parties. In the early 1960s Terry would become a strong advocate for otherwise undocumented Egyptian and Greek landing in Australia, but as far as can be ascertained he made no significant observations about the region at this time (Barnard 1987; Terry 1974).

Although the email only referred to "a large artificial landmark," the map link was centered on the face image. The lack of locational context and scale assists in allowing the face to be identified among the other landforms. No information was collected from email recipients on whether they immediately recognized that the face was the subject of the email, but incidental remarks make it clear that it was readily seen by those who opened the link.

The recognition that this natural feature resembles a face is a cognitive response known as *pareidolia* (from ancient Greek, literally "a mistaken image"). Seeing faces or shapes in clouds, geological formations, or even burnt toast is a normal function of the brain seeking to find patterning in random or unstructured data. It is understood as a fundamental neurological process that has obvious evolutionary advantages (Hadjikhani et al. 2009; Reed 1972). However, even the very young recognize that resemblance is usually entirely coincidental and implies nothing about the nature of the object. In situations when the viewer argues in the reality of such images, or sees significance in the resemblance beyond coincidence arising from random patterning, then such reasoning is often referred to as magical thinking. Examples would include interpreting such faces as being expressions of divine presence, reflecting the operation of otherwise unknown processes, or being generated by stimuli from the viewer. Magical thinking is generally well correlated with many other aspects of belief in the paranormal, although it remains unclear whether it is causative (Riekki et al. 2013; Zusne and Jones 1982).

Although many toponyms around the Earth reflect how geographical features resemble things to a vast range of cultures, perhaps the best-known example of *pareidolia* is the phenomenon commonly called the Face on Mars. In July 1976 the Mars exploration satellite *Viking* took photos of the Cydonia area in Mars's northern hemisphere. In 1979 the first suggestion appeared that a large Martian mountain had been sculpted into a face, and the following year DiPietro and Molenaar presented a paper to the American Astronomical Society on the claim (Carlotto 1997). Their paper discussed the potential of image enhancement techniques to generate additional pictorial and topological data that would test whether the face was natural or artificially created. The paper introduced the general public to the Face on Mars theory, which claimed that it was a deliberate modification of a natural terrain feature to represent a Martian face and was evidence of the existence of an advanced civilization on the planet. The skeptical position was that it was entirely a fortuitous combination of natural unmodified landforms, shadows, and human imagination (McDaniel and Paxson 1998).

A number of subsequent Martian exploratory missions added more general information on the object, without providing any conclusive evidence in support of either position. Researchers sought different ways to improve the quality of the digital images of the face and other features that appeared to be pyramids or artificial landforms in the same region. It was only in 1998 when NASA undertook a detailed photographic survey with an average pixel size of 4.3 m that most of the previous supporters of the Face on Mars theory accepted that it was a natural landform. The remainder, however, argued that the data were deliberately falsified by NASA (Matthews 2002; McDaniel and Paxson 1998).

The face image identified by Mitchell in Central Australia does not withstand close analysis. Although the Bonzle projection appears to show a face, there is no such resemblance in the comparable and readily accessible Google Earth terrain model or in independently produced government air photo coverage. The detailed topography also is inconsistent with an attempt to achieve bilateral symmetry, which would be required. It is entirely the result of a chance combination of digital modeling and terrain data produced by a particular company and not present in other images. Mitchell clearly saw a face on the screen, as have almost all people who have been asked to view the image since then. There is no doubt that this perception can be achieved by all observers, but it is the meaning assigned to it that places it in the category of pseudoarchaeology.

Authorship

Is it a genuine email or a hoax? Is Phillip Mitchell real? How can we tell?

Hoaxes with malicious intent, for personal amusement, or to demonstrate a valid point about critical processes of evaluation are all well-known in science, and archaeology has contributed Piltdown Man as one of the most enduring and celebrated examples. Most hoaxes aim to test the idea that the experts do not necessarily know as much as they think they do, and any new discovery claim should at least consider the prospect that a hoax is at play (e.g., Schnabel 1994).

The status of Mitchell as a real individual cannot be independently confirmed from his initial email. His Internet service provider operates mainly in Queensland and the Northern Territory, which is consistent with his interest in the find area and awareness that permission was required from the Central Land Council to access the site. Despite my attempts at the time, Mitchell never responded to a request to take part in further discussion. My emails have remained unanswered for more than five years. However, one original academic recipient of Mitchell's email who replied to him did receive a response from Mitchell. This individual specifically raised the issue of the similarity of Mitchell's claim to the Cydonia Face on Mars and its status as a *pareidolia* effect. The academic received a response that suggested Mitchell is a genuinely motivated individual who was aware of commentary on the Martian face. In responding to my survey (which I will discuss shortly) two academics also thought it prudent to explicitly ask whether

I was also Phillip Mitchell. For the record, I am not, and I had no role in sending out the email.

The potential remains for Mitchell to be either an alias or a fiction, designed to elicit a particular response from academics and the media. However, it is likely that he is a real person and has reflected on the responses he received and withdrawn his claim or at least not raised it again.

The Recipients

The 120 recipients of the email were mostly academic archaeologists and historians in Australian, British, or American universities; the remainder were news media organizations and contacts. Australian addresses predominated among the recipients (59.2 percent of total) and include both academic and media addresses. No national, state, or territory heritage or conservation agencies or Aboriginal cultural organizations are represented and neither are any consultant archaeological practitioners. There were no Central Australia–based recipients in any category. Although it remains uncertain, this analysis assumes that there were no blind copies included in the total distribution.

A breakdown by category is presented in Table 7.1. Australian academic recipients make up nearly half of the total at 48.3 percent, with the next largest category being internationally based news media organizations.

Of the Australian recipients approximately a quarter of the university contacts are either general departmental or nonteaching staff email addresses, as well as two students identified as archaeological society contacts, whose emails are listed in the online departmental directories with the academic staff. The mixing of academic and other addresses suggests that they were gathered without close attention to recipient details or a clear understanding of roles within tertiary institutions.

The international academics also do not appear to have been systematically selected for any particular connection to Australia or the site. They include historians of religion and medieval Europe and China-focused archaeologists, but none of the considerable number who may have relevant experience in Australia. Also unrepresented are archaeologists who figure in the study of pseudoarchaeological issues, such as Kenneth Feder and Garrett Fagan, both authors of major critiques of pseudoarchaeology, or an archaeologist such as Alice B. Kehoe, who would be seen as sympathetic to some claims not supported by the profession generally (e.g., Fagan 2006b; Feder 2014; Kehoe 2008). No potential researchers in other relevant fields, such as anthropology, astrobiology, geography, or geophysics, were included. Overall, there is a strong sense that both Australian and international academic contacts were put together through a fairly haphazard Internet surfing process.

Table 7.1. Recipients of Initial Email, by Category

	Category		*Number of email recipients*	*Category total (%)*
AUSTRALIAN	*Academic*		58	48.3
		Academic staff	45	
		Departmental	13	
	News media		13	10.8
		Media officers	8	
		News agency	4	
		Online news	1	
		Newspapers	0	
OVERSEAS	*Academic*		21	17.5
		Academic staff	20	
		Departmental	1	
	News media		28	23.3
		Media officers	0	
		News agency	3	
		Online news	14	
		Newspapers	11	
	Total		*120*	*100*

Note: The Australian universities represented are Australian National University (3 recipient addresses), Flinders (12), La Trobe (18), Sydney (14), University of Western Australia (10), and University of Wollongong (1). The international universities represented are Harvard (4), Oxford (14), and Yale (3).

The categorization of the 41 news media contacts (both Australian and overseas) is more complex than it is for the academics. One distinct subgrouping is eight University of Sydney media officers, who are all listed on the same web page and who were each contacted with the claim. Apart from these the remainder were a combination of traditional newspapers, television news programs, exclusively online sites, and news agencies, although this categorization is problematic, simply because the Internet has blurred once-clear distinctions between ways of delivering news (e.g., Küng et al. 2008). Therefore, the breakdown in Table 7.1 is only indicative on the relative frequency of the different media types contacted.

There also seems to be no systematic approach to the way in which the media were contacted. As shown in Table 7.2 some newspapers of national standing received the email, but no Australian broadsheets did. Multiple

Table 7.2. Media Organizations That Received the Initial Email

International media	*Number of emails sent*	*Australian media*	*Number of emails sent*
CBS News	3	Australian Associated Press	4
Fox News	1	Crikey.com	1
Hindustan Times	1	Sydney University Media Unit	8
Jornal Copacabana	1		
Los Angeles Times	3		
Manchester Evening News	2		
MSNBC/NBC UNI	6		
New York Times	3		
News Limited	2		
Newsweek	1		
Rense.com	1		
Stranger [Seattle]	1		
Times [London]	1		
Washington Post	1		

messages were sent to local offices of the Australian Associated Press, an independent news agency, and News Limited, the umbrella for a range of media interests including the *Australian* newspaper. The only Australian online news site that received the email was Crikey.com. Many international television and radio news programs, however, received the letter. The eclectic nature of the sites chosen is demonstrated by the inclusion of the *Stranger*, a free Seattle street-press magazine, and *Jornal Copacabana*, a small English-language Brazilian tourist paper.

Perhaps the most likely media outlet to have published Mitchell's claim is Rense.com, a website for the controversial American radio broadcaster Jeff Rense, which has a strong focus on UFOs, conspiracy theory, and anti-Semitism in its content (see Ballinger 2011). However, nothing relating to the Central Australian Face has appeared on any of the media organizations contacted by Mitchell.

Responses to the Email

Survey Rationale

One of the original recipients forwarded Mitchell's email to me because it seemed to relate to my interest in the politics of archaeology and pseudo-archaeology. After reading it and verifying the location through Google Maps, I sent copies of the Google and Bonzle images compared side by side on the same page to Mitchell, with a comment to the effect that the image was not present in the higher-resolution coverage and was better explained as a *pareidolia* effect. I never received a response from Mitchell.

On further reflection, Mitchell's claim clearly provided an opportunity to explore in more detail how other professional archaeologists had reacted. All addressees of the initial email were known, and their response to receiving it and reacting to it could effectively be documented in real time. This had the potential to map how a typical pseudoarchaeological claim was received and responded to by a broad range of archaeologists and media organizations. Although there have been many studies of pseudoarchaeological claims (see references in Fagan 2006a; Feder 2014; Williams 1991), they only present general information on the early stages of their dissemination and without any detail as to why archaeologists make a decision to ignore or oppose a claim and to what purpose.

It remains an open question as to whether challenging or ignoring a claim will be more effective in preventing its propagation. The argument against a response is that any recognition adds legitimacy to the claim, reinforces the credibility of the claimant, wastes professional time, and is likely to mire the professional in further futile interaction. The opposing position argues that refutation of the evidence and arguments can work, especially when claims are modest and have not gained "traction" by broader exposure.

The Survey

I sent an email to all 120 of the addressees of the original email from Mitchell in late February–early March 2010 requesting that they answer a few simple questions. Nonrespondents were sent a reminder and the collection of data was closed off two weeks after the reminder. In total 30 addressees, a quarter of the total, responded. Most survey responses came within 48 hours while the final person contacted responded after returning from fieldwork three months later. The email asked the recipients a number of questions designed to find out their response to Mitchell's email in particular and more generally how they handled contacts from pseudoarchaeology advocates. The following section provides a commentary on the responses received. Table 7.3 lists the number and percentages of responses by category.

News Media Responses

Only two responses were received from media organizations—one from an Australian news agency and one from an international newspaper. Because of the low response rate, all of the media organizations were subsequently monitored to the end of 2011 to see if they aired the story, but it appears that none did (no social media or news service did either).

Table 7.3 Responses to Survey Questionnaire within Each Contact Category

	Category		Email recipients (No.)	Survey responses (No.)	Response within category (%)
AUSTRALIAN	*Academic*				
		Academic staff	45	25	55.5
		Departmental	13	1	7.7
	News media				
		Media officers	8	0	0
		News agency	4	1	25
		Online news	1	0	0
		Newspaper	0	0	0
INTERNATIONAL	*Academic*				
		Academic staff	20	2	10
		Departmental	1	0	0
	News media				
		Media officers	0	0	0
		News agency	3	0	0
		Online news	14	0	0
		Newspaper	11	1	9
	Totals		*120*	*30*	*25*

It is not clear whether any of the media organizations opened or read the original email. Both media responses to the questionnaire reported deleting it immediately. The lack of response from media organizations to Mitchell's email is understandable given that it needed to stand out from the large quantity of unsolicited material received by these contact points daily. A journalist for the Sydney-based news agency wrote, "We get thousands of emails a day and have a nanosecond to decide whether to action them." The same journalist also noted that messages from individuals, containing links that needed to be opened or are poorly worded, receive much less attention than those with a recognizable institutional affiliation, relevant images embedded rather than linked, and a clear statement of what they are proposing.

The story's apparent newsworthiness would also have restricted media interest. The likely risk, given the evidence presented, was that the story would not go anywhere versus the considerable effort implied in following it up and researching and reporting it. Arguably, the sector of the media least likely to be interested in such claims because of their irrelevance to their audience profile would be general news desks, major newspapers, and television programs. A greater likelihood of being chosen for publication may have resulted from picking regional magazines, those focusing on alternative news interest, or those that rework privately generated material without independent fact-checking.

Academic Responses

In my survey, the recipients of Mitchell's email were asked a number of questions to map out how they responded to the email. There were 27 responses containing quantifiable information from academic staff and one student listed as an archaeology society contact. The first four questions asked whether they remembered receiving the email, what they did with it, and whether they replied to Mitchell. The results are discussed below.

1. Do you remember receiving and reading Mr. Mitchell's email when it arrived?
2. Did you open the link or was the email text sufficient to give you an idea about what he was proposing?
3. What did you do with the email [e.g., deleted it, passed it on to friends or colleagues, saved it for considered response, etc.]?
4. Did you reply to Mr. Mitchell at all? If so, with what purpose and what did you say?
5. Over the past 12 months how many similar email contacts regarding pseudoarchaeological topics have you received, either directly or forwarded by others?
6. In general terms do you think there is any benefit to responding to such contacts from the public? Should a response come from individual archaeologists who have been contacted or a centralized point such as a national archaeological society or the relevant state heritage agency?
7. Is a response from an archaeological professional more likely to change people's minds about their belief or entrench their opinion? Is this based on your own previous experience?
   Separately to this contact would you be interested in receiving a more detailed questionnaire on archaeological responses to pseudoarchaeology, once this has been developed?

Tertiary institution staff contacted by Mitchell ranged across the teaching spectrum from professors to contract lecturers. The only survey response received from departmental addresses came from the student representative. There was some difference in the response rate by different institutions, with Australian universities ranging from 0 to 66 percent (average 39.5 percent) and overseas institutions averaging 9.2 percent. There may have been a distortion in the Australian numbers as a result of the survey email going out at the start of the academic year when a large number of the addressees were still on leave or away doing fieldwork.

Both of the international academic respondents asked me whether I had written the first email in order to elicit a response. No Australian researchers made similar suggestions or otherwise indicated that they thought there was an element of hoaxing to the authorship. I know many of the Australian respondents and they may have not felt it appropriate to venture the idea of a hoax.

Managing the Email

Most recipients (24 or 88.9 percent) remember receiving the email, although two qualified this by saying they only vaguely remembered it. Three recipients did not remember the email at all, and one of those is certain that he did not receive it. No information was collected about what could be called the email environment, the total number of emails that land in each day's inbox, the effectiveness of spam filters in culling these, or the relative number of unsolicited contacts through email.

Fourteen recipients (51.9 percent) remembered opening the link, while the remainder who remember reading the email did not open the link. Stated reasons for not proceeding with the link included that the text of the email allowed them to make up their mind about it. Two of these mentioned the words "nutter" and "out there," but the overall tone of responses in this category is that they were simply too busy and the subject of the email was irrelevant to them. One reply also expressed concern about possible computer viruses.

One who opened the link did so because "morbid curiosity got the better of me." Another with a government agency background opened the link on the basis that "having received similar emails in the past from the public with legitimate information," she felt obliged to at least see where the link led.

Only two responses mentioned any similarity to the Face on Mars phenomenon. This is not surprising as my request for information specifically asked about the recipient's management of the email and asked them to set aside any commentary on the merits of the claim.

Twenty-one recipients reported deleting the email and five said they saved it. Three of those who saved it specifically mentioned keeping it for possible teaching use. As noted, one of the latter passed it on to me because of its relevance to my research. One also used the locational information to relocate the image on Google Earth as I did.

Only one academic—an Australian professor—responded to Mitchell, specifically mentioning the Face on Mars and NASA's evidence rebutting its artificial origin. Mitchell wrote back "claiming the NASA analysis was not valid." This tells us several things. First, it is the only indication that Mitchell is likely to be a real believer rather than a hoaxer. Second, it shows that he is aware of at least some of the commentary about the Face on Mars and the argument that it is likely to be naturally caused. His use of the term "artificial landmark" suggests that he has been influenced by the Face on Mars commentary, which may have also directed the way that he recognized the Central Australian Face and interpreted it as being of "significance to human history." The ambiguous wording also leaves open the possibility of a nonhuman, that is, extraterrestrial, origin for the Central Australian Face.

In summary, while most of the recipients of the original email remembered receiving it, only about half read it and explored the link. The remainder deleted it without opening the email or without clicking on the link. The tone of the email and the lack of information within the body of the text seem to have been a strong disincentive to many of the recipients. Only a small proportion saved the email, mainly as a possible teaching tool and only one replied to the sender, receiving a negative response. If this is representative of the entire group of email recipients, then it is likely that Mitchell received only one or two replies to his email deluge from a community of 65 academics who were personally contacted, plus another from me.

It is somewhat surprising that the email was not forwarded to more people. There is a vigorous tradition of passing on funny or unusual emails in most workplaces; I remember this occurring in pre-email days as well as with correspondence or news clippings dealing with pseudoarchaeological claims received in government departments being photocopied and posted to colleagues with requests for "immediate action by your agency" (e.g., Seal 1989 on office faxlore).

Dealing with Pseudoarchaeological Claims

Additional questions in the survey asked more generally how many similar claims the addressees each received in a year, how they responded to them in principle, and, importantly, whether they thought that a response by archaeologists was useful as a way of correcting pseudoarchaeological claims. Related to this, the email recipients were asked whether the responsibility for dealing with pseudoarchaeological claims was with the individual contacted, their institution, or another group.

Respondents were asked how many similar email contacts they had received over the previous 12 months, either directly or forwarded by others. The results were not reliably quantifiable into an average as many respondents replied in general terms. Eight respondents reported receiving none over the previous year, while 13 recipients received between one and five over a year. This includes replies of "not many," "maybe 2 or 3," and "a few." Three recipients estimated that they received about six per annum. Of this group, a maritime archaeologist received many emails relating to the Mahogany Ship claims and another received a regular stream of emails from a specific individual obsessed with African American history.

Overall the trend is for academic recipients to get one to three per annum, but the range varies from zero to six. The results indicate that email contacts regarding pseudoarchaeological claims are still very few in number, despite the ease with which they can be sent to multiple addressees. Although it is not strongly brought out by the data, there is some indication from those who receive large numbers of emails about pseudoarchaeological claims that they may have attracted attention to themselves through their role as a spokesperson about a particular pseudoarchaeological phenomenon, such as the Mahogany Ship, or they may have encouraged a particular enthusiast to think of them as a ready audience for their ideas. This concern about being drawn into further unfruitful or vexatious contact was also apparent in replies to later questions.

Addressees were asked whether there was any benefit to responding to such contacts from the public. The majority response was in the affirmative. There were 10 definite and 2 qualified "no" responses, as opposed to 8 definite and a further 8 qualified "yes" responses. Many of the affirmative responses were also apologia, giving reasons why they wanted to respond but had not in this case. There were also two nonresponses on this question. This is consistent with the earlier observation that only one of the 30 people who provided information to me actually replied to Mitchell and emphasizes the difference between what respondents thought should be done and their actual conduct.

The reasons cited in support of not responding were varied but included:

- it was a waste of time as the information would be ignored and the claim unchanged, as such claimants are unlikely to change their minds;
- "the world is full of crazy people" and other variations questioning the mental capability of claimants and their ability to deal with criticism;
- responding would legitimize the claim;
- there was a risk of being drawn into further unwanted correspondence, including the risk of possible aggression;
- universities do not recognize the time invested by staff in public communication.

Those who thought that responding could have a positive effect identified the following outcomes:

- claimants need to be made aware of any relevant heritage legislation or appropriate channels regarding access to land;
- it would reduce the perception "that academics are only interested in protecting academic turf";
- it would show respect for their enthusiasm and interest in the past;
- it could counter misperceptions and beliefs that have political implications, such as "this proves that Aboriginal people weren't here more than 500 years ago—and I've already contacted the media to tell them this."

There was a slight correlation between respondents who had worked in the public sector (state agencies and museums) and belief in a positive response. One respondent specifically stated that if he were at his former institution, a museum, there would be an expectation that all correspondence received a response, regardless of content.

Apart from some relationship to the final positive point, no respondents articulated what are often cited as the key concerns of archaeologists who identify pseudoarchaeology as a significant concern. These include the archaeological profession's ethical responsibility as stewards of the past to ensure that it is not misrepresented, that standards of scientific rigor are observed, and that all evidence of the past is consistently conserved following professional ethics.

In answer to the survey question regarding who should address such claims—the individual contacted, a body such as a national archaeological society, or the relevant state heritage agency—respondents provided a broad range of answers, with none predominant. There were 19 multiple responses. Ten thought that the response should come from a relevant state or national agency, and only seven thought that if the individuals contacted were academics they should be the ones responsible for such actions. Two thought that only a society or professional organization had this role.

Some who thought it should be an individual response implied that it was the polite thing to do as the person contacted. Several thought that an academic response would provide some credibility over that of an agency or society. One noted that the response should not be "official" in order to deny legitimizing any claim. The same respondent also wrote that "all archaeologists should have the capacity to deal with these sorts of inquiries." Those advocating a state agency response thought this was better because there could be specific heritage legislation at issue or because this was part of their role—they were paid to communicate with the public. Several respondents thought that a claim that was made publicly, rather than in the form of contact with individual archaeologists, should receive a public response by a heritage agency, with information on their website. Others thought there was confusion in the public mind about where to look for answers or advice on these topics. On this latter point, the eclectic range of Mitchell's emails may be a reflection of such difficulty to an outsider.

Further survey questions explored whether a response from an archaeologist was likely to change minds or, as mentioned at the beginning of this chapter, all too often seemed to affirm and solidify the initial opinion. Respondents were also invited to share their own experience. Sixteen responded that there would be no change of opinion, only one of which was a qualified answer, compared to seven who responded that such interactions could shift opinion toward that of the profession (Figure 7.1).

While the positive responses were phrased cautiously to recognize that not all interactions would result in change, the negative responses often focused on the most reluctant to change their opinion. "In my experience, NOTHING changes their minds" is typical of these, while a number of them alluded to mental issues, such as "it does alter opinions and outlooks with the exception of those individuals who have some form of mental or behavioral issues."

The linking of pseudoarchaeological claims to mental health issues is not at all new. Flinders Petrie's admonition of those who saw various cabbalistic, numerological, and revelatory significance in the dimensions of the Egyptian pyramids illustrates the same attitude (Derricourt 2012b).The psychology of magical thinking remains an area of active exploration and much has been done in correlating beliefs with a lack of experience in critical thinking (Lindeman 1998; Lindeman and Aarnio 2007). Archaeologists would, however, need to be careful not to use outdated and offensive language that depicts anyone who does not accept their opinion as having mental illness.

Discussion

The analysis reveals an inconsistent approach among academic archaeologists regarding their personal and collective role in advocating their professional view as well as wide differences of opinion in how seriously they should treat pseudoarchaeological claims and a lack of awareness of which strategies may be most effective in maintaining this professional divide.

The Digital Image

My initial assessment of many Australian pseudoarchaeological claims suggests that many natural features have been mistaken or misidentified as artifacts, but this has generally been at the level of small items, such as an un-

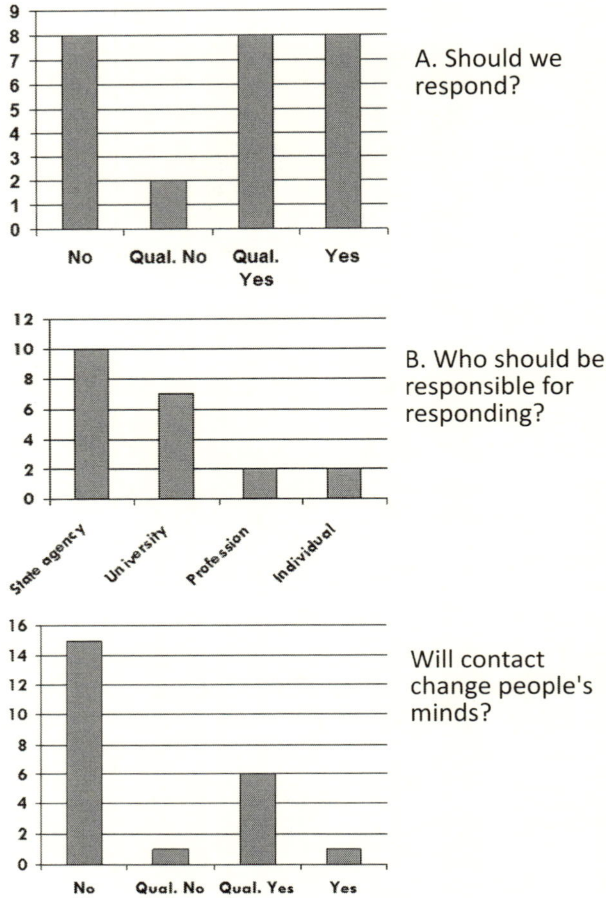

Figure 7.1. Results from survey follow-up to Mitchell email. Courtesy of Denis Gojak.

usual rock that fits in the hand nicely = stone ax, natural igneous outcrops = stone arrangements, and so on. The phenomenon of identifying extremely large terrain features as being cultural is relatively new and certainly encouraged by the availability of essentially free air photo coverage. Martin Gibbs (personal communication with the author) has suggested that the Central Australian Face may be an example of a new form of digital pseudoarchaeology, which results from the ability to scrutinize large amounts of landscape data, whereas previously bespoke aerial and satellite photo coverage was expensive and made at scales more useful for land survey.

One of the respondents reminded me that Australian archaeologists were making significant discoveries of unknown archaeological sites in Afghanistan and elsewhere, precisely because tools like Google Earth had become available. Much of the Earth's surface is now available for inspection in this way and we should expect that there will be both positive and negative results arising from its widespread use in the decades to come.

As seen with the Face on Mars, the ability to manipulate, enhance, remodel, and generally play with digital data provides a superficially strong validation of claims that there is actually something represented in these images. This remains a false premise, because the baseline argument should be that the interestingly shaped rock is nothing more than that. If *pareidolia* encourages us to see it as a face, for example, then digital manipulation is very unlikely to remodel it sufficiently to no longer see the image that has already been primed in the viewer's mind. As psychologists point out, once you have had pointed out the similarity of the features to a face it is virtually impossible to look at the object again without seeing it immediately (Liu et al. 2014).

Academic Responsibilities for Response

If the 28 academics are representative of how university-based archaeologists deal with pseudoarchaeological claims, the examination of their responses presents some issues of concern. There is considerable disagreement evident within this professional group over how to deal with pseudoarchaeology, with inaction being the consequence. A considerable majority consider there to be no point in engaging with such claims, either as dialogue or to critique the ideas. Even those who did feel it was important to do so did not articulate any of the major arguments that have been presented in the past two decades regarding pseudoarchaeology as reasons for their response. In short the issue has not been recognized, let alone articulated, and therefore a diversity of approaches can be expected from within the profession.

Very often the pseudoarchaeological claim is established and consolidated before much evidence has been accrued, and a proponent's further investigation is aimed at gathering supporting proofs rather than identifying testable propositions that may nullify or challenge the hypothesis. While this is a failure to understand and implement a basic scientific method that promotes hypothesis testing, it is also a failure to recognize that hunches, "common sense," and what appear to be self-evident conclusions, often based on overt similarities of objects, can be wrong. This is seen among scientists as much as among people with other types of training (Friedlander 1995).

The expectation that pseudoarchaeologists will not necessarily respond to any corrective statement or information provided by archaeologists is likely to frequently be correct. There are two related but distinct reasons for this. First, there is the well-studied psychological phenomenon of cognitive dissonance (Festinger et al. 1956). When people with a strong belief are confronted with evidence that is likely to show that their worldview is mistaken, rather than changing their minds, they are likely to entrench their beliefs and look for arguments that undermine the validity of the criticism. In Festinger et al.'s original study of a group that believed the end of the world would come on a certain date, the group built a series of rationalizations around insufficient prayer, God testing the believers' faith, and so on when that date came and went. In this and other cases a range of extraneous arguments were used to justify the failure of the predicted outcome. Similar behavior is often shown among various believers in alternative phenomena, such as water dowsing, when they cannot perform under experimental conditions (Randi 2013).

The second reason that pseudoarchaeologists fail to accept archaeological evidence is their increasing belief that there is an explicit or tacit desire among archaeologists and historians to suppress alternative evidence and theories about Australia's history, not just on factual grounds but because it challenges their status and power as part of an orthodoxy that controls perceptions of the past. While not all pseudoarchaeologists regard the poor reception of their ideas as resulting from "conspiracy thinking," it has become part of the repertoire of some such advocates to position themselves in opposition to the orthodoxy—mavericks who want to tell truths that are unpalatable to the Establishment. This disengagement with archaeologists is also strongly reciprocated by the profession, as shown in further results that will be discussed shortly. Aaronovitch (2009) argues that the final decades of the twentieth century saw a rapid increase in conspiracy thinking, his term for a widespread acceptance that deliberately concealed human agency is commonly responsible for the outcome of events rather than random variation, human error, and coincidence.

Some of those advocating pseudoarchaeological ideas are increasingly aiming to distinguish themselves from orthodox archaeology with specific language while trying to maintain that they are undertaking legitimate archaeological research. Maintaining the trappings of science without any commitment to its method or structure is usually cited as one of the defining elements of pseudoscience (e.g., Park 2000; Shermer 2002). Some advocates therefore carefully describe themselves as "field archaeologists," implicitly in opposition to desk jockey and ivory tower archaeologists (e.g., Gilroy and Gilroy 2003:164). Increasingly photographs illustrating articles are likely to have a scale or a reasonably drafted diagram to help provide an aura of scientific method (e.g., Strong and Strong 2014 and links therein).

Pigliucci (2012) notes that archaeologists' reluctance to participate in public outreach is not limited to their field; such reluctance is well embedded in all branches of science. Archaeology continues to be, alongside astronomy, one of the few fields where a motivated amateur can realistically make a significant research contribution. Sociologists who have examined how professionals and the public have interacted have noted a shift over time in the exclusion and downgrading of the contribution of the amateur or avocational investigators and researchers (Stebbins 1992; Taylor 1995). Such shifts are interesting, particularly in light of the increasing visibility of public archaeology as a response to the exclusion of indigenous and marginalized groups by mainstream archaeology.

Past Approaches

While the approach of ignoring the pseudoarchaeologists and hoping that they go away has been the predominant mode adopted by Australian archaeologists over the past four decades since the rise of the profession, it has not been marked by any apparent success. The results of my research suggest that the pseudoarchaeology of Australia is stronger than it has ever been, supported by an Internet-based propagation of a range of different claims.

However, Australian archaeologists have directly confronted some claims from pseudoarchaeologists and alternative historians. During the early twentieth century claims that Australia was discovered by the Spanish or Portuguese were hotly contested by professionals. There was a strong emphasis on presenting counterarguments to these claims in the same forum and publishing to reach the same audience (Gojak 2007). For example, Lawrence Hargrave published in the *Journal of the Royal Society of NSW* a claim that a ship lost from Mendana's 1595 expedition to the Solomon Islands ended up in Sydney Harbor (Hargrave 1909). Detailed rebuttals were published in the same journal in the following year by experts (Haddon 1910; Mathews 1910). The same pattern took place in the debate between George Collingridge, an advocate for the Dieppe maps showing earlier Portuguese voyaging, Cardinal Moran, who sought to place de Quiros's 1606 landfall in Australia rather than Vanuatu, and historian George Arnold Wood and a range of other professional and amateur scholars.

This took place in the context of the rise of academic Australian historical study during the period from the lead-up to Federation and the Great War. The approach of rigorously contesting alternative historical claims seems to have been successful, as there was very little further discussion of this from the start of the war until their resurrection by K. G. McIntyre's book (1977) on the topic, which reiterated many of the earlier arguments for Spanish voyages. Since then there has been little direct confrontation between pseudoarchaeological claimants and their deniers, and very little of it aimed at what could be considered the same audience.

Australian archaeology has done little to acknowledge the presence of alternative views of the past outside of indigenous experience and very explicitly differentiates its attitude toward them. Hiscock (1996) is one of the few who has, but he addresses an academic audience and places his argument in the context of alternative time scales used by different cultures and belief systems.

Getting the Message

One of the anonymous reviewers of this chapter challenged me to think beyond the email as specific content and to consider how this discussion would be placed in the context of the overall daily toll of emails that most of us receive. This is an important aspect that could have been included in the initial analysis, at the risk of becoming an altogether much larger study.

Most jurisdictions regard emails received and sent from work addresses as public documents, in the same way as a letter, and subject therefore to all workplace expectations for the nature of their content, accessible under freedom of information searches and so on (e.g., NSW Government—email use). However, when emails appear directly in an in-box, unfiltered and addressed to an individual, they take on the tenor of a phone call, an altogether more personal communication.

In understanding how individuals responded to Mitchell's email, we could ask whether they saw it as spam, in the same category, as the reviewer suggested, as "Nigerian banking scams, personal information phishing, and male genital enhancement spam." This could have been a profitable line of inquiry, but in general terms, the negative attitudes that academics and professionals display toward the fringe as revealed here would be expected to strongly influence their opinion. A category of spam as unwanted, unsolicited, and actively discouraged material provides an additional, more subordinate category in which to place such messages. As a result they do not even enter the modern forwarded/retweeted equivalent of "faxlore" (Seal 1989).

Effectiveness of Challenging the Claim

The survey that tracked responses to the Central Australian Face claim demonstrates that archaeology is failing to effectively engage with pseudoarchaeological claims and claimants. Almost no archaeologists contacted by the claimant responded to him, despite the range of critical comment that they could have leveled against his proposal about the face.

Mitchell declined to discuss either his claim or the response from the archaeological community with me. This reluctance is difficult to understand given his willingness to announce the claim to the world news media and the international archaeological community. It is hard to interpret it as a response to the collective silence of those contacted, but a direct factual response by two archaeologists may at least have resulted in his further reflection on the evidence.

Responsibility for a Response

We may ask whether academic archaeologists should continue to shoulder an added responsibility as the spokespeople of the profession. Even though most receive few such emails per annum, many are concerned that responding may deflect from their workload. I believe there is some justification to this. The argument that a state heritage agency should respond has some resonance among the academic community; fewer believe that a professional association should undertake the task.

This disagreement shows, though, that there is no mechanism within the archaeological community to understand the issues, to reflect on past practice, and to identify what has worked and what has not. There is strong evidence to support the argument that the current system is ineffective, as pseudoarchaeological claims are as prevalent as they have ever been. A change in approach is warranted, but the reaction is to move the problem. Despite acknowledging overwhelmingly that response is not an option, the majority also thought that responding individually should be undertaken. The survey reveals a disjunct logic, where the problem and the solution are barely connected.

The lack of clarity between the roles of the different branches of the profession—academics, consultants, public sector heritage managers—and the distinction among individual, collective (society or association), and corporate (state/territory heritage agency) roles are not limited to how pseudoarchaeologists are handled. This blurring of roles has been a characteristic of archaeology in Australia since at least the rise of cultural heritage management.

It is arguable whether professional archaeology ever had an exclusive mandate to represent the voice of the past in Australia. This was a role carried quite uncomfortably by academics such as John Mulvaney. The empowerment of Aboriginal communities both politically and as representative agents for the archaeological past has severely cut back that authority. Increasingly as well in the wider community the role of archaeologists and historians in being the primary custodians of the past has been questioned.

If it is accepted that there is an innate public good in an accurate understanding and acceptance of human history based upon evidence, then archaeology needs to respond to pseudoarchaeology in a different way from how it has until now.

Pseudoarchaeology has always been present but is now increasingly attractive and accessible to the wider audience. It is clear that the nonengagement by archaeologists over the past 40 years since the profession was established in Australia with its first academic positions has done nothing to diminish the strength or extent of belief in pseudoarchaeology.

The Media Silence

Focusing on the archaeological response in this study was necessary as almost no response came from the media to my survey. As far as can be determined there was no response to Mitchell's initial email, and only two media representatives responded to my survey. A third of the emails sent out were to media, so archaeology should not perhaps be portrayed as excessively unresponsive.

Without doubt Mitchell was naive if he thought his email would gain media attention. His letter reflects the average person's lack of familiarity with what constitutes the news-making process—from the eclectic and largely redundant selection of outlets, the mixed message (A new discovery! . . . will be made), and the lack of useful detail for busy journalists to pin a story on.

The rise of individual commentary blogs, "churnalism" (a neologism for reposting stories until the volume of their appearance provides credence), and other phenomena facilitated by the rise of the Internet have considerable potential to provide an alternative pathway for pseudoarchaeological claimants such as Mitchell (Fuchs 2013). It is surprising that he did not, either before or after he sent the email, post on any of the many bulletin boards, discussion groups, or blogs that could have sustained discussion about it. My experience has been that once claims have transferred to these sorts of forums it is extremely difficult to provide a contrary archaeological response. The audience is generally not interested in such a response, and some see their role as defenders of the alterity of their site against orthodoxy.

Colley's (2013) recent survey of social media use by archaeologists suggests that they are conservative in exploiting its potential. My blog—The Secret Visitors Project (https://secretvisitors.wordpress.com/)—aims to provide a more direct focus on addressing specific claims. The effectiveness of any of these critiques on people who still believe in the authenticity of the Egyptian scarabs, hieroglyphs, and other claimed evidence found in Australia remains to be tested.

Conclusions

This chapter documents a survey intended to map how responses to a genuine pseudoarchaeological claim were responded to by an audience predominantly of academics and media outlets. Of the respondents, half effectively ignored the email. The survey was able to track the opinions of both those who did this and the remainder who opened it. Only one of the survey respondents wrote that he got back to the man who sent it. None of the other archaeologists in the sample did.

The actual contents of the claim could be readily dismissed as the result of *pareidolia*, seeing a face in a meaningless array of elements. This was communicated back to the sender and seems to have stopped the further propagation of the idea. It is reasonable to conclude that this was effective in preventing the belief being communicated to a larger group.

Although a single event, it highlights that the current stance of Australian archaeology is to ignore such claims, in the hope they will go away. This has demonstrably not worked into the present. The respondents, almost all academics, feel that they should not be responsible for this role, which really should belong with a state agency. At the same time they acknowledge that response is likely to be ineffective, in that it will probably not change anyone's opinion. When probed, none of the archaeologists offered a reason for responding that identified the concern at a professional level.

The survey clearly showed that the absence of a coherent understanding of pseudoarchaeology and its effects prevented the formulation of a coherent response, either at the level of the discipline or at the level of individual action. Hanen et al. (1980:viii) note that "pseudoscience purports to be scientific and yet is denied that status by practitioners of science. Thus, understanding pseudoscience becomes central to understanding what the scientific community regards as properly scientific."

Archaeology is similarly positioned. Acknowledging the alternative views of the past held by indigenous people is a continuing challenge, and the way we treat the ideas of members of the general community that differ from our own needs examination is as well. Regardless of whether we consider such beliefs wrong, contestable, or benign, we need to understand how to make archaeological messages more effective.

Acknowledgments

I would like to thank the people who responded to my somewhat unusual email and were willing to share information about their practices. I would particularly like to thank Jane Ainsworth, who convened the Advocacy in Archaeology session at the 2010 ASHA Conference, Brisbane, where a version of this chapter was first presented, and the audience for incisive comments and questioning afterward.

Dave Anderson and Jeb Card invited me to present to their SAA session and Dave presented the paper in my absence. I would particularly like to thank them for the effort they made to extract the final version of the chapter from me and the patience with which they did this. The chapter benefited from the constructive comments of two anonymous reviewers, who suggested other perspectives to be drawn from the analysis.

8
The Proliferation of Pseudoarchaeology through "Reality" Television Programming

EVAN A. PARKER

Attention is being directed toward reality-driven media representations from an ever-wider array of sources: journalistic, literary, anthropological. It may well be that the marginalization of the documentary film as a subject of serious inquiry is at an end. After all, the key questions that arise in the study of nonfiction film and video—the ontological status of the image, the epistemological stakes of representation, the potentialities of historical discourse on film—are just pressing for an understanding of fictional representation (Renov 1993:1–2).

All reality television, or factual programming, as it is sometimes called, is ultimately derived from the more traditional documentary film genre with which archaeologists are most familiar. This chapter discusses the alignment of more traditional archaeological documentary filmmaking practices with the genre of reality television. The past decade has witnessed the proliferation of programs in this new fusion genre, which has often been labeled infotainment or docudrama (Figure 8.1) (Kilborn 2003). In this chapter, I discuss five archaeologically oriented television programs that largely epitomize this bourgeoning trend in American television: *Chasing Mummies*, *Digging for the Truth*, *American Digger*, *Diggers*, and *Nazi War Diggers*. Each show contains elements typically found on reality television programs, including an emphasis on celebrity, the imposition of a scripted narrative in the midst of real-life events, and frequent depictions of action and drama. These elements are certainly present throughout the history of documentary filmmaking, yet the balance between factual representation of the past and the

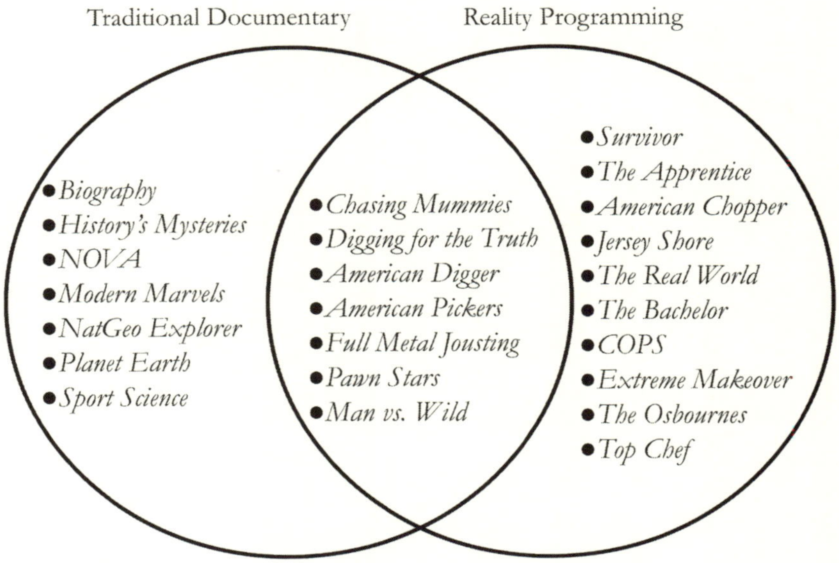

Figure 8.1. Fusion of traditional documentary and reality programming into infotainment. Courtesy of Evan A. Parker.

need to entertain is becoming increasingly skewed with the advent of these programs (Kilborn 2003; Lafollette 2013). Furthermore, the proliferation of these programs becomes problematic when we consider that they are purported to be educational and lay claim to authenticity and scientific truth. This presumption of an authoritative voice is an issue that archaeologists have long faced in light of the development of nonscientific theories regarding the prehistoric development of humanity. Furthermore, Erich von Däniken, one of the progenitors of modern ancient alien theories, has had significant exposure in a host of media productions. But what are the implications for archaeology when the lines between informing and entertaining become blurred? Serious problems arise when nonarchaeologists (and even some real archaeologists) don the mantle of authenticity and claim that "this is what archaeology really is" without having to answer to the broader archaeological community.

This disjuncture between the aims of educational documentary programs and the frameworks imposed by the genre of reality television has serious implications for how archaeology is perceived and understood by the viewing public. Understanding why this genre has arisen in American television productions and how archaeologists should respond to and capitalize on these new televisual formats is another goal of this work.

Case Studies of Programs

Sample Selection

The programs selected for discussion in this chapter each needed to share formatting commonalities with reality television programming. Certainly there is no shortage of television programs filmed in documentary styles that feature pseudoarchaeology. The most commonly panned and regrettably popular among these is the History Channel's *Ancient Aliens*. While the show has greatly popularized many typically pseudoarchaeological claims, it is not filmed in the conventions of reality television. However, a new program premiered in 2014 on the History Channel called *In Search of Ancient Aliens*. Rather than relying upon the more traditional documentary format of *Ancient Aliens*, this newer program instead features the program's host, Giorgio Tsoukalos, as he travels around the globe outfitted in Indiana Jones garb and searches for aliens, Atlantis, and the other traditional fare of pseudoarchaeology. While not fully employing the format of reality television, *In Search of Ancient Aliens* does incorporate some aspects of reality programming, perhaps a testament to the growing importance of the format in the preferred programming of various networks.

Another aspect of the sampling strategy is that only programs produced and televised in the United States were examined. Archaeological television programming has enjoyed a longer history and greater appreciation in Europe than in the United States (Brittain and Clack 2007; Holtorf 2007). In spite of this, most of the television shows adopting reality formats are based in the United States. Furthermore, the bulk of scholarship that examines archaeology and the media has principally focused on television programs in Europe as opposed to the United States. European media corporations produce a plethora of television programming outside the traditional documentary format that focus on archaeological issues. European nations also have a long history of incorporating famous archaeologists into media productions. Given the national archaeologies and localized origins of European populations, many of these programs directly address several key issues related to European identity, including ethnic and national origins and the roots of material and intellectual traditions deep in prehistory (Dietler 1994; Kohl 1998).

The history of archaeology in the Americas and the nature of ethnic identity in the United States did not generate similar nationalist archaeologies that would later be assimilated into media productions. As such, archaeology in the United States has almost exclusively focused on "The Other," given the history of the conquest of the New World. In turn, this bred a disassociation between the national identity of Americans as a people and their own ethnogenesis (Gosden 2001). As a result of the history of American archaeology, the disjuncture between archaeology and nationalism in the United States could not be bridged by the media as it did in Europe. This disconnect may partially explain why such sensationalized and ethically questionable media productions have enjoyed popular success in the United States.

Although this chapter may be critical of many media practices, especially the representations of archaeologists or archaeology in a particular light, it does not condemn the practices of the reality television format itself. Scripting, confession-booth style interviews, and imposed action narratives are simply part of the genre. They are inherently neither good nor bad, but when such conventions and formats are utilized in the obfuscation of true archaeological practice or the promotion of ethically questionable archaeological procedures, then they are subject to some criticism.

Chasing Mummies: The Amazing Adventures of Zahi Hawass

The TV series *Chasing Mummies: The Amazing Adventures of Zahi Hawass* premiered in 2010 on the History Channel. The program follows Egyptian archaeologist Zahi Hawass and several other archaeologists as they visit various archaeological and museum sites in Egypt. However, rather than focusing on ancient Egyptians and their past lifeways, the show instead centers on Hawass and his "adventures" at various archaeological sites. Accompanying Hawass are several archaeological neophytes, students learning the ropes of how archaeology is done. Any examination of the show by an experienced archaeologist reveals that it is anything but educational or tied to how archaeologists actually are educated. For example, in the first episode, Hawass receives a phone call while at a book signing. He learns that one of the graduate students on the program, Zoe, has somehow managed to become locked into the famed Pyramid of Djoser and faces mortal peril. Rather than contacting the authorities or having someone nearby the archaeological site release her, Hawass instead races to the pyramid and frees Zoe at the eleventh hour. In the fourth episode, Hawass vents his rage at his archaeological students while traveling to Saqqara. In the scripted universe of reality television, no visit to an archaeological site is without its perils. Their truck breaks down in the middle of the desert, forcing them to walk to the archaeological site in the desert heat until they just happen to run across a Bedouin group who lend them horses and camels to complete the journey.

Several elements of reality television programming are evident in *Chasing Mummies*. First, this is a show about celebrity and personality. The program features Zahi Hawass starring as Zahi Hawass. Indeed, one must question his intentions: Is he educating the public about ancient Egyptian culture, or is he seeking to enhance his own brand? While intentionality ultimately is unknown, the effect of celebrity and its accompanying dramatic conventions seem to be present as a foundational aspect of the program.

Rather than following actual archaeological investigations and presenting scientific hypotheses and conclusions, the show instead is heavily scripted and features scenes of action and danger in place of carefully controlled and safe legitimate archaeological pursuits. In many regards, the show is similar to the hit reality series *Survivor* in that the three students of archaeology accompanying Hawass must face the same fabricated rigors and dangers of Egyptologists. Failing to do so leads to expulsion from the program, a common occurrence for the students featured on the show. Although archaeological fieldwork does involve some hardships and dangers, no graduate student would end up locked in a pyramid or be forced to walk through the desert with a lack of essential supplies under orders from a supervisor. That such elements are included in the show highlights the central roles of scripting and genre in a series that espouses education about the past. In the words of one critic, "Dr. Hawass, having studied his Simon Cowell and Donald Trump, has concluded that American audiences want to see underlings browbeaten. But there's a big difference between enjoying Mr. Cowell's antics in the artificial construct of *American Idol* or [Donald Trump's in] *The Apprentice* and seeing the same thing out in the real world, where college kids are just trying to learn, and film crews are just trying to film" (Genzlinger 2010). These antics may entertain some and possibly even draw interest to the field of archaeology, but they offer a false sense of the nature of archaeological research. While archaeology can be dramatic, entertaining, and exciting, it can also be frustrating and boring. In a worse sense, such depictions may discourage younger viewers from becoming archaeologists in an effort to avoid such hazing and trials. Archaeology requires teamwork, and although directors of various archaeological projects each bring a unique management style to the workplace, at the very least subordinates must cooperate so as to run a viable and sustainable project.

Growing unrest in Egypt and charges of corruption led to the resignation of Hawass as minister of antiquities in February 2011 in the government of Hosni Mubarak (Taylor 2011a). Hawass was then reappointed by the new prime minister, Essam A. Sharif, in March 2011 (Taylor 2011b). His reappointment was short-lived, however, as Hawass was sacked in mid-July and no longer maintains any affiliation with the Egyptian government (Diab 2011).

Digging for the Truth

Digging for the Truth premiered in 2005 and ran for four seasons. During its first two seasons, it received the highest ratings of any History Channel program, indicative of its potential influence for framing and generating metanarratives of archaeology for general audiences (Morrison 2006). The show features Josh Bernstein as a host. After graduating with a degree in anthropology from Cornell, Bernstein resided in Jerusalem for a year, where he studied mysticism and ancient texts, and later served as the CEO of the Boulder Outdoor Survival School. In each episode, Bernstein travels to various parts of the world in an effort to solve ancient mysteries. In many cases, he pursues answers to excellent archaeological questions, such as what life was like in ancient Pompeii, how the ancient Maya conceived of the underworld, or how the ancient Egyptians constructed their pyramids (this episode featured Hawass, albeit in a much more scholarly and subdued role). In several of these episodes, Bernstein examines scientific and pseudoarchaeological claims, and in most cases he does select legitimate archaeological explanations as "the truth." Most episodes end with Bernstein unable to find truths, and this is most apparent in episodes with pseudoarchaeological qualities. These particular episodes include the typical pseudoarchaeological fare, such as quests to find Atlantis, the search for the Holy Grail and Lost Ark, and a journey to find El Dorado. Yet what makes *Digging for the Truth* different from other pseudoarchaeological programming?

Arlid Fetveit (2002:130) explains, "Reality TV comes with a unique promise of contact with reality, but at the same time it promises a secure distance." Unlike the format of traditional documentaries, each episode of *Digging for the Truth* features Bernstein engaging in death-defying stunts to uncover mysteries. In an interview, Bernstein even states, "And finally, there's the 'activity factor.' Or, as the producers ask it, the 'What's Josh got in his hands?' factor. We want the show to be driven by an archaeological mystery, yet supported by my doing things like scuba-diving, rappelling, paragliding, etc. to keep it interesting and active" (Hirst 2007). "Active" is a key word here. Indeed, *action*, *doing*, and *experience* are key elements of the reality genre and are in opposition to the *exposition*, *informing*, and *observation* seen in more traditional documentary practice (Kilborn 2003). Bernstein has become the intermediary between the archaeology and the viewer, bringing them into contact with the archaeology and the presumed dangers associated with it, all while enabling the viewer to maintain a safe distance. He has combined the archetypal archaeologist embodied in Indiana Jones with the survival skills of Bear Grylls. Yet hosts of documentaries have long served as the interlocutors between science and the public, and they have often been selected more for their ability to entertain than for their expertise in a particular field. However, with the advent of reality television, the terms have changed. A host no longer offers observations or guides viewers through the current state of archaeology; instead, the host is the one doing the archaeology. Veiled with the authority granted to archaeologists for properly investigating the past, reality television stars can now dictate to audiences what passes as valid interpretations of the past.

The rise of reality television is also emblematic of ongoing parallel processes in American and mass-mediated culture as a whole. This process is the emergence of the experience economy and performative labor. Consumer experience and performative labor have become increasingly important not only in retail industries but in media productions as well. Performative labor is "the rendering of work by employees as akin to a theatrical performance in which the workplace is construed as similar to the stage" (Bryman 2006:103). In both *Chasing Mummies* and *Digging for the Truth*, the hosts utilize archaeological sites as stages for their portrayal of what an archaeologist does. Performative labor seems like a redundant and counterintuitive concept when describing an actor's performance, but it differs from traditional acting roles and mirrors contemporary reality television performances in that reality and experience, rather than only narrative, must be conveyed in the production (Bryman 2006). In other words, the engagement of the viewer through the performative labors of the host/actor becomes paramount in the digital age. In answering the challenges of pseudoarchaeology, we must acknowledge the power that viewers wield with regard to determining program content. Archaeologists must also be prepared to revise their approach to how they interact with the media, especially when viewers no longer demand traditional documentary programming but more experience-focused formats. More research on this contradictory dichotomy between authentic experience and the distance that viewers desire is certainly warranted. Even if audiences grasp the inauthenticity of such programs, it does not diminish many of the negative externalities generated by the scientific claims made by hosts.

American Digger

The March 2012 premiere of the Spike television program *American Digger* generated substantial controversy and outrage in the archaeological community. The program stars Ric Savage, a retired professional wrestler who now runs an "artifact recovery company" in the United States. He and his crew request permission from private landowners to excavate areas that contain archaeological artifacts that he then sells for profit. No attention is given to proper methods of excavation or the recording of contextual information that accompanies typical investigations. In countries with more stringent heritage preservation laws, such excavations would be considered looting and punishable by law; on this show, audiences are treated to fully documented looting expeditions.

The show is filmed and scripted in typical reality television format. Much like *Chasing Mummies*, the program draws heavily on the importance of celebrity. Members of the archaeological community and organizations such as the Society for American Archaeology and the American Anthropological Association are striving to mitigate the consequences of this production and address the issues it is raising.

American Digger is not a unique program. The past few years have seen a rise in object-oriented or object-centric television shows. On the one extreme, there are traditional programs such as *Antiques Roadshow*. On the other, programs such as *Pawn Stars*, *American Pickers*, *Cajun Pawn Stars*, and *Storage Wars* have gained increasing notoriety. All of these shows are concerned with historical and archaeological objects and, most important, how valuable they are. That a show such as *American Digger* would arise is quite unsurprising given the popularity of these object-centric programs.

American Digger also falls into the category of occupation-based reality television shows such as *Deadliest Catch*, *Dirty Jobs*, *Cops*, and *Hell's Kitchen*, which focus on the detailed aspects of particular occupations of notable gravitas. While these programs do depict professionals working in their respective fields, they still employ many of the devices of reality programming, such as scripting and injection of construed drama into the plot.

A reality show such as *American Digger* contains "much potent information about a society's contemporary view of itself and how it understands its own, usually fairly proximal, historical origins" (Taylor 2007:189). Commoditization, success, individual agency, wealth, and power have become focal points for contemporary American narratives regarding current politics and the nation's mythic origins. The founding of the United States serves as a marker of legitimacy for the unbridled accumulation of wealth and consumption of material goods. *American Digger* taps into this recently generated historical consciousness. Savage's company is simply a commercial enterprise, but in this case, history has become the commodity. The acquisition and peddling of historical artifacts have become quite common in American television, a trend from which media executives are drawing increasing profits. Savage repeatedly states that it is his right by law to excavate and sell these artifacts (Carter 2012). Such gall resonates with American viewers and has led to the increased production of object-centric shows. Silberman (2007:184) argues that "the direct, sensory—rather than merely intellectual or educational—involvement of visitors in public heritage interpretation has become part of an essential marketing strategy." Object-centric television programs—especially those in reality format—not only draw upon the direct and sensory as traditional documentaries do but even grant the individual viewer the assumed authority and skill to participate in this profitable enterprise themselves. This is one reason why a pseudoarchaeological looting team filmed in a reality format poses such a threat to the archaeological record.

Diggers

Much like its Spike TV counterpart *American Digger*, the National Geographic Channel program *Diggers* has raised ire among archaeologists, historians, and preservationists, less over the commoditization of historical objects and more over the complications that can arise from amateur metal detecting. The reality-formatted show follows two metal-detector hobbyists, "King George" Wyant and Tim "The Ringmaster" Saylor, as they visit various historical sites across the United States in search of historical artifacts. Unlike *American Digger*, the hosts of *Diggers* do not keep their finds for later sale but instead return them to landowners.

Regardless, the show still casts the metal detecting as a search for "buried treasure," or as they call it, "nectar." The two avocational metal-detector enthusiasts have traveled to various locations throughout the United States. Historical sites visited during the course of the show include the Civil War battlefield at Vicksburg, army encampments from the French and Indian War, the Gettysburg battlefield, historic New Orleans, the California Trail, and an army encampment in Tubac, Arizona, dating to the period of Pancho Villa's raids into the United States. The most treasured items are typically coins, especially ones minted from precious metals such as gold and silver. Historic weapons, ammunition, and soldiering equipment and attire are also prime finds for the group.

With regard to format, the show typically opens with a brief introduction to the area and its associated historical events. Camera operators accompany the diggers as they survey fields and yards. Uncovered artifacts are excitedly examined and appraised both monetarily and for historical significance. However, after the initial outcry by various archaeological associations and historical societies, the producers of the show no longer offered monetary appraisals for the most valuable objects discovered (e.g., gold coins).

Unlike *American Digger*, this particular program offers a view into a hobby that is easily accessible to the public. No backhoe or dynamite is necessary for metal detecting; an amateur can easily acquire the necessary tools for less than $1,000. The primary impediment is obtaining permission from private landowners or government agencies that oversee public lands.

Upon announcing the premiere of the program, the National Geographic Channel was immediately confronted with stern protest from a variety of organizations that advocate stewardship of the past. In a letter to the CEO of the National Geographic Society, the Society for American Archaeology president Fred Limp wrote that the show ran afoul of archaeological ethics and encouraged the destruction of the archaeological and historical record (Limp 2012). In a similar statement, the Society for Historical Archaeology president Charles Ewen (2013) noted that over one million viewers tuned in for the *Diggers* premiere and that the program exposed more people to its own archaeological message than he most likely would ever reach in all of his writings and presentations.

The bourgeoning outcry stimulated the National Geographic Society to convene a conference with material culture advocates, ultimately culminating in a revision of the practices and format of the program. These revisions included only filming in areas where heritage was threatened by development, increased air-time for local professional archaeologists and historians who assist with the ultimate identification of objects, employing an associate producer with archaeological experience who acts as a supervising archaeologist, the valuation of objects by historical significance rather than monetary value, and the publication of a website with information on ethical metal detecting (Meeting on Archeological Preservation, Avocational Metal Detecting, Ethics of Archaeology).

Even in light of the changes imposed to the format of the program, Dan Sivilich, president of the Battlefield Restoration and Archaeological Volunteer Organization, has argued that the changes to the format of the show are still not adequate to ensure the preservation of historical objects or ethical metal detecting (Ewen 2013). While observing the filming of an episode of *Diggers* at a New Jersey Revolutionary War site, he saw that there was almost no artifact mapping, noting of contexts, or publication of a site report. Among the repercussions, Sivilich argues that New Jersey State Park Police will have to place additional units of patrol at the sites of these battlefields because of increased interest in metal detecting wrought by the program. Of course, such an assertion is unsubstantiated, but the valuation of items such as musket balls does commercialize historical objects. Increased focus on the process of doing archaeology and portraying proper archaeological method with metal detecting could very well eliminate the infotainment aspect of the program. Most likely, the reality television components of the program would have to be dropped.

Nazi War Diggers

The bourgeoning outrage over the commercialization of historical objects and mistreatment of cultural and human remains reached its apex upon the March 2014 announcement by the National Geographic Channel of a new reality television program, *Nazi War Diggers*. The program's promotional material that aired online generated so much outrage among professional archaeologists and historians that National Geographic Channel announced later that month that the program would be shelved for the foreseeable future.

The planned four-episode program appears to have been filmed in reality television format. The program focused on the work of American Craig Gottlieb, a dealer of Nazi artifacts from World War II and weapons expert for the History Channel program *Pawn Stars*. The program also features three amateur metal-detector hobbyists from the U.K., Stephen Taylor, Kris Rodgers, and Adrian Kostromski (Brockman 2014). The program, set in Poland and Latvia, focuses on the search for and excavation of Red Army and German soldiers' graves and artifacts from World War II battlefields. In the initial press releases issued by the National Geographic Channel, Gottlieb was quoted as saying, "I feel that by selling things that are Nazi-related and for lots of money, I'm preserving a part of history that museums don't want to bother with" (Mashberg 2014a). This is a sentiment expressed in all three metal-detecting programs surveyed for this chapter. The perceived inability of archaeologists to quickly excavate and display historical objects serves as justification for the recovery of these objects by hobbyists and dealers. That such sentiments are explicitly presented in these programs is certainly one of the more insidious outcomes of presenting the past through a reality television format.

The promotional video that sparked the initial protests by archaeological associations featured one of the program's hosts removing a German soldier's femur from the ground at a battlefield in Latvia and then speculating as to how the soldier may have died (Brockman 2014; Mashberg 2014a). National Geographic acknowledged it was a poor choice for a promotional clip and that viewing it out of context made it appear even worse. The producers of the program have repeatedly noted that all of their actions have been conducted lawfully, yet as Brockman (2014) notes, excavations can occur lawfully but that does not mean they are conducted under the ethical strictures of archaeology. Regardless, the airing of the clip prompted the Society for American Archaeology, the Society for Historical Archaeology, the Archaeological Institute of America, the American Anthropological Association, the European Association of Archaeologists, and the European Association of Social Anthropologists to compose a letter condemning the program for its callous treatment of human remains and the commercialization of the battlefield artifacts (Altschul et al. 2014). The organizations also expressed concern over the incorporation of the word "Nazi" in the program's title, asserting that the choice of title was driven more by the desire to raise viewer numbers than with any concern for the actual history being portrayed: "We also strongly suspect that the TV show will leave the audience with the impression that metal detecting and archaeological excavation can be done without supervision and without being part of a larger archaeological team. We fear that instead of encouraging the interested public to work with archaeologists to recover in a respectful and systematic manner human remains, artifacts, and information about critically important and emotionally charged historical events, the show will have the exact opposite effect: to encourage individuals to buy metal detectors and loot World War II battlefields and other archaeological sites" (Altschul et al. 2014). As a result of the outcry raised by archaeologists, historians, and preservations, the National Geographic Channel canceled the program before it even aired (Mashberg 2014b).

Time Team and *Time Team America*

As a foil to the previously discussed programs, the British program *Time Team* stands as a commendable example of how the reality television format and archaeology can be successfully combined. Each episode of the program focuses on the work of archaeologists in the field undertaking problem-based research. Archaeologists cooperate with local avocational enthusiasts in working at a particular site. Throughout the excavation process, the archaeologists are queried by the show's host, Tony Robinson, regarding the importance of particular finds, why they make particular decisions, and why consensus between archaeologists is rarely achieved. In other cases, Robinson explains in nonprofessional terms what the archaeologists are doing. Sensationalism is minimized, and confession-booth style interviewing with archaeologists is a limited as well.

Time Team not only solely focuses on the archaeological and historical significance of a site but also devotes time to discussing how the research process works. In other words, *Time Team* covers the full range of the scientific method while also imparting a sense of authenticity and accuracy regarding even the quotidian aspects of archaeological research.

In 2009, a group of professional archaeologists in the United States, with funding from the National Science Foundation, created a new television program that bridged the reality television format with more traditional factual programming. *Time Team America* was produced by Oregon Public Broadcasting and aired over the course of two seasons in 2009 and 2014. The program features a core group of six professional archaeologists who travel to various prehistoric (as early as pre-Clovis) and historic (as late as Civil War prison camps) archaeological sites and conduct survey and excavation. Unlike *Time Team*, the archaeologists of *Time Team America* join existing archaeological projects in the field to aid and supplement ongoing research. One of the explicitly stated goals of the program is to bring specialized equipment and scientific techniques to various archaeological projects that may otherwise lack such resources. For example, a geophysics team led by Meg Watters typically identifies subsurface features that can then be excavated.

In a typical episode, the core group of archaeologists for *Time Team America* arrives at an archaeological site currently undergoing investigation. They then invest three days of a combination of geophysical survey and excavation in an effort to supplement or advance researchers' knowledge about a site. A three-day window for excavation may appear to be yet another egregious example of entertainment value taking precedence over scientific method with regard to format, but it was for exactly this reason that the creators chose to supplement the efforts of ongoing projects.

Thematically, the program focuses on larger debates within North American archaeology, such as the Clovis first debate. In addition to aiding ongoing projects, perhaps the more salient goal of the program is to engage and educate youth who may not be fully aware of the STEM applications of archaeology. An informal science education grant awarded by the National Science Foundation funds the program and allows the producers and archaeologists to more explicitly focus on the educational aspects of archaeology without necessarily having to appeal to investors or studio executives. With no pressure to achieve profitability, as in the cases of programs produced for Spike and the History Channel, *Time Team America* can produce factual reality programming that is not reliant on celebrity or scripting to the same degree as other programs. Episodes typically focus on aspects of daily life in the past and feature in-depth examinations of domestic lifeways and vernacular architecture. Sensationalizing of the past is limited.

A central tenet of the producers and the archaeologists on the show is that archaeology in and of itself is sufficiently interesting to provide entertainment value without necessarily having to rely on celebrity personalities or gratuitous scripting. Furthermore, rather than relying on attracting viewers through making heritage connections as is often the case in Europe, *Time Team America* instead investigates historical sites that may have a more prominent connection for most Americans, or they note that investigations of prehistory are not solely limited to exotic locales around the globe but instead can be found almost anywhere in the United States. In addition to the program itself, *Time Team America* also leads field schools for students, hosts educational outreach activities, and created an interactive website, all of which are designed raise awareness of the role of STEM in archaeology. An evaluation conducted by the consulting company Rockman et al. (2013) on the program's efficacy with regard to opening archaeology to a wider audience was tremendously positive, with reviewers concluding that viewers of the show were significantly more educated on archaeological ethics, archaeological method, and the role of STEM in reconstructing the ancient past.

Discussion

When discussing why these types of shows are appearing, what they mean for archaeology as a discipline, and what they can tell us about how we as archaeologists need to frame our research for broader consumption by the public, the simplest explanation lies in the profitability of such shows. In the United States, reality programming regularly earns the highest ratings for the majority of half-hour primetime American television programming (Hill 2005). That these types of programs are so cheap to produce also contributes to their favorability among media production corporations. Increasing commoditization of all genres of programs combined with the decline of public broadcasting firms such as PBS has led to a waning in the prevalence of documentary in favor of more profitable yet highly contrived forms of factual programming that draw heavily on the prescriptions and proscriptions of the reality genre (Kilborn 2003). In other words, infotainment has replaced documentary. The accrual of increased power by purportedly educational networks such as the History Channel means that new programs must adhere to the conventions set by the standards of profitability, that is, the ability to entertain, even at the risk of misinforming. This means higher ratings for each broadcast are required. A producer generates higher ratings by increasing the accessibility of the program in an attempt to draw a wider audience. Traditional documentary filmmaking, unfortunately, is no longer suitable for fulfilling media executives' demands for greater viewership and, therefore, higher profitability (Kilborn 2003). Ouellette and Murray (2009:4) note that "although the current wave of reality TV circulates ideologies, myths, and templates for living that might be called educational in nature, it eschews the twin expectations of unpopularity and unprofitability that have historically differentiated 'serious' factual formats from popular entertainment." This recombinant strain of television has garnered the moniker "infotainment," and it possesses great potential in opening avenues for pseudoarchaeological claims to gain traction, all in the name of ratings and profitability. An additional side effect is that educators are increasingly called on to infotain students, who are increasingly presented with information that blurs the lines between fact and fiction. At this critical junction, archaeology needs television to remain a sustainable enterprise much more than television needs archaeology. This implies the necessity of coexistence and the need for some type of integration with these televisual formats. The greatest promise lies in that "'alternative' and serious archaeology can be merged together in a programming format that, by combining the interests of each party, would ultimately rationalize mistaken belief into responsible practice" (Brittain and Clack 2007:19).

The emergence of celebrity in factual programming is not a new phenomenon but is instead part of a larger trend beginning in the 1950s, in which boundaries between factual and fictional discourse have become increasingly blurred. While early documentaries did audition people to assess their suitability for a role in a project, producers in the 1990s began to search for semiprofessional performers who were aware that their casting resulted from their need to be entertaining rather than be scientists or experts (Kilborn 2003:12). As such, three hosts of the programs previously discussed have all been part of the construction of celebrity. As Marshall (1997:65) argues, "Celebrities represent subject positions that audiences can adopt or adapt in their formation of social identities. Each celebrity represents a complex form of audience-subjectivity that, when placed within a system of celebrities, provides the ground in which distinctions, differences, and oppositions are played out. The celebrity, then, is an embodiment of a discursive battleground on the norms of individuality and personality within a culture." If these celebrities embody discursive struggles for the norms of individuality in American society, then it is becoming increasingly apparent that the individual possesses increasing autonomy in deciding who is allowed to do archaeology and why we should do archaeology. Certainly such circumstances may not always produce negative outcomes, but when a celebrity endorses destructive practices such as looting or embracing pseudoarchaeological theories while under the protection of presumed scientific authority, real archaeologists face the problem of being reduced to a universal personality type that is not conducive to preserving and interpreting the past.

In the 1950s, one of the prime movers toward the combining of celebrity with factual programming was Walt Disney Studios, which was already producing nature documentaries when the television era began. These documentaries were purportedly unscripted, with nature as the screenwriter (Lafollette 2013). The series *True Life Adventures* starred anthropomorphized animals (a trend that continues in Disney documentaries today, seen in the recent movie *Chimpanzee*). These documentaries were edited to heighten the drama and draw connections between animal actions and "motivations": "Disney's fictionalizations of nature constructed a tidy world devoid of mess, chance, and human error, and upheld 1950s-style environmental stewardship, which emphasized domination and control, punctuated by sentimental wonder, as the appropriate relationship between humans and other species" (Lafollette 2013:48).

Following the success of Disney programs, the Bell Telephone Corporation began to develop a line of documentaries on various scientific subjects. The need to entertain while also informing led Bell to cast a host who was not a scientist but could serve as an entertaining, recallable face for the public. The role of Dr. Research was filled by Frank C. Baxer, a professor of literature at Trinity College, Cambridge. Scientists criticized the program heavily because of its reliance on conventions of entertainment that supposedly diminished the validity of the science in the program. High ratings rendered scientists' criticisms mute, however, and the program continued unchanged.

One reason why entertainment has overrun informed scientific exposition in documentary is due to changes in the production of these programs. New FCC regulations in the 1970s allowed broadcast and cable television series to become highly intertwined. Before this, educational organizations such as the Smithsonian and National Geographic Society were unsure as to their role in this new system, leading them to cut back television production for mass audiences (Lafollette 2013). The entrance of new commercialized educational networks such as The Learning Channel, the History Channel, and Discovery filled the void for more popular forms of documentary broadcast. However, as Richard Kilborn (2003:8) notes, "one of the most tangible consequences of the growing commercialization of the whole broadcasting sector is that all established TV genres have, to a greater or less extent, become commodified. In practical terms, this has meant that programs within the larger domain of the factual/documentary are required, in the language of broadcasting executives, to 'earn the right to be there.'"

Another critical issue that has surfaced with the rise of the reality format is the necessity for the programming to incorporate entertainment and drama. For example, the cavalier attitude of the producers of *Nazi War Diggers* toward historical objects is certainly an egregious example of how all of these reality television programs and infotainment strip dignity from the past. Of course, the commercialization of artifacts and the mishandling of human remains in archaeological contexts demand outrage from both preservationists and the public. The commercialization of artifacts by these programs is caused partially by their object-centric focus but also derives from the format of reality television. Certainly one of the most common themes of all of the programs discussed is the elevation of the banal, a phenomenon Bourdieu (2001) has likened to a form of symbolic violence that is tacitly accepted between producers and viewers. The sensationalism that accompanies traipsing about World War II battlefields both attracts the notice of the viewer to a particular phenomenon while paradoxically diverting our vision from it. In a sense, the banal obscures the precious. In the case of elevating the banal elements of "unearthing history," the reality television format obstructs the importance of proper documentation and curation of historical materials. In some cases, an even more problematic issue revolves around the repatriation of objects to local and/or descendant communities. Touting the fact that the past is preserved by selling these artifacts is pointless if the question as to whom these objects are being preserved for cannot be answered or addressed.

The productive dialogue with measurable outcomes that has been established between the National Geographic Society and various archaeological organizations is promising for the future of the relationship between archaeologists and the media. But the ethical quandaries surrounding artifact collecting by hobbyists will continue to surface while such programs persist. Pitblado (2014) suggests that it is ethically imperative that archaeologists engage with and cooperate with artifact collectors and hobbyists. Such an imperative is driven by two principles: the necessity to engage in stewardship of the past, and the effort to prevent the commercialization of prehistoric and historic objects. While the ethical ramifications of cooperating with artifact collectors is beyond the scope of this chapter, it is important that archaeologists consider how their interactions with the media promote stewardship of the past while reducing the commercialization and sale of prehistoric objects. As such, archaeologists may be ethically obliged in some cases to address questionable practices by media productions. The outcome of the dialogue between archaeological associations and the National Geographic Society was viewed as less than satisfactory by some, but it arguably represented an improvement for the preservation of the past. Regardless, archaeologists are obligated to either cooperate with or criticize producers of archaeological documentaries, whether or not the format is reality television.

How can we as archaeologists cooperate with the public such that a viable, sustainable archaeology free of scientific illiteracy can be attained? Brittain and Clack argue that new media forms represent a "violent deconstruction process of the traditional foundations of archaeological thinking, looking to break away from author-centered interpretation and instead explore the potentials of a multiplicity of interpretation, reflexivity, and intertextuality" (2007:27). The phenomenological aspects of factual programming centered on archaeology actually offer archaeologists new ways to connect the public to the past. Viewers can become empowered to reposition themselves to the past through phenomenological television formats. The problem we face is presenting the data in such a manner that avoids the unqualified extraction of archaeological data and interpretations that stray too far from the bounds of science while also fulfilling the demand for narrative, drama, and entertainment that are currently necessary for the success of any program. Drama and narrative are not our enemies as archaeologists, but overdramatization that skews reality is a problem. Any mutual engagement must come to terms with why many people watch television—to seek new information but also to be told a story. Considering the importance of narrative and storytelling in human prehistory and our penchant as archaeologists for examining ancient narratives in minutiae, there is great benefit and future for the media and archaeology but only if both sides understand the needs of the other. In our environment, we need to find ways to tell stories that are compelling/dramatic without tipping into celebrity worship and drama for its own sake. Reconciling new dramatic forms within factual programming with the goals of archaeologists and educators has become the new imperative. Fictional representation can no longer be disentangled from reality, and it is becoming increasingly clear that fictional representation will have to serve as a conduit through which audiences receive legitimate information about the archaeological past.

Acknowledgments

I would like to thank David Anderson and Jeb Card for the invitation to contribute to this volume, as well as for a considerable amount of guidance during this process. Many thanks to Curtis Coats, who offered helpful comments from the field of communication studies. The comments of two anonymous reviewers also greatly improved the final draft. Any errors or omissions are my sole responsibility.

9
Lessons Learned from *Lost Civilizations*

KENNETH L. FEDER, TERRY BARNHART,
DEBORAH A. BOLNICK, AND BRADLEY T. LEPPER

The Lost Civilizations of North America is a video documentary released as a commercial DVD in 2010. It has been shown in a variety of venues and was featured prominently and favorably on Glenn Beck's television show on Fox News in August 2010. The film purports to tell the story of the mounds of eastern North America—their ancient and more recent histories. It has high production value and includes interviews with respected archaeologists, anthropologists, and historians. It appears to be a credible contribution to the public's understanding of a neglected chapter of America's past. The video even won an award for the Best Multicultural Documentary at the 2010 International Cherokee Film Festival. Nevertheless, we, who are among the scholars interviewed for the program, hold a different opinion. In this chapter, we present the story of our involvement with this film, explain why the final product is so problematic, and offer some words of advice for others who hope to avoid similar experiences.

How We Got Involved in This Video

Add archaeological video documentaries to the list of things (along with laws and sausage) whose production is perhaps best left unexamined. Though they sometimes appear on channels with well-known pedigrees, many archaeological video documentaries are actually made by independent production companies, essentially subcontractors for distributors like the History Channel or National Geographic Channel. Production companies are commonly told the kind of documentary to make and, we suspect, the approach to be employed. They are in the business of making entertaining films and may not be engaged in such work as part of a commitment to archaeological education or science literacy.

However, things may get substantially murkier when the creators are not on contract, as was the case with the documentary *The Lost Civilizations of North America*. In such situations, the filmmakers are producing a show on spec, ultimately hoping to get it on one of the major cable channels. More important, they are producing it to promulgate a particular perspective or worldview. That view in this case was the "diffusionist" belief that the mound-building people of North America were Hebrew migrants who came from the Middle East about 2,000 years ago.

To support this view the film relied on artifacts known to be fraudulent, such as the Newark Holy Stones (Lepper and Gill 2000), and interviews with a variety of "independent scholars" or individuals without institutional affiliation, formal training, or archaeological experience who are nevertheless confident in their interpretations of the archaeological record and genetic data. The documentary also included interviews with academic scholars such as ourselves, which perhaps made the film appear more credible.

How, you might wonder, did the filmmakers convince each of us to take part in this documentary? Unfortunately, it was very easy. When the producers asked to film each of us—and indeed, during the filmings themselves—they never said a word to any of us about the underlying theme of their documentary. Though in hindsight we wished we had been more circumspect, how could we have turned down their request for our participation? Opportunities to share our work with a wider audience unlikely to read scholarly publications or sit in campus lecture halls are infrequent. When such opportunities present themselves it is difficult to decline, especially regarding a subject about which one has passionately invested a considerable amount of time and energy and that directly appeals to one's professional ethic as a public archaeologist, historian, or geneticist. Truth be told, there is more than a little ego involved, too. Flattering attention by those who purportedly share your interests and value your work will favorably dispose you toward them. Nowhere is that more true than when you are interviewed at the conclusion of a well-attended and successful symposium at which you have just given a paper on the subject presumably in question. Your guard is down and your sense of accomplishment and self-satisfaction is up. You are vulnerable and at risk!

While our naïveté as interviewees played a part in this affair, the most important factor was the failure of the interviewer to disclose the central hypothesis of the film. At no time was a "diffusionist" agenda mentioned. There were no questions regarding archaeological frauds or the problems associated with authenticating anomalous finds. Nor were there any inquiries about potential migrations to the American continent a few thousand years ago or about the indigenous peoples found here in the fifteenth century. Instead, we were asked more general questions about the Hopewell and other Native American societies, their remarkable technological achievements, and their genetic histories. Our interviews were then selectively edited, making it appear that we agreed with the idea that the North American Moundbuilders were descended from Hebrew immigrants. If we had been asked about these topics, we probably would not have given the answers that the producers sought, but we would have discussed them frankly and candidly. Yet therein lies the rub. The producers did not inform us of their perspective or goals and we are not convinced that they were interested in including our honest opinions in the film.

The Diffusionist Perspective

It is instructive to place the diffusionist perspective of the producers in broad context. Kenneth Feder was interviewed by the producers of *Lost Civilizations* on the general topic of how archaeologists in North America assess hypotheses concerning the exploration and settlement of the New World after the migration of northeast Asians at the end of the Pleistocene and before the Columbus voyages beginning in 1492. Some of his comments were included in a prerelease copy of the video. That interview was cut entirely from the version of the documentary that was ultimately made available to the public—a fact for which Feder is eternally grateful. It is revealing, nonetheless, to summarize how the producers misinterpreted Feder's contribution in regard to the scientific method.

In his interview Feder used the example of the Norse settlement of the New World as a model for how skeptical archaeologists and historians have been convinced of the historicity of a claim related to the exploration and settlement of the New World before Columbus. The example of the Norse is instructive on a couple of levels:

1. The material evidence of a pre-Columbian Norse presence in North America, as exhibited at L'Anse aux Meadows (Ingstad and Ingstad 2000) and a number of other Canadian locations identified by archaeologist Patricia Sutherland (2000) and others, provides a benchmark for the kinds of archaeological data that would be expected,

and even required, by historians and archaeologists assessing claims of the pre-Columbian presence of Hebrews or other Old World people in ancient Ohio (and elsewhere).

2. The Norse example proves conclusively that "mainstream" archaeologists have been willing to consider claims of a pre-Columbian Old World presence in the New World and accept them as valid, contingent, of course, on how convincing the data are. This fact negates claims that mainstream scientists are unyielding in their rejection of such scenarios.

Mainstream archaeologists were largely skeptical of the historicity of a Norse settlement in the New World when that claim was based primarily on the Norse written record—specifically, the *Greenlander's Saga* and *Eric the Red's Saga*, both of which were recorded about two centuries after the events they describe (Magnusson and Paulsson 1965). Such an approach is a requirement in a scientific approach to the issue. Until supporting evidence is forthcoming, any hypothesis, historical or otherwise, must be viewed with skepticism. Not surprisingly, archaeologists prefer data in the form of diagnostic artifacts, features, and sites to confirm such claims. Archaeologists may be skeptical about the claimed exploration and settlement of the New World in antiquity by Europeans, Africans, Hebrews, the Chinese, and so forth, but skepticism is not the same thing as rejectionism.

Unfortunately, the producers of *Lost Civilizations* did not draw that conclusion from the Norse example that Feder provided. Instead, they interpreted the Norse example—both their settlement of the New World and the way in which the assertion that they had been here more than five hundred years before Columbus was treated by scientists and historians—through the lens of what Carl Sagan (1979:64) has called the "they laughed at" perspective ("they laughed at Columbus, they laughed at Fulton, they laughed at the Wright Brothers," etc.). If the mainstream was wrong about Columbus or Fulton, they might be wrong about everything else. The producers interpreted Feder's comments to mean that since mainstream thinkers were "wrong" about the Norse they might also be wrong in their skepticism concerning the hypothesized presence of Hebrews in ancient Ohio.

Is skepticism ever wrong in the initial assessment of a hypothesis? Is it wrong to be skeptical and demanding of proof before that proof is offered? We think not. Assertions, claims, and hypotheses are not like accused people afforded their day in court and who are, in American jurisprudence, presumed innocent until proven guilty. It is quite the opposite in scientific reasoning. Assertions, claims, and hypotheses are, in a scientific approach, presumed wrong until proven otherwise. Archaeologists were not wrong to be skeptical about a pre-Columbian Norse presence in the New World before physical evidence supporting that scenario was presented. And they are not wrong to be skeptical about ancient Hebrews building burial mounds in Ohio without any evidence to support that claim. Unfortunately, *Lost Civilizations* does not demonstrate this basic tenet of the scientific method and did not present any convincing evidence that the Moundbuilders were ancient Hebrews. They present no village sites or burial sites or quarry sites with artifacts and features that are diagnostically those produced by ancient Hebrews. Instead of sites with context and association, the producers present a series of "one-offs," individual artifacts, typically with questionable archaeological context, most of which have been conclusively proven fraudulent.

Fabricating History

> On several occasions, I have taken the trouble of calling the attention of the Society to a series of archaeological impostures, that have found a place in our newspaper press—chiefly in the newspapers of the West, where there seems to be a morbid tendency in this direction. Most of them are too transparent to deceive any man of ordinary intelligence, but some are rather adroitly conceived and have led some very clever students into a painful kind of semi-credence.
>
> Ephraim George Squier (1871:92)

One of the many problems with the *Lost Civilizations* video is the degree to which it presents authentic artifacts, such as the magnificent animal effigy pipes of the Hopewell culture (Otto 1984), alongside demonstrably fraudulent ones, such as the notorious Michigan Relics (Halsey 2004). According to the video's narrator, the conflation of authentic and spurious artifacts was deliberate. It was done "in part, to underscore the difficulty in determining authenticity, and also to illustrate a conflict that exists between mainstream anthropologists, and those who have been termed 'diffusionists.'"

The suggestion that the Michigan Relics are worthy of being placed alongside the Hopewell animal effigy pipes as equally likely to be representative of the indigenous cultures of eastern North America is absurd. Moreover, the claim that the reason for this obfuscation was to illustrate the conflict between diffusionists and "mainstream" archaeologists conflicts with the fact that the mainstream archaeologists interviewed for the project were never given the opportunity to present their views on these objects, while the diffusionists were free to offer their ideas unopposed. Showing such artifacts side by side without allowing the so-called mainstream view to be presented elevates fraudulent or dubious objects to an unearned respectability by al-

Figure 9.1. The Decalogue Stone, one of the so-called Newark Holy Stones discovered in and near Newark, Ohio, in 1860. Ostensibly found by antiquarian David Wyrick, the stone presents the Ten Commandments in a unique form of Hebrew, which, though it gives the appearance of being ancient, actually has been shown to be derived from the modern Hebrew alphabet. The figure in the center of the stone is identified as Moses. The Holy Stones were interpreted by some as proving a connection between biblical Hebrews and the Moundbuilders of the American Midwest. Photograph by Kenneth L. Feder.

lowing them to bask in the reflected glow of the halo of authenticity of the legitimate artifacts.

The inauthentic artifacts given the most screen time in the documentary are the Newark Holy Stones (Figure 9.1). The narrator expressly refers to the controversy surrounding these artifacts as a case study that "demonstrates the division between some diffusionists and most mainstream archaeologists." But if the producers of the documentary wanted to teach the controversy, why did they not present the views of the mainstream archaeologist (Lepper) they interviewed who has extensively researched and published on these objects (Lepper and Gill 2000)? One might have expected that the producers were at least passingly familiar with the research and writing of the archaeologists and historians whose participation they had requested. As such, one might have hoped that they were aware that one of those archaeologists, Brad Lepper, has written extensively on the topic of the Newark Holy Stones (Lepper and Gill 2000). Would it not have made sense to at least question Lepper during the interview session about his skepticism concerning the authenticity of the artifacts in question, even if his interpretation was ultimately rejected?

Lepper et al. (2011) exhaustively critique the documentary's error-filled presentation of the Newark Holy Stones, but the most egregious mistake made by the producers and others who champion the Holy Stones as authentic relics of antiquity is the lack of understanding of the cultural context in which these objects appeared. Why were curious stone carvings bearing Hebrew inscriptions found so readily by nineteenth-century researchers (David Wyrick discovered the two principal Holy Stones within four months of each other at sites more than 12 km apart), whereas twentieth-century archaeologists have found nothing of the kind despite decades of survey and excavation in the region? Diffusionists seem to think that such artifacts are still being uncovered but that there is a conspiracy of professional archaeologists to conceal the evidence from the general public. Anyone who could make such a ludicrous claim does not know any professional archaeologists. The discovery of ancient Hebrew artifacts in a demonstrably pre-Columbian archaeological site in America would make the excavator famous.

Matthew Canfield Read, writing about the Holy Stones in 1888, had the right of it. He understood that "such forgeries will always in some way represent the ideas of the time of the forgery" (Read 1888:105). In 1860 when the Holy Stones appeared, the most important scientific debate centered on the question of human unity, that is, whether non-Europeans and especially Africans and American Indians were fully human or not. The United States was about to rip itself apart over the political implications of this debate. Lepper and Gill (2000) argued that the Holy Stones were tailor-made to undermine key arguments put forward by advocates of the doctrine of polygenesis, which stated that Africans were not fully human and therefore their enslavement was justifiable. Finding an object bearing a Hebrew inscription beneath an enormous stone mound in Ohio placed America's mounds solidly within biblical history, thus supporting monogenesis, the view that Africans were sons and daughters of Adam and therefore their enslavement was reprehensible. After the American Civil War rendered the political side of this debate moot and the publication of Darwin's *On the Origin of Species* did the same for the scientific side, there was no more need for Holy Stones and they were largely forgotten.

Why then are the Newark Holy Stones and related frauds and forgeries being revived and featured in twenty-first-century periodicals, such as the *Ancient American* (e.g., Deal 2010) and in documentaries such as *The Lost Civilizations of North America*? The answer is that some biblical or Book of Mormon literalists see the Holy Stones as "scientific" proof that American prehistory can be accommodated within the narrow confines of their doctrinal frameworks. These groups accept American Indians as fully human but deny them an independent history. Some extreme diffusionists, in contrast, have a darker agenda, viewing the Holy Stones as proof that the indigenous peoples of America did not build, perhaps because they were not capable of building the architectural wonders of this continent. Instead, one or another "lost race" of white people is invoked to account for virtually every important cultural achievement in this hemisphere, including the domestication of plants, the development of writing, and the appearance of monumental architecture (Williams 1991).

Naïveté and an obdurate will to believe likewise informed the protracted controversy over the alleged authenticity and significance of the Grave Creek Stone (Figure 9.2). Excavators of the well-known Grave Creek Mound in present-day Moundsville, West Virginia, reportedly discovered the celebrated stone in the spring of 1838. Antiquaries on both sides of the Atlantic bestowed a prodigious amount of literary effort in either assailing or defending the genuineness of the stone and the supposed meaning of its enigmatic characters. Several nineteenth-century authorities accepted the stone's inscription as authentic while others were equally vocal in denouncing it as a fraud. Virtually all of the early accounts of American antiquities made reference to it, generating nearly a half century of debate among scholars of repute.

Henry Rowe Schoolcraft, Ephraim George Squier, Edme Francois Jomard, Charles Whittlesey, Wills De Hass, Daniel Wilson, Matthew Canfield Read, and Cyrus Thomas all commented upon the stone's claims to attention either pro or con—the majority opinion being decidedly in the negative. The Grave Creek inscription appeared to some as confirmation that a people possessing an ancient European alphabet had visited the American continent before Columbus. The circumstances attending the stone's appearance, and the various theories that emerged over the years concerning the presumed meaning of its inscription, are indicative of the trials and tribulations of American archaeology as an infant discipline. The Grave Creek controversy provides insights into the methods, theories, and personalities of several of the most prominent figures in nineteenth-century American archaeology, but it substantiates no theory regarding supposed Celtic or Phoenician colonists in the New World (Barnhart 1986).

Figure 9.2. Ostensibly recovered during excavation of a large Adena burial mound in Grave Creek, West Virginia, in 1838, this small pebble—it is only about 5 cm across—presents a nonsensical inscription in no particular written language. Aspiring epigraphers who have examined the stone have come up with not just slightly varying interpretations but entirely different translations and cannot even agree on the language represented. The inscription as it has often been interpreted is an impossible medley of what purport to be old-world alphabetic characters. The mound in which it was found was excavated—"mined" is a far more accurate term—as part of a commercial venture in which investors were promised fabulous ancient treasures. When these were not forthcoming, and once investors began to lose interest, the inscribed Grave Creek Stone was "discovered" in what likely was a cynical attempt to reignite the money-making potential of the project. The photo here is of a facsimile of the object. The original disappeared sometime after 1910 and its whereabouts are unknown. Photograph by Kenneth L. Feder.

Interpreting the DNA Evidence

Just as "mainstream" archaeologists were never asked about fraudulent artifacts like the Michigan Relics, the Grave Creek Stone, or the Newark Holy Stones, the "mainstream" anthropological geneticist in the film (Deborah Bolnick) was never given the opportunity to comment on the hypothesis that the North American Moundbuilders were genetic descendants of Hebrew migrants from the Middle East. Bolnick was interviewed because she had analyzed ancient DNA from the remains of 73 people buried at two prehistoric mound groups in Illinois and Ohio (Bolnick and Smith 2007). The interviewer asked her about her general findings, about the genetic relationship between the two burial populations and how they were each related to other human populations, and even about whether any genetic evidence supports the Solutrean hypothesis (the idea that Solutrean tool makers from France or Spain migrated to North America 17,000–21,000 years ago, with their technology eventually giving rise to Clovis lithic technology).

The interviewer never mentioned possible genetic connections between the Moundbuilders of North America and Hebrew populations in the Middle East. Had the interviewer asked, Bolnick would have been well qualified to comment because she previously coauthored a genetic study investigating whether the Lemba of southern Africa were descended from Jewish migrants from the Middle East (Thomas et al. 2000). That study established the kinds of genetic patterns that are necessary to support a genetic relationship between the Middle Eastern Jewish population and others, such as the presence of multiple shared genetic lineages (i.e., the same genetic variants should be found in the Jewish population and the putative descendant population). Because the Lemba exhibited several genetic lineages that are found in Sephardic and Ashkenazi Jews, but not in other South African populations, Thomas et al. (2000) concluded that the Lemba may very well be descended (in part) from Jewish migrants who left the ancient Hebrew population in the Middle East and moved to southern Africa.[1]

This example demonstrates that "mainstream" geneticists do not simply dismiss hypotheses about ancient Hebrew migrations out of hand. Rather, such hypotheses are taken seriously and tested scientifically. The Lemba example also illustrates the kind of genetic evidence that is needed if one wants to assert that the Moundbuilding peoples of North America were descended from Hebrew migrants who moved from the Middle East about 2,000 years ago. However, no such evidence exists. The maternally inherited mitochondrial DNA (mtDNA) that was extracted from burials at the Pete Klunk mound group in Illinois and the Hopewell mound group in Ohio shows that these Moundbuilders were most genetically similar to populations in east Asia (Mills 2003; Bolnick and Smith 2007). This finding fits with the scientific consensus, based on more than 150 studies of Native American genetic variation, that Native Americans are descended from an Asian source population (or populations) that migrated to the Americas via Beringia (Kemp and Schurr 2010; Reich et al. 2012). This consensus reflects the observed patterns of mtDNA variation as well as studies of paternally inherited Y-chromosome markers and biparentally inherited autosomal markers.

Furthermore, the genetic evidence clearly indicates that there are no close biological relationships between the Moundbuilders and Middle Eastern populations. The Moundbuilders that have been studied exhibit mtDNA lineages that are different from those present in the Middle East (in Jewish or non-Jewish populations). Because none of the genetic lineages that are common in Middle Eastern populations have been found in these Moundbuilders or in other pre-Columbian Native Americans (Raff et al. 2011), the genetic data provide no support for a direct migration from the Middle East to the Americas in pre-Columbian times.

The *Lost Civilizations* documentary suggests that the presence of a particular mtDNA lineage ("haplogroup X") in one mound group is evidence of a pre-Columbian migration of Israelites to the Americas. This assertion is based on the diffusionists' claim that haplogroup X originated in the "hills of Galilee" in Israel and began to disperse out of the Middle East approximately 2,000 years ago. However, haplogroup X was found in only one of the 73 Hopewell burials studied (around 1 percent), and it is not a marker of Israelite or Hebrew ancestry: it is found throughout the Middle East, Eurasia, and northern Africa; it is not especially common in Israelite or Jewish populations; and scientific studies do not suggest that it originated in Israelite or Hebrew-speaking populations (Brown et al. 1998; Reidla et al. 2003; Behar et al. 2004; Shlush et al. 2008). Furthermore, the forms of haplogroup X that are found in the Middle East are not closely related to the particular form of X found in the Moundbuilders or in other Native Americans, as Bolnick et al. (2012) explain in detail. Finally, DNA studies do not suggest that haplogroup X began to disperse out of the Middle East only 2,000 years ago, as Rod Meldrum claims in the *Lost Civilizations* video. Rather, the most recent and comprehensive studies of mtDNA mutation rates suggest that haplogroup X began to diversify and spread much earlier, about 31,800 years ago (Howell et al. 2003; Soares et al. 2009). The genetic data therefore provide no support whatsoever for a migration of Israelites to eastern North America approximately 2,000 years ago.

Answering Pseudoarchaeology: A Historical Perspective

> The task of fool-killer is not, however, a pleasant one, nor yet that of clearing away the dead wood of falsehood and ignorance. It is far easier to inculcate a truth than to eradicate an error.
>
> Ephraim George Squier (1871:92)

Answering pseudoarchaeology is a difficult task. The persistent popularity of several of the extraordinary claims made in the *Lost Civilizations* video begs for historical perspective. The contentions of the archaeological fringe in our own time had their direct antecedents in the nineteenth century. Old controversies dating from that era periodically reopen and old battles are refought as they move forward in time. Others, now largely forgotten, still define the lineaments of fringe archaeology in any era. But they must be answered when they resurface lest silence give them credibility.

Human gullibility regarding the remote past springs from many sources: faith, fantasy, innocence, lack of caution, and above all the willingness on the part of some to suspend disbelief in the pursuit of romantic and exotic theories of lost tribes, lost races, and lost civilizations. Cult archaeology, indeed, has remained remarkably persistent on that score. Time and again enthusiasts enter its ranks as if nothing has ever been established or settled. The predisposition or will to believe trumps all other considerations among true believers. A few examples from archaeology's past will suffice to illustrate the problem. These are hardly random examples but rather those that speak directly to narratives and speculations such as those made in *Lost Civilizations*. The nineteenth century is replete with examples of those who never let facts get in the way of a good story.

Josiah Priest's *American Antiquities and Discoveries in the West* (1833) is a notable precursor of pseudoarchaeology. Priest's widely read book appeared in several editions between 1833 and 1858. According to the author, it went through three revised editions within the first year of its publication. Priest had this to say in presenting the third revised edition of *American Antiquities* to the public in 1833: "If we may be permitted to judge from the liberal subscription this work has met with, notwithstanding the universal prejudice against subscribing for books, we should draw the conclusion, that this curious subject, has not its only admirers within the pales of Antiquarian Societies." The title page of the fifth edition, moreover, states that the Albany publishers Hoffman and White printed 22,000 copies within 30 months and once again for subscribers only. And therein lay the problem for those trying to establish archaeology as something more than hearsay evidence or the pipe dreams of armchair antiquaries (Priest 1833:title page, iii–iv).

Priest's *American Antiquities* exceeded the author's expectations. It directly appealed to popular interest in the subject and perhaps also to a desire on the part of some for further investigations. Priest examined what he supposed to be evidence "that an ancient population of partially civilized nations, differing entirely from those of the present Indians, peopled America many centuries before its discovery by Columbus." What is more he imagined that he had proven it. Priest ventured opinions as to what nations may have settled in America and built the mounds and conjectured about what may have happened to them. He thought it highly probable that not only Asiatic nations colonized the New World soon after the flood but that other ancient nations also migrated here during different time periods. His reading of American prehistory was as accommodating as it was fanciful. The Polynesians, Malays, Australasians, Phoenicians, Egyptians, Greeks, Romans, Israelites, Tartars, Scandinavians, Danes, Norwegians, Welsh, and Scots all colonized America at different points in time. He further attempted to establish that America was peopled before the deluge and was "the country of Noah, and the place where the ark was erected."

Priest attempted to square the existence of the mounds and their architects with his own literal interpretations of Genesis 6–9. Arguably, Priest's book did as much as any nineteenth-century production to entrench the idea that the mounds had not been built by indigenous Americans but by a presumably lost race. Whatever the actual origin of the Moundbuilders, Priest was certain they had been one of the groups mentioned in the Bible who had presumably peopled the New World sometime after the flood. The most likely candidates in Priest's speculative tapestry were the Ten Lost Tribes of Israel. Priest's work reflected many of the biases and racist assumptions about Native Americans that were deeply woven into the fabric of nineteenth-century American society and culture.

A set piece with Priest's flights of fancy are those found in the three additions or printings of William Pidgeon's *Traditions of De-coo-dah and Antiquarian Researches* (1852, 1853, and 1858). Pidgeon's work represents Moundbuilder mythology at high tide. There were several myths and often variations of the theme within each, but Pidgeon's is among the most original. The author's narrative loosely blends Pidgeon's travels with many wonderful embellishments and tall tales fabricated whole cloth. De-coo-dah, Pidgeon's 89-year-old informant, is purportedly a member of the extinct "Elk Nation." He is the last of his tribe, or at least the last of its prophets, from whom he is said to be descended. It was his people and other ancient tribes who built the mounds before being amalgamated into later groups of North American Indians. De-coo-dah then instructed Pidgeon as to the origins and uses of the mounds based on traditions handed down through his family. Pidgeon at one point floats the idea that the mythical Elk Nation, and presumably other mound-building groups, were descended from Europeans or possibly from Egyptians, but he never produces supporting evidence. The underlying assumption is clear: the mounds were built by someone other than the ancestors of the North American Indians known to history, who had presumably replaced the lost tribes, the mounds in the Upper Mississippi Valley monuments to their former existence. Theodore H. Lewis demonstrated in 1886 that Pidgeon fabricated much of his supposed research and distorted what he actually had undertaken. Indeed, Pidgeon's inspired narrative is so mind-boggling and beyond belief that it is not altogether clear whether he intended the book to be taken seriously or consciously wrote it in the tradition of a farce. Nevertheless, as Robert Silverberg (1986) has noted, several credulous writers in the 1870s and 1880s uncritically cite Pidgeon's hardly creditable narrative without question or comment (Lewis 1886; Pidgeon 1858).

Unbridled theorizing about ancient colonists in the New World illustrates what Stephen Williams (1991) has described with good humor and good purpose as "fantastic archaeology," a province of thought where the imagination runs far ahead of the evidence. W. Lester Hunter (1983) has aptly referred to the persistence of this phenomenon concerning the alleged existence of Old World alphabets in the New World as "cult archaeology strikes again." Further examples from archaeology's past and present could be multiplied. The entire *Lost Civilizations* experience, indeed, is highly reminiscent of what Robert Wauchope (1962) once so brilliantly termed a contest between "Dr. Phuddy Duddy and the Crack Pots"—Wauchope's metaphor for the tension often existing between professional and avocational archaeologists who champion archaeological evidence they believe has been systematically suppressed by the archaeological establishment.

A notable instance of this occurs in the *Lost Civilizations* video in the treatment accorded John Wesley Powell. A conspiratorial tone runs throughout Powell's place within the narrative. Powell set the tone for the archaeological and ethnological fieldwork conducted by the Bureau of Ethnology established in 1879 (renamed the Bureau of American Ethnology in 1894 until its merger with the Smithsonian's Department of Anthropology at the United States National Museum in 1964). It was necessary that he did so given the inordinate amount of unprofitable speculation that centered on alleged archaeological finds bearing mysterious alphabet inscriptions.

Witness, for instance, Powell's critical commentary on interpreting pictographs as evidence of pre-Columbian colonization, speculation that had fueled interest in the supposed existence of Old World texts ("hieroglyphics," as they were often described in the press). Anthropologists needed to think in different terms if they were ever to free themselves from such fanciful theorizing about the pre-Columbian colonization of North America by Phoenicians, lost tribes of Israelites, Celts, or the Welsh: "Hence, it will be seen that it is illegitimate to use any pictographic matter of a date anterior to the discovery of the continent by Columbus for historic purposes; but it has a legitimate use of profound interest, as these pictographs exhibit the beginning of written language and the beginning of pictorial art, yet undifferentiated; and if the scholars of America will collect and study the vast body of material scattered everywhere—over the valleys and on the mountain sides—from it can be written one of the most interesting chapters in the early history of mankind" (Powell 1881:75). Powell argued that it was "illegitimate" to interpret pictographs as a form of written history as that phrase was usually understood, yet he considered them to be of enormous importance as representing the first steps in the development of written language.

The problems of archaeological fraud and associated extravagant theories have attracted considerable attention. William Broad and Nicholas Wade (1983:8) observed in *Betrayers of the Truth* that the study of scientific frauds is important in identifying scientific inquiry "as it is, as distinct from how it ought to be." Science is an imperfect and far from foolproof endeavor, widely held beliefs about objectivity notwithstanding. The pursuit of science is hardly exempt from the basic attributes of human nature. Science aims to be value free, but that is difficult to achieve. It is a laudable goal all too easily corrupted by the desire to establish careers and reputations. Science is a "human process governed by ordinary human passions of ambition, pride, and greed," and "the step from greed to fraud is as small in science as in other walks of life" (Broad and Wade 1983).

Thus the problem of authenticating archaeological materials has beset American archaeology from its very inception. A predisposition to accept the fabulous and fantastic at face value and the corresponding problem of archaeological fraud have been the subject of comment by Caleb Atwater, Albert Gallatin, Charles Whittlesey, Ephraim George Squier, Matthew Canfield Read, John Wesley Powell, Frederic Ward Putnam, Désiré Charnay, and Charles Conrad Abbott, among others. Whittlesey (1876:1) wryly noted that the supply seems to be fully equal to the demand, while Powell attributed the root of the problem to the public's manifest "craving for the marvelous," much as Gallatin had before him (Whittlesey 1876:1). Putnam made a concerted effort to alert unsuspecting archaeologists, museums, and private collectors about the pervasiveness of the problem and, without naming names, was nevertheless very specific in identifying the particular type of artifact that was being manufactured in what locations. When such spurious articles found their way into museum collections, as many already had Putnam was sorry to say, the integrity of those repositories was compromised. The problem is no less acute today even if archaeologists have learned from their history. They are more aware of the problem and ever vigilant in guarding against it (Putnam 1883, 1887:184–85; see also Wauchope 1962; Williams 1991; and Feder 2014).

Conclusion and Recommendations

None of us is happy with how our interviews and research were made to appear that we agreed with the ideas espoused in the film, yet we do not recommend a knee-jerk avoidance of all opportunities to work with filmmakers—even those who are not affiliated with an established source of quality documentaries, such as National Geographic (even the National Geographic Channel has the potential to produce disappointing programming, as demonstrated by its grotesque glorification of looting in the reality show *Diggers*; see Parker, this volume). Lepper, for example, had a wonderful experience working with an independent filmmaker who produced the documentary *Searching for the Great Hopewell Road* on Ohio's Mound-building cultures that eventually aired on many public television channels especially in Ohio and Oklahoma. These sorts of programs can have a very positive impact on the public understanding of archaeology and Native American history, and we think archaeologists, anthropologists, and historians should do their best to encourage and support such documentaries.

However, based on the lessons we have learned from our experience with the *Lost Civilizations* documentary, we would like to offer a few suggestions for reducing the risk of a bad experience when you are asked to participate in a film. First of all, try to get to know who you are going to be working with before you commit to the project. Ask for a list of their previous films. Find out who the producers are working with. And look them up online! If we had looked at the web pages of the producers of the *Lost Civilizations* video we might have noticed some red flags. For example, two of the producers had worked on *Demographic Winter*. This video champions the claim that "below replacement fertility rates in many countries and the decline of the natural family are leading us to a demographic 'tipping point' which threatens catastrophic consequences."[2]

Second, try to get something in writing from the filmmakers regarding the project. A statement of purpose, an outline—anything that will allow you to judge how the content you are providing will fit into the overall goals of the project. Reputable filmmakers will be happy to provide this sort of thing. And do not hesitate to ask questions if you see gaps in the "plotline." One archaeologist in the film, Sonya Atalay, asked for a set of sample questions before her interview, and the production team provided those. In hindsight, the producers provided very vague sample questions and the verbiage they used to describe the documentary film project seemed equally vague. Had Atalay responded to the producers by probing further about the lack of specifics in the sample questions, perhaps the likely nature of the final product would have become more obvious.

Third, it is critically important to ask the right questions of the documentary production company. It is instructive to point out that while we may have been naive, none of us approached the documentary completely unaware of the potential for problems or with our eyes sealed shut. Feder, in fact, clearly remembers his hackles raising when the term "lost civilization" was used in an initial correspondence. In the world of alternative archaeology, that phrase is code for "Atlantis" or related concepts, so, reasonably enough, he asked if the producers were claiming that the cultures of native North America had been inspired by refugees from that lost continent. He was relieved when the producers assured him that this was not at all the theme of their documentary. Unfortunately, Feder mistakenly assumed from this that the "lost" in *Lost Civilizations* was figurative and referred only to the fact that the glories of the Moundbuilders were "lost" on most Americans. Perhaps by asking the producers more directly what they meant by "lost," the film's theme would have become clearer.

Of course, even had we asked further questions, there is no guarantee that we would have been happy with the result. In a previous instance, when the producers of a different documentary expressed the need for an archaeologist to testify as to the historicity of Atlantis, Feder responded that he was not the guy they wanted because of his skepticism on that point. The producers reassured him that he could be his usual skeptical self on camera, explicitly stating that they could edit his remarks to make it sound like he was firmly ensconced in the Atlantis camp. Needless to say, Feder was appalled, not reassured. But such editing may not be unusual. Indeed, in *Lost Civilizations*, selective editing played a crucial role in cultivating the impression that the testimonies of the five of us supplied clear support for the underlying theme of the documentary.

This brings us to our fourth recommendation: try to maintain some control over what the producers do with your interview. Examine the consent or release form carefully. Insist that the producers provide you with a copy of your quotes as they will be used in context within the film or that they provide a complete transcript of the product. This type of request should be written into any consent form that you sign. If it is not there, ask that it be added. If the producers will not add such a clause, do not agree to an interview. If you are at all concerned about the release form being too broad, check with a lawyer. Be wary of being filmed in front of a green screen! Green screens give filmmakers complete control over where you appear to be and allow them to put whatever imagery they want behind you (such as ancient Greek marble tombs, fraudulent artifacts, or Egyptian hieroglyphics—all of which were used by the producers of *Lost Civilizations* to help bolster their claims).

Finally, if you have any concerns about the project or find yourself in a situation where you or your work is being misrepresented, get good legal advice. Bolnick worked closely with a university lawyer after seeing the advance copy of the *Lost Civilizations* documentary, and he helped her to get the filmmakers to correct some of the most egregious problems with their editing of her interview.

Following these suggestions will not guarantee a positive outcome, but they give you some basis for making an informed decision about the risks of getting involved.

It is worth noting that the outcomes of this project have not been entirely awful. It has provided a "teachable moment" that has allowed us opportunities to present our views on these issues to a wide general public. We have published three articles in the magazine *Skeptical Inquirer* addressing the various fallacies presented in the documentary. We disseminated a shorter statement about the documentary and our participation in it via the web, and a blog post relating to the documentary on the Ohio Historical Society's Archaeology web page is currently the most-viewed post by far in the history of the blog. We have also individually given presentations on the documentary and the history it discusses for various audiences.

Notes

1. It should be noted that Thomas et al. (2000) also identified some of the same genetic lineages in non-Jewish (Arab) populations in the Middle East, so it is also possible that the Lemba's Middle Eastern ancestry is derived from Arab (or both Jewish and Arab) sources.

2. http://www.familyfirstfoundation.org/, accessed October 13, 2015.

10
Ghost Hunting as Archaeology
Archaeology as Ghost Hunting

APRIL M. BEISAW

> We tell each other stories all the time; it is the way we are taught to communicate. We do not, as archaeologists, as scholars, necessarily tell each other stories in such a way that anyone outside of our rather small profession wants to hear.
>
> Barbara Little (2000:10)

London's *Times* newspaper recently published an article proclaiming that "archaeology is at its most gripping when it uncovers enigmas for which there is no explanation" (Morrison 2009). However, archaeologists are in the business of investigation and (ideally) explanation of human behavior, not documenting unsolvable mysteries. When the public is interested in real archaeology, their attraction seems centered on "a fascination with origins, the lure of buried treasure, the challenge of interpreting evidence, and the thrill of discovering artefacts and monuments of past societies" (Moshenska 2006:91). The expectation of thrills and challenges sets a high bar that our archaeological site tours, museum displays, and other forms of public engagement have a difficult time meeting.

In our age of personalized on-demand entertainment with instant answers to common questions at our fingertips, archaeology has lost some of the audience it once had. The archaeologist's tale used to revolve around travel to exotic locations, searches for forgotten civilizations, and the reward of seemingly priceless artifacts. Now our tales are about driving up to a manicured lawn, digging where we are pretty sure we know what we are going to find, and recovering small fragments of objects whose importance will be revealed after some data analysis in the lab. We talk about ethics instead of adventure and required training instead of luck and bravery. Others, including ghost hunters, have filled the void for those seeking to know the past through adventure.

During ethnographic fieldwork with ghost hunters, Michele Hanks recorded the thoughts of one ghost tourist: "You get to know a lot of history doing this. . . . Certainly more than I learned at school" (Hanks 2015:130). Ghost tourists are people who travel to historic sites to participate in hunts or walking tours in search of some connection with the past. For the less adventuresome, ghost hunting–themed television programs and movies allow viewers to follow along while brave ghost hunters assume most of the risk and all of the travel expense. With any luck the hunters, and their audience, will get to encounter something or someone from long ago. Tales of ghost hunters are full of suspense and everything else that archaeology used to offer. Ghost hunting is also more accessible than archaeology in that it can be done virtually anywhere and by anyone. Training manuals and equipment are relatively inexpensive and one can become a ghost-hunting professional within a matter of weeks. How easy is it for an amateur archaeologist to become a professional?

To the nonprofessional participant, a ghost hunt or tour is not much different from an archaeology site tour. Upon arriving, a professional gives visitors a quick overview of the site's history. Then the visitor is led around the site and is told stories about specific locations and/or objects. Both may offer the visitor an opportunity to try out professional methods of hunting or excavation. In either case the visitor may or may not discover something and the professional will explain how it does or does not fit within the known history of the site. The superficial differences are that the ghost hunt usually occurs at night, and in the dark, while the archaeology experience occurs in the daytime and is more likely to soil the visitor's clothes.

In many ways ghost hunting is archaeology and archaeology is ghost hunting. The real differences are in the ways that each tells its stories and the nature of its data. This chapter does not address the scientific validity of one approach over the other or advocate for or against a belief in ghosts. Instead this essay compares the ways in which each approach can educate nonprofessionals about the past and suggests ways that archaeologists can improve their storytelling skills by learning from the success of ghost hunters. Those who firmly do not believe in the paranormal and discount ghost hunting as pseudoscience may have the most to gain from this discussion. Ghost hunters have an enviable way of capturing the attention of their audience, and if it is all a scam, then they are master storytellers.

Storytelling

In some ways archaeologists have always been storytellers; those of the late nineteenth and early twentieth centuries published their findings as tales of discovery (i.e., Moorehead 1904). Such stories captured the attention and imagination of nonarchaeologists, young and old. Then, as archaeology moved toward the jargon-filled practice of developing linear culture histories, we began to lose our audience. Instead of explorer and adventurer, archaeologists became the keepers of chronology and our tales revolved around artifact typologies that meant little to anyone outside the local group of professionals. The scientific revolution of processual archaeology put even more distance between us and our audience; significant discoveries were now often made behind computer screens instead of in dusty exotic locales. Even those who understood our artifact typologies might not share our excitement for calculating carrying capacities and modeling settlement patterns. Archaeology, once the stuff of exciting stories (Holtorf 2010), took on the unfathomable labels of "boring" and "tedious."

Recently archaeologists have wrangled with their role as storytellers. In 1998 and again in 2000, the journal *Historical Archaeology* published special issues on storytelling that featured examples of historical fiction created by archaeologists. For example, Beaudry (1998) created diary entries for some of the women who inhabited her site using the real diaries of others who lived there, her knowledge of women's history, and the archaeological data as recovered: fact and fiction were mixed by an expert whose goal was to create more compelling stories about the past than what archaeology normally provides. These special issues also featured discussion pieces written by archaeologists, critiquing their colleagues' historical fiction as well as the place of storytelling in archaeology.

One archaeologist advocated storytelling as a way to enhance archaeological practice by presenting possible explanations along with much-needed imagination (Lewis 2000:7). Another archaeologist suggested that the fear of seeming unscientific has kept archaeologists from developing better ways of speaking to and writing for the public (Majewski 2000 18). This fear is reflected in the position that archaeological storytelling should not be presented as "truth." Clearly archaeology-based historical fiction can help us tell less-technical stories about the past, but we also need to create compelling stories that the public wants to hear.

Archaeology is not where nonprofessionals turn when they want to learn facts about the past. Instead, those who venture to an archaeological site (real or virtual) are usually looking for an experience—a way to connect with past places and people, with their "thoughts and feelings" (Holtorf 2010:382). They want to become engulfed in a plot that has meaning for their present-day lives, one that might even make them reconsider their own values and priorities (ibid.:388). They might be looking for commonality or insight into seemingly timeless human issues, such as unexpected tragedy, unrequited love, seemingly inescapable socioeconomic statuses, or the mental or physical health of loved ones. They are looking for the "magic" of archaeology, interesting methods of solving mysteries through *meticulous* (not boring or tedious) analyses (ibid.:384). Unlike professionals, nonarchaeologists are not concerned with accuracy, yet they do not want to be intentionally deceived.

Producing historical fiction from archaeological data does not necessarily address the main issue—archaeologists have become disconnected from their audience because we do not always tell the stories they want to hear. To produce historical fiction about our sites changes our main genre from technical writing to creative nonfiction, but it does not provide us with a means of sharing the archaeological magic. We have devoted our lives to solving mysteries yet we seem to selfishly keep that part of archaeology to ourselves as we disseminate accounts of methods and results that are devoid of the never-ending stream of questions and misdirections that characterize our work. (Misdirection is the stuff of great stories.) To truly share archaeology, not archaeologically derived knowledge, with the public we need to learn how to connect with nonexperts, to teach method and theory, and to share examples of their application. Ghost hunters, and the ghost stories they tell, are just one model of successful interaction between experts and their audience.

Few can deny the power of a well-told ghost story. Even if the listener does not believe in ghosts, a ghost story is usually welcome entertainment. Deetz (1998) points out that a good story is one that is remembered, has meaning, and leaves readers with new questions for thought. Ghost stories do all of this and for that reason they have been the subject of academic research. The paranormal in general seems to provide a playful space for reflection where the audience can fetishize the past as a way of resisting an undesirable present (Boddy 1994:417). But ghost stories in particular allow us to rethink what is normal and help us understand tragic ruptures in daily life (Harlow 1993).

Many ghost stories are actually warnings of things that might happen, or might happen again, providing listeners with worse-case scenarios and vague instructions on how to avoid them (Goodenough 1966; Santino 1988). As such, ghost stories are perceived as having educational value for real-world situations. For that reason belief in a ghost story is often situational, and ghost stories are usually reserved for the context in which they have the most meaning to the listener (Santino 1988). For example, Tucker documented stories of ghosts in mirrors and other reflective surfaces as told by college dormitory residents. She found that these stories provided a safe way of discussing sensitive issues, like teen suicide, with the ghost serving as an example of what could happen if certain choices are made. Once the ghostly encounter has passed, the participants or listeners move on with their own lives "strengthened by a richer perception of life's boundaries" (Tucker 2005:198). Ghost stories, especially those rooted in historical events, are therefore not meaningless and ghost hunting provides an audience with more than just entertainment.

One prominent writer of ghost stories, M. R. (Monty) James, was a "serious-minded academic" (Clarke 2012:121) with strong ties to archaeology. James published his ghost stories in the early twentieth century, and his masterpiece was written shortly after participating in an archaeological excavation (ibid.:124). The main character was a skeptical scholar who finds a mysterious object. Archaeologist Gabriel Moshenska has studied James's life and works and concluded that his stories worked by juxtaposing the everyday with the uncanny, with artifacts and ancient monuments serving as the supernatural triggers (Moshenska 2012). Horror films also use archaeology as a common plot device to introduce some discovery that must then be confronted by both story characters and audience (Carroll 1981:23–24). As James once said, good ghost stories should leave the reader thinking, "If I'm not very careful, something like that may happen to me" (James 1930 as quoted in Moshenska 2012). The links between archaeological artifacts, sites, ghost hunting, and audience participation are nothing new.

Ghost Hunting as Archaeology

Today's version of a democratized ghost hunting, as site survey with equipment that can be performed by anyone with little training and no special powers, has been traced back to Andrew Green and his *Ghost Hunting: A Practical Guide* (Green 1973; Clarke 2012). Before publication of that guide, most ghost hunts were led by psychics or mediums, who claimed abilities to communicate with the departed, or skeptics, who sought to debunk them. In contrast, many of today's ghost hunters see themselves as part of an oppositional popular culture (Mayer 2013:373) that reimagines "the nature of epistemic authority in knowing the past" (Hanks 2015:126). By positioning themselves as knowledge producers, ghost hunters reclaim historic sites, museums, and other public spaces for the non-elite members of society that they see as under- or unrepresented in museums. For example, during her ethnographic work, Hanks found that ghost hunters "foregrounded the ghosts of obscure or forgotten members of the working class or the poor" (2015:171). But the emotional experience of encountering the ghost was more important to them than creating a historical narrative of the forgotten. Ghost hunters also use a good deal of humor in their work to cast their investigations in a more rational light and simultaneously occupy the positions of skeptic, believer, and scientist (Hanks 2014).

This more egalitarian version of ghost hunting is, at its core, a site-specific history lesson conveyed in an experiential/participatory way, even if the participation is reduced to watching it on television. The really interesting thing about ghost hunting, as I have experienced it through these television programs and by leading students on ghost hunts of a college campus, is that they are often not much more than dimly lit site tours. A successful ghost hunt includes a shadowy figure or unexplained noise, but it does not need to. As long as participants can envision past inhabitants walking up the stairs or sitting by the fire, there is a palpable excitement as they move throughout the historic site, armed with a variety of instruments ready to detect a slight change in temperature or electromagnetic field. The sense that anything can happen is bolstered by the historical knowledge they received at the start of the hunt.

Ghost hunting always begins with a backstory, elements of which are often repeated as way of explaining otherwise unexplained phenomenon. Participants pay close attention to these tales because they know their experience depends on them. These stories do not start at the obvious beginning, when the building was built (most ghost hunts are indoors). Instead they start with the answer to the all-important question of "who cares?" *Residents report seeing the figure of a small boy in this hallway.* Now the tale moves to who the boy might have been—*a boy named John died in the upstairs bathroom.* Names and dates are optional, as they can be inferred from the setting, or they are relational. *After his death the house was abandoned and no one has lived in it for the last 100 years.* Additional details may be withheld until they are useful—*caretakers often hear the name "John" whispered in this bedroom; it is clearly a female voice, perhaps his mother, Elizabeth, the daughter of the couple who built this house in 1884.*

Just before or just after actual hunting begins, participants get trained in the methodology of ghost hunting. Instrumentation is presented—*this meter measures electromagnetic fields, which ghosts can manipulate, but it also responds to areas with poorly insulated wiring.* Procedures are explained—*when you hear a whisper ask if that was Elizabeth calling her son. When you go into the bathroom use this recorder to try to pick the voice of John.* Etiquette is conveyed—*keep quiet and travel in small groups.* Here information is provided only when it is needed and participants pay close attention because they feel that anything done incorrectly might spoil the hunt.

Suspense builds and new stories are told as participants move through the building—*this was John's room, those are his toys still left where they were the day he died.* Certain details are repeated as they become relevant—*John's mother, Elizabeth, was only 20 years old when he died.* The hunt ends, the lights come on, the evidence is evaluated and fit within the original story—

we may have seen John and heard his mother but we also heard a man's voice. That may have been John's father or it may have been the worker who died when the house was under construction. The results are never conclusive but the participants usually leave with an experience they want to tell others about and a newfound interest in this place and its ghosts, supernatural or phenomenological.

Archaeology as Ghost Hunting

Some archaeologists have embraced phenomenology as a means of conveying how peoples (past and present) experience the places we study. One prominent example is Tilley's (2004) book on Stonehenge. Others have addressed the role of performance in the creation, excavation, and interpretation of archaeological sites. The most notable example of this is Pearson and Shanks's book *Theatre/Archaeology* (2001). Archaeology as ghost hunting is a way of combining phenomenology and performance to create engaging site-specific history lessons, without summoning the dead or creating tall tales with no truth value. Archaeology as ghost hunting is a means of invoking the ghosts of place (Bell 1997) in a way that makes them visible to our audience.

Bell's ghosts of place are phenomenological, conveyed by the ability to sense people who are not physically present but can still be perceived through memories, either individual or collective. This perception of a site's former inhabitants fills it with a sense of past aliveness, not actual spirit entities. Certain places can take on a positive aura that reminds us of our social relations, creates a sense of wonder, and commands respect—*this is where John used to play with his two siblings.* Other places take on a negative aura that reminds us of the profane, creates a sense of fear, and either commands respect or contempt—*this is the bathtub that John's father drowned him in because he was crippled.* In a few places we can even envision the ghosts of ourselves or those we care about there, creating a sense of ownership that conveys belonging—*this is the ballroom where the local community gathered every December 31 to ring in the new year, before John's death.*

Ghosts of place are often exorcised when we occupy a new space, through rituals such as cleaning, painting, or redecorating, that allow us to forget that our new place was once someone's old place—*after John died Elizabeth locked the door to his room and forbid anyone from entering, leaving his room as a time capsule for us.* Sometimes we intentionally leave a few reminders behind in the form of heirlooms that have their own associated ghosts—*when she died in 1973, Elizabeth was buried with a locket that contained some of John's ashes.* When spoken of this way, it is easy to see how archaeology can be a form of ghost hunting, for it is the past aliveness of a site that we seek to recapture, understand, and ultimately convey to an audience.

The ghost story interwoven through the text above is based on artifacts. It tells a compelling tale about what happened here without providing unnecessary details. It leaves open spaces for our listeners to fill—*what happened to the construction worker?* It allows for the telling of multiple narratives—*where did the family move to after John's death? Was John's father charged with murder?* It speaks to common human issues such as the loss of a child or a sibling—these things happen and mothers carry on but never forget. It is memorable and it leaves the listener with something to reflect on—*Elizabeth should have protected John. I hope she protected his siblings from that monster. What would I have done if I were her?*

As Bell (1997) points out, historic sites have long attempted to summon their ghosts of place for tourists. Preserving the condition of the site to the time about which stories are told helps visitors envision the ghosts, while a poor state of repair conveys the passage of time. Costumed guides sometimes fill the role of ghosts to help stoke the imagination. These ghosts of place, paranormal or human stand-ins, are products of imagination and social constructions (Bell 1997:831) that appear because we conjured them. But many historic sites fail to conjure their ghosts. I find living history museums to be awkward, for those all-too-human manifestations prevent me from conjuring my version of the place's ghosts. Living history reenactors often instruct visitors in the mundane details of weaving or bread making but make no attempt to address Holtorf's themes (2010) of tragedy, love, and social class. It is no wonder that historic sites are often criticized for making the past seem meaningless and leaving visitors bored (Potter 1981:156). The best way to prevent boredom is to maintain a visitor's senses of discovery and suspense.

Archaeology as ghost hunting resists any attempts at creating or telling static tales about the past, opting instead to bring the audience along on the process of imagining a past and trying to detect its signatures in the present day. Archaeological ghost stories do not need to be fleshed out with historical facts (and certainly do not need historical reenactors) for ghost hunting works best when the stories are simple and incomplete, allowing each listener to fill in the blanks with their own imagination or by asking questions. "What was that noise?" is replaced with "How was that thing used?" and "What does this shadow mean?" is replaced with "What does that soil color mean?" The space for these questions can only be created by the lack of a scripted narrative, the sheer presence of which assures the audience that they should not have questions and if they do they probably were not paying attention. Like ghost hunters, let's tell our audience just what they need to know to get started. Let's let our audiences decide what else they need to know. Let's give them the opportunity to conjure their ghosts of our shared places.

Archaeology as ghost hunting starts its stories in unexpected places. This prevents us from telling stories that our audience has already heard and encourages us to tell familiar stories in a different way. Use archaeology as a safe way to discuss sensitive issues that have meaning in the lives of the visitors and that make sense for the context of this site (Tucker 2005). Look for the timeless human issues (Holtorf 2010) or ruptures in normal life (Harlow 1993) that this site exemplifies. Construct the archaeological story such that it provides instruction on how such events can be avoided (Goodenough 1966; Santino 1988). Allow the past to be a playful space for reflection (Boddy 1994). End the story when visitors have an awakened curiosity. Remember that a good story is one that is remembered, has meaning, and leaves readers with new questions for thought (Deetz 1998). Give visitors a reason to seek out additional information on their own.

Archaeology as ghost hunting does not insult or bore its audience through the use of unnecessary jargon. The magic of archaeology is the way we use techniques to solve mysteries (Holtorf 2010). So jargon should be reserved for the technical names of equipment or techniques, which the audience wants to learn about. Even then the jargon is explained using real-world examples and the technical terms are repeated on a regular basis so that the listener remembers without making a conscious effort to do so—this is an EMF meter, it detects and measures electromagnetic fields. It is believed that ghosts can manipulate electric fields and therefore changing EMF levels suggest a ghost is nearby. It also responds to areas with active electric currents. See how the values change by this fuse box? In ghost hunting the story is always limited to exactly what is relevant to the listener given the current situation, and demonstrations help solidify content in the mind of the listener. This method of communicating technical information reduces the chance of boring or insulting the listener by assuming they know more or less than you think they know. Any additional detail about how an EMF meter works might insult an electrician or engineer or bore anyone who is not an electrician or engineer.

Archaeology as ghost hunting is just an approach to telling good archaeological stories, especially those where a nonprofessional audience is meant to interact with an archaeological site either in person or through media. Archaeology as ghost hunting is about phenomenology and performance, not about the paranormal. It is a call to share with our audience the elements of adventure, exploration, and discovery that make archaeology special. Archaeology as ghost hunting is about doing what we do but uses imagination to enhance what we do (Lewis 2000).

The Educational Power of Ghost Hunting

While teaching at a small liberal arts college in Ohio, I experienced the educational power of ghost hunting. As soon as I arrived on campus, several local residents asked if I could use my archaeological expertise to help save some historic buildings in the surrounding town. I teamed with the historical society to conduct archaeological excavations in the yard of their headquarters. The event was advertised as part of the state's archaeology month activities and volunteers were welcome to come excavate with us. We had two people sign up and visitors were limited to those who knew me or were already part of the historical society. I failed to capture the interest of the general public, despite an aggressive advertising campaign.

Not long after this disappointment I was asked to help save another historic building. This one had been donated to the college and was within view of the administration building, a classroom building, and a dormitory. This time I took a multifaceted approach, constructing a course around discovering the history of the building and placing it within the context of the lives of my students and fellow faculty members. The building had been built by one of the college's founders, who also taught there. Later it was home to a beloved dean who held Halloween parties there. Then it was used for student housing and as an apartment house for nonstudents. The history of this house was suddenly relevant to the entire community as each group could see people like themselves in its past.

On the first day of the course I brought the students to the house and asked them to write down what they thought of it. Most students had never noticed the distinctive octagon-shaped building (Figure 10.1) that they walked past to arrive at our classroom. They wrote down that it was an old building in such need of repair that it should be demolished. Some said it probably was once a beautiful place. No one wrote down that the Octagon house was an important place. For the next several weeks my students and I conducted oral history interviews with former residents of the house, searched the college archives and the county library's local history section for interesting stories, conducted small-scale archaeological investigations of the property, and studied the architectural history of the building using insurance maps for the exterior and critical thinking to assess the interior. Once we thought that we knew a lot about the Octagon house we scheduled our ghost hunt.

Figure 10.1. The Octagon house on the campus of Heidelberg University, Tiffin, Ohio. Photograph by April M. Beisaw.

By design the ghost hunting would take place at night. By luck it was thunderstorming, which only added ambiance to our activity. Small groups of students, three or four, arrived one at a time for just 20 minutes of hunting. I distributed equipment obtained from a ghost-hunter website: flashlights, thermometers, and EMF detectors. I supplied a mini-cassette recorder (which my students did not know how to use) and Ouija board (which they did know how to use). I let the students choose their tools and lead the hunt as I recorded them with a digital video camera.

The students were adventurous, agreeing to be left alone in dark places with the cassette recorder in an attempt to contact past residents. In doing so they recited aspects of the site history from memory, asking the professor who built the house if he was there and questioning the dean about her Halloween parties. A leaking roof provided eerie dripping noises, and the chirping of a smoke detector in need of a new battery was challenged as a possible attempt by the ghosts to communicate. Those who used the Ouija board received messages with no immediate clarity, but students saw the initials of the house's past residents in them. They asked what the room our séance was used for. They sought out the ghosts of place to learn more about the building they had come to care about.

Not long after the ghost hunt each student was asked to create a 10-minute site tour. Their instructions were that the tour had to tell stories about the house that they believed were true, each story was to be relevant to the room that it was told in, and the tour had to move from room to room in a predictable fashion to allow multiple tours to proceed at once. Last, the tour had to be done from memory, no scripts allowed. I reviewed and commented on a draft of each student's tour but did not require a revision or final version as a way to encourage creativity. Without a planned script, students were free to respond to each tour group's interests without the anxiety of needing to say exactly what they planned.

We advertised the site tours on campus and to the local community. After my experience with the archaeology month excavations I quietly kept my expectations low. The students arrived at the house with great enthusiasm and a little trepidation. We opened the doors. Within a few minutes we were swamped with guests. Tour groups ranged in size from 2 to 12. As many as 5 tour groups were in the house at once and as soon as a student was done with one group he or she took on another. Some tourists chose to do a second tour with a different student because they wanted to learn more. I stayed outside to coordinate the tours and to solicit feedback from visitors. Most visitor comments can be summed up as follows: "This place needs to be saved and I would like to help." College students, who often get characterized as self-centered and disconnected, asked about organizing workdays to make repairs to the building. The same building that had stood empty for years now teemed with life. The ghosts of that place were out that day.

On the last day of class I asked the students if they wanted to go to "our house" one last time. The entire class took me up on the offer and students took pictures of each other in the rooms and outside on the porch. One student hugged the wall, saying that she would miss this place. Another student told me that she and some friends started coming to the house to sit on its porch on the weekends. Two students asked me about starting a historic preservation group on campus. The college administration assured us that money to repair and renovate the house would be added to the college budget.

Several other archaeologists and institutions have begun incorporating ghost tourism into their public programs. In 2011, the University of Pennsylvania Museum of Archaeology and Anthropology hosted their first ghost-hunting event: "We See Dead People." During that event, 166 visitors used ghost-hunting equipment to explore the museum (Xie 2011). In 2013, the

Ohio Statehouse's "family-friendly" ghost tours sold out. In 2014, Michigan State University's (MSU) Campus Archaeology Program teamed up with the MSU Paranormal Society to host an "Apparitions and Archaeology" tour of their campus. Archaeology was the main focus of the tour, but each archaeological story was paired with a ghost story for the same site. Over 70 students attended the one-night program (Meyers Emery and Goldstein 2014). Students touring their own campus to learn about its archaeology—that is the educational power of ghost hunting. MSU plans to make this an annual event.

Conclusion

Archaeologists can learn a lot about telling compelling stories from ghost hunting. Archaeology as ghost hunting is about public education—the goal is to teach nonspecialists about the past and specifically about what happened in a particular place by (1) capturing and conveying the ghosts of place, (2) retaining the magic of discovery that lies at the heart of archaeology, (3) leaving many questions unanswered to spur thought, (4) limiting details and jargon to only what the audience will use during their experience, (5) starting stories in unexpected places and allowing the audience to dictate where it goes from there, and (6) connecting past events to common themes.

All that remains is a clear way of merging ghost stories and archaeology in a way that does not offend those who are concerned with the truth-value of that which is labeled "archaeology." Bell's (1997) ghosts of place is just one example of the social theory we can use to explain how humans can perceive ghosts in places that are special but only after we are told stories about it. Every good ghost hunt starts with stories so that the things we sense can be interpreted within that context—a shadow becomes a little girl, a whisper becomes a command. With a little practice we can translate that power to our sites and artifacts—a tobacco pipe becomes the communal property of tavern guests, post molds become a house built by a group of Native Americans who once called this place home. The contexts should raise important questions in the minds of our audience—"What was personal hygiene like in a colonial tavern?" and "Where did the Native Americans go?" (Hint: They did not disappear and their history is not enigmatic.) Once our audience sees archaeologists as brave guides who can lead them on explorations of a past that they do not already know, we will once again succeed in conveying our explorations of the past and nonprofessionals will better understand the need to preserve and study past places. Archaeology is not about enigmas, it is about understanding.

Acknowledgments

This chapter was inspired by work undertaken with the support and assistance of students, faculty, administrators, and staff of Heidelberg University in Tiffin, Ohio. Although any criticisms should be directed toward me, the chapter greatly benefited from many discussions with Jeb Card about weird things and why they are both fascinating and informative.

11
Answering Pseudoarchaeology

KENNETH L. FEDER

We archaeologists are blessed and, to be frank, at the same time cursed by the popularity of our discipline. Peruse your local TV listings and you will not see many documentaries focused on organic chemistry, quantum mechanics, or the Boer Wars. Ancient aliens, lost continents, and paranormal Aztec (or is it Maya? or Inka?) crystal skulls, however, are ubiquitous and these topics generate a tremendous amount of interest online. Google any of these topics and you will produce a depressingly large number of hits. Students likely register for our introductory archaeology and prehistory courses at least in part as a result of assertions on cable and the Internet about a fantastic human antiquity heretofore hidden from the public. Perhaps the arcane truth about the human past will be revealed in that intro arch course at the same time a general education requirement is being fulfilled. It is a win-win situation all around.

It is a challenge we face every day as professional archaeologists and educators. Even if they do not raise their hands to ask questions about these and similar topics in our classes, our students certainly are aware of and likely intrigued by cable shows about ancient astronauts, rogue artifact diggers, and the Maya apocalypse. Outside of the classroom, as soon as we are introduced as "an archaeologist," we are peppered with probing questions about the Mars Face, pyramids, Stonehenge, and on and on. Should we respond? And, if so, how? The authors of the chapters of this book answer the first question with a resounding: "Yes!" The authors answer the second question: "In myriad ways."

Labels

Before we discuss the ways in which archaeologists ought to consider how to respond to, well, um . . . how exactly do we label the specific claims the contributors to this book address? Some prefer the term "fantastic archaeology," coined by Stephen Williams (1991) from the Peabody Museum at Harvard, which was the title of his wonderful book. That term, or a variation, was later appropriated by Garrett Fagan (2006) for his edited volume *Archaeological Fantasies*. There is always "alternative archaeology," which some prefer. I view that as a bit too noncommittal. It is not enough to characterize the "archaeology" underpinning the ancient astronaut psychosis as being an "alternative" to standard scenarios of antiquity, in much the same way that it is not quite enough to characterize cyanide gas as, simply, "alternative" air.

How about "inauthentic archaeologies," from Troy Lovata's terrific 2007 book by that title? I will throw myself into the mix here, having written the one-volume *Encyclopedia of Dubious Archaeology* (Feder 2010). The organizers of the SAA symposium that inspired this book elected to characterize this phenomenon as "esoteric archaeology" and who could argue with that? Of course, there is always "pseudoarchaeology" or "pseudoscientific archaeology," both of which can be found in the literature.

Then there is John R. Cole (1980) and his term "cult archaeology," which he used to characterize not so much particular claims being made about the human past but the cult-like behavior of the claimants. In Tera Pruitt's intriguing contribution to this volume, she uses the terms "performative inventing" and "performing science." These are exactly what Cole was referring to: superficially replicating the performance of science by, for example, collecting samples for radiocarbon dating, sending those samples out to labs, holding meetings and delivering papers where the results are presented but with no discussion and no demonstrable understanding of issues like stratigraphy, context, or association; oh well. The goal is not to do good science but to look good while appearing to be doing science. Khakis and fedoras are required.

Similar examples of science performance can be seen in popular presentations of cryptozoology in television programs like *Finding Bigfoot*. (By the way, when will the producers of that program, in the spirit of complete transparency and full disclosure, rename it to the far more accurate *Not Finding Bigfoot*? Come on guys; it's been five years!) The performers/researchers in that show use infrared detectors and night-vision goggles. That is pretty sciencey, right? Similarly, only marginally authentic-looking science performances can be seen among paranormal investigators in shows like *Ghost Hunters*, where they preface their investigations with plenty of technical-looking preparations with EMF detectors, thermal imaging cameras, and even Geiger counters (are ghosts radioactive?). The elaborate set-up scenes provide great visuals and scream: Hey, this is real science! We use cool, very techy-looking equipment.

I do not find any of these terms—including the one I used in my encyclopedia—nearly as satisfying as the descriptor applied by British prehistorian Glyn Daniel (1979), who, in his Presidential Address to the Royal Anthropological Institute of Great Britain and Ireland, used the far more colorful—and appropriate—phrase "bullshit archaeology." In fact, that was my choice for the title of the aforementioned *Dubious Archaeology* encyclopedia, which, by the way, is intended for high school libraries. For reasons not entirely clear to me, my publisher opted for the milder title.

Whatever We Call It, What Should We Do about It?

Whatever we end up calling it, the far more substantial issue is one wrestled with by the contributors to this book: What is the best strategy for archaeologists in dealing with "fantastic-alternative-cult-inauthentic-dubious-esoteric-pseudo-pseudoscientific-bullshit" archaeology?

Some of our colleagues in archaeology seem to believe that the best response to nonsense is no response at all, that it is preferable to ignore extreme claims about the human past—including ancient aliens, lost Maya manuscripts, Lost Tribes of mound-building Israelites, lost continents, gleaming ancient White Cities nestled on mountain tops, 12,000-year-old pyramids in Bosnia, and giant carved faces in Australia—for fear that a naive public may believe that any kind of a response by professional archaeologists elevates the claims to a level of seriousness that is undeserved. In other words, the assumption here is that the public will interpret any response by professionals as an admission that there is a genuine controversy and a meaningful debate to be had on these topics. Denis Gojak's statistics (this volume) concerning the professional response to a circulated email proposing the existence of a giant carved face in Australia are as informative as they are frustrating. Half of his academic sample did not even read the email, and while there was a general, though weak, consensus that a response was needed, it appears that, with the exception of a single individual, no one actually took the time to respond.

Obviously the contributors to this volume, as shown by their participation in its publication, would disagree that it is best not to respond at all to emails, letters, phone calls, or media treatments of ancient aliens, psychic archaeologists, giant faces carved in the desert, and the like. I would add that in almost every instance, a conscious decision to ignore extreme claims made about the human past is irresponsible and elitist, surrendering public discourse about the human past to those who are not in any way committed to its honest and objective study and appraisal. I admit to refusing to respond to an email communication I received from a correspondent who, after viewing me in a television documentary about Atlantis (I think), sent me a thoroughly insulting email, which he closed with the statement: "You sir, are full of shit." However, the writer asked me not to respond to this because, as he put it, he was using his mom's email address and she would not understand. Point taken.

Ambivalence and Equivalence

This certainly is not the only instance in which I have felt the hate. At one time or another, most of us who have publicly commented on issues related to extreme claims made in the name of human antiquity have borne the brunt of attacks on our intelligence, our knowledge, and, in some cases, even our parentage. A recent experience has given me some insight into this particular issue.

Immediately following a public presentation on the topic of archaeological frauds at a local historical society, I was approached by a gentleman brandishing a thick volume that turned out to be a photo album. The album contained page after page of mostly underexposed photographs, all taken in southern New England, of what appeared pretty clearly to be glacial erratics. Some were quite impressive and interesting but otherwise unremarkable and standard examples of an extremely well-known category of glacial features. Most were large boulders positioned on exposed bedrock, some were resting on forest soil, and a few were firmly perched on top of smaller erratics.

"Do you think *these* are archaeological frauds?" he good-naturedly inquired of me. "No, of course not," I responded. "These appear to be geological features called erratics, boulders plucked from their bedrock sources by ancient glaciers during the Ice Age or Pleistocene Epoch. The ice pushed them along, sometimes great distances from their point of origin. Erratics are very cool and their discovery and identification played a key role in the recognition by scientists in the nineteenth century that parts of the world that are now free of ice were, at one time, covered by large, moving, frozen rivers. The moving ice pushed the boulders around, sometimes even raising them up to the tops of mountains. You've got some awesome photographs of a bunch of terrific examples."

I thought I had been pretty polite and, I hoped, informative. I also was confident, given the limited information I had, that my diagnosis was correct. My newfound friend thought otherwise and responded in an extremely revealing way: "Well," he said, "I don't know anything about geology . . . but I'm sure these are not erratics."

It was truly an amazing response when you consider it. How can an otherwise quite pleasant and seemingly intelligent and reasonable person begin a sentence by admitting complete ignorance about the topic under discussion, yet then go on to make an apparently definitive diagnosis? How does that thought process work? "Well, I'm an archaeologist and I don't know anything about neurosurgery, but I'll give it a shot and suggest that your headaches are the result of a brain tumor. Let me sharpen my Marshalltown and we can take a look." Would anyone consider that a prudent course of action? Shouldn't an admission of ignorance about a subject result in a reluctance to share a strong opinion about it, at least out loud? If you disagree, remind me to share my take on string theory with you sometime.

The gentleman proceeded to lecture me about the boulders. They were, he maintained, "not natural" and had been carved and placed "in straight lines," impossible through any natural agency, he assured me. He went on to suggest that the boulders had been carefully positioned by an ancient, unidentified race of people for reasons that were not well explained to me and that continue to remain rather obscure in my mind. He seemed unimpressed—and unconvinced— by my description of erratic boulder trains deposited in straight lines along lateral moraines.

After a little more back and forth we essentially agreed to disagree about the boulders. Before we went our separate ways, I gave him the email address of a geologist colleague of mine (who in all likelihood will never forgive me) and he gave me a business card that included his name and contact information. The professionally printed card also had boldly emblazoned across its center the gentleman's focus of interest: ARCHEOLGY. I am aware of a couple of alternate spellings of "archaeology" but I am reasonably sure that this is not one of them.

I think the entire experience reflects the ambivalence the "pseudos" feel about mainstream science similar to what Card and Anderson refer to in their introduction to this book. I had the clear impression that my friend's statement that "I don't know anything about geology" was both an admission and, at the same time, a point of pride. He might have wished for the greater heft that would have been afforded his argument had he possessed a degree, maybe even a PhD in geology, but at least his interpretations had not been corrupted by geological orthodoxy. I think he felt unburdened and unbridled by geological theory or consensus. His interpretation was therefore pure and innovative, his creativity unconstrained by the shackles of traditional explanations. Nevertheless the question is begged: If a maverick researcher does not need experience or knowledge in the field in which his research is conducted, why share his groundbreaking results with a mainstream scientist? Was he picking a fight? I did not get that impression at all. Was he looking for my validation? Maybe, but I do not think he was counting on it or even expecting it. He certainly was not depending on it. I believe, instead, he was looking for a kind of equivalence and collegiality in the strict sense of that term. Look at the two of us. We may have attained our status as researchers and thinkers through alternate routes, but our routes were equally valid, each with its own advantages and disadvantages. We might disagree about the significance of the photographed boulders, but we are nevertheless mutually respectful colleagues sharing our opinions concerning a scientific phenomenon. I do not think he was looking for agreement or vindication, at least not vindication of a particular perspective. I believe he was hoping for a far more powerful experience: personal validation. Perhaps this desire for personal recognition, attention, and equivalence is universal among the pseudos. This might explain the level of vitriol they aim at academic archaeologists when we fail to provide it.

What Are We to Do?

Perhaps we will never convince very many of the dedicated purveyors of archaeological pseudoscience that their reconstructions of human antiquity are erroneous. Oh well. That leaves us with the key challenge of crafting the best strategies for debunking nonsense for a public merely fascinated by the possibilities of ancient aliens, lost continents, and the rest but who are not committed, intellectually or emotionally, to their validity.

One reasonable approach may be called "confrontational-reactive," which is just a fancy way of saying that some archaeologists will take the time to respond but often only when prompted to and on a case-by-case basis. In other words, as the result of a student question, a particularly egregious local newspaper piece, or an awful cable show (as Evan Parker has shown in his contribution here, the term "awful cable show" is a redundancy) we respond with a discourse in class, write an impassioned letter to the editor, or make an angry call to the cable station but only in direct response and limited to the particular claim being made at the time. The chapter by Feder, Barnhart, Bolnick, and Lepper reflects this strategy. In response to a documentary asserting that the burial mounds of Ohio and elsewhere were built by ancient Hebrews, they responded with three articles published in *Skeptical Inquirer* (Bolnick et al. 2012; Feder et al. 2011; Lepper et al. 2011).

Mind you, this type of response is absolutely essential but I fear that it represents a game of intellectual "whack-a-mole," the carnival game where mechanically animated stuffed moles randomly pop up out of simulated mole holes and you need to whack them into submission. Of course, as soon as you whack one back into the ground, another one randomly pops up and the one that you have already whacked is just as likely to pop back up as not. Imagine the moles being ancient astronauts, Bosnian pyramids, the Newark Holy Stones, lost cities, lost continents, and so on, and you get the picture. I do not question the necessity of whacking moles when then appear. I do, however, question whether mole whacking is a sufficient response.

The next response category can be called "proactive." In this approach, we recognize that there is a vast reservoir of fascination about the human past on the part of the public and a great interest in hearing our stories about the veritable past revealed through archaeological research. We can attempt to satisfy this interest through popular books, newspaper columns, Internet sites, and blogs. I would like to single out Brad Lepper (2005) of the Ohio Historical Society for his popular book *Ohio Archaeology: An Illustrated Chronicle of Ohio's Ancient American Indian*, his regular column in the *Columbus Dispatch* (http://www.dispatch.com), and his blog on the Ohio Historical Society website (http://apps.ohiohistory.org/ohioarchaeology/). Most of Brad's pieces are proactive, sharing the discoveries of genuine archaeology, exemplifying how the "mysteries" of the past are addressed through archaeological research. From time to time Brad is also confrontational-reactive, responding to specific, popular, and current claims that fall outside of the mainstream of science, but here his readers can view those responses in the broader context of how archaeological research in general can answer questions about human antiquity.

The Anthropology of Pseudoscience

In the overall context of the professional response to esoteric archaeology, in their separate chapters, Christopher Begley, Tera Pruitt, Stacy Dunn, Jeb Card, and David Anderson make the crucial point that we cannot understand claims or beliefs—and, therefore, we cannot construct effective strategies for responding to them—if we ignore the cultural contexts of these claims and beliefs. As they point out, from an anthropological perspective it is just as important to understand the cultural contexts, significance, and meaning of ancient cities occupied by the gods, of pyramids older, larger, and more sophisticated than those found anywhere else in the world, and of ancient curses, witches, and aliens, as well as the skin color of ancient Egyptians (break out the Munsell color chart), as it is to address the historicity of these claims. In other words, it is not enough simply to debunk claims; it is important to recognize and understand the historical and cultural contexts of alternative pasts to the people who promulgate and embrace them. Particularly in the case discussed by Pruitt (the Bosnian pyramids), the pseudoarchaeology being presented is not merely an intriguing topic for conversation. Believers have a strong emotional bond to a construct of the past that archaeologists view as irrational, and we need to understand the nature of that bond if we are ever to effectively address it.

Dunn's chapter raises a vexing and similar issue: Are we wrong to react as scientists to nonsense about the past when that nonsense is being espoused by native people who are descendants of those who left behind the archaeological materials on which the nonsense is based? For example, when writer, lawyer, and activist Vine Deloria, Jr. (1995) launched his assault on archaeology, specifically denouncing the consensus opinion that the native population of the New World arrived here from northeast Asia via the Bering Land Bridge (in his book *Red Earth, White Lies*), should archaeologists have remained silent because, after all, Deloria was a Native American and his perspective and opinion were somehow privileged? Do we give certain categories of people a pass on their embrace of archaeological pseudoscience because they are historically and emotionally connected to the artifacts, sites, and history encoded in those artifacts and sites? As Dunn indicates, is that not patronizing in the extreme, assuming that certain groups of people cannot handle interpretations of the past revealed and supported by the archaeological record?

Other Ways of Responding

Evan Parker has done a terrific job in his contribution to this volume of summarizing some of the more egregious examples of what passes for archaeologically themed programming on cable. As bad as the ones he mentioned may be, there certainly are some wonderful examples of cable responses to bad archaeology, and not always where you might expect them. For example, it would be great if I could report that the definitive documentary response to the ancient astronaut nonsense has been broadcast by a television channel with a general commitment to science education. Certainly there have been some worthwhile treatments of the topic. Some may remember the 1978 BBC Horizon documentary titled *The Case of the Ancient Astronauts* and, more recently, National Geographic's 2007 episode "Ancient Astronauts" in its *Is It Real?* series. However, neither of these was as succinct or as brilliantly done as the November 9, 2011, episode of Comedy Central's *South Park*. There, in the episode titled "A History Channel Thanksgiving," to avoid doing any actual work on a Thanksgiving assignment, the boys turn to the History Channel's *Ancient Aliens* series, where they learn that ancient astronauts attended the first Thanksgiving feast and introduced to earthlings the alien technology necessary for the production of stuffing. As Eric Cartman puts it: "Who needs to read a bunch of stupid books when we've got History Channel?" The show is absolutely spot-on in its parodying of cable documentaries in general, and the *Ancient Aliens* show in particular in the hyperventilated prose of the narration, the breathless presentation by interviewees, and the questionable academic credentials of on-air consultants. In a bizarre turn of events, fourth-graders Stan and Kyle actually become the experts interviewed on a follow-up episode of *Ancient Aliens*. I promise, you will never look at stuffing the same way again.

Archaeologists as Storytellers and Entertainers

In responding to pseudoarchaeology, should we, as April Beisaw suggests in her chapter, take a page from the book of the folks who label themselves as "ghost hunters" and tell far more detailed stories about the past, stories that may be viewed as more engaging, more interesting, and more exciting by the general public? Part of me rejects this suggestion as, in a sense, it appears to raise the white flag to sensationalism. Even with the most sophisticated methodologies at our disposal, you have to admit that we cannot compete with folks who claim to base their stories about the past of a building, a graveyard, an archaeological site, or a person through a paranormal back channel. Why dig at all if we truly had a psychic "way-back machine" (yes, that is a reference to the cartoon *Peabody's Improbable History*)? However, Beisaw makes an important point. Archaeologists are, from the perspective of an interested public, storytellers. We tell stories about some fascinating and unexpected stuff: Egyptian pyramids, Maya calendars, prehistoric migrations, ancient astronomical knowledge, and so on. The burden is on us to tell our stories based on actual evidence in a way that engages the public at least every bit as much as the stories told by the pseudoarchaeologists.

That is difficult, but it is an important challenge that raises a key question: Do most people view traditional and genuine archaeology as boring or, at least, not nearly as interesting as the archaeology and prehistory presented by the pseudoarchaeologists? Maybe. Several years ago in a television documentary focusing on the Bermuda Triangle, the author of a book that wholeheartedly accepted the myth of an inexplicable force responsible for the disappearance of thousands of travelers through the region was interviewed about the evidence on which he based his discussion. At the time, researcher Lawrence Kusche (1975) had recently written a book assessing primary and eyewitness reports, none of which supported the claim that anything in particular was happening in the Triangle. When author Richard Winer (1974), who had written an extremely credulous book on the subject, was confronted in the documentary with the entirely prosaic explanations that Kusche had tracked down concerning purportedly inexplicable disappearances in the Triangle, Winer responded: "If I didn't try to make my books mysterious, I would have another book like Kusche's, is [*sic*] just a bunch of facts and incidents and what most of the reviewers say is just plain dull reading. I try to make my books interesting."[1] It was an interesting and appalling rationale for ignoring evidence, but it reflects an important problem that we all face. If nonarchaeologists find archaeology to largely be water-cooler fodder, who cares about historicity or authenticity? Are most people primarily interested in a good story, the truth of which is a secondary concern? If that is the case, we certainly need to be able to tell good stories in an effort to expose people to what science has revealed about the human past.

That raises yet another challenge. Pseudoarchaeologists are not confined in their storytelling by the need for evidence and logic. Their speculations are not going to be tempered by peer review. We all might put on a brave face when confronted by extreme claims, responding that the real archaeologically and scientifically based scenarios we construct are far more interesting than the nonsense promulgated by the lost continent/psychic archaeology/ancient aliens crowd. But is that really true?

Take, for example, the internal ramp hypothesis for pyramid building as proposed by Bob Brier and Jean-Pierre Houdin (2008) in their popular book *The Secret of the Great Pyramid*. It is novel, intriguing, and well researched, and it appears to explain many of the technological mysteries, both big and small, presented by the construction of the largest of the Egyptian pyramids. On a scale of 1 to 10 for archaeological hypotheses, for me it is a 10. But suppose another archaeologist working at Khufu's pyramid uncovered indisputable evidence for the presence and participation of extraterrestrial aliens in ancient Egypt. That does not solve just the mysteries of pyramid construction. That changes fundamentally our understanding of life in the universe and maybe all of human history. On a scale of 1 to 10, that is a 50! As interesting as the real deal is here, I do not think it can compete (at least on a scale measuring earth-shaking, mind-blowing significance) with the fantasy.

But there is no reason to despair. Of course people are going to be intrigued by such claims and might be less skeptical than they ought to be. Archaeology will always be faced with that. However, as much as people are drawn to fascinating claims that change the way they think about the world, most folks also have an aversion to being fooled and dislike being made to look foolish.

This is an important point. My impression is that while many people are intrigued by extreme claims made about the human past—and many would like to believe them—all but the most committed understand that the claims have not been proven and they are not emotionally wedded to them. In Elizabeth Bird's (1992) anthropological analysis of readers of supermarket tabloids, she found that most of those readers did not take the absurd headlines and stories very seriously. While they admitted that the articles were fun to read, consider, and talk about, it was a guilty pleasure at best and those same readers asserted that they knew most or all of the stories were untrue. Maybe that applies to the large audience of *Ancient Aliens*.

There are statistics that show that even among those interested in extreme claims made about the human past, those deeply committed to such claims represent a small minority. Every survey I have conducted among students since 1983 focusing on their level of acceptance of pseudoarchaeological claims (Feder 2014) shows that, though a depressingly large proportion of them express a mild degree of belief, a similarly high percentage admit that they do not know, and only a very small percentage, for example, strongly agrees that ancient aliens helped build the pyramids or that there was a lost continent of Atlantis. They admit to watching *Ancient Aliens* but recognize the silliness of it. If we can extrapolate from my student samples, there is a large reservoir of public interest but great uncertainty about extreme claims related to the human past. People are interested in the possibility of ancient aliens, lost cities, and lost continents. They enjoy documentaries that present such claims and they like reading about them, but the vast majority are not sure that they are real and strongly suspect they are not. That presents archaeologists with an opportunity to change minds and to shift the conversation. It also means that if we fail to rise to the occasion and respond to pseudoscience, the purveyors of nonsense will monopolize public discourse about the human past.

Their Own Worst Enemies

Occasionally the proponents of extreme claims do us the favor of being so over the top that even fervent supporters are turned off. A student who has expressed an "open-mindedness" about the ancient aliens hypothesis came into class recently, thoroughly depressed by his newfound insight that it was all nonsense. How did he come to this realization? Was it my brilliant lectures? My fabulous and articulate deconstruction of ancient astronauts in my *Frauds* book (Feder 2014)? Nope. It was the *Ancient Aliens* show itself! A recent episode suggested that the genius of Albert Einstein was inexplicable and could not have been the result of hard work or just human intelligence. No, instead, his brilliant mind was ascribed to the genetic intrusion of extraterrestrial DNA: Einstein was a human-extraterrestrial hybrid. Even a gullible follower of the show like my student understood that this was simply crazy and caused him to seriously question the central thesis of the entire ancient aliens worldview.

The Ebb and Flow of Fantasy

Epiphanies like my student's combined with the fact that Erich von Däniken's ancient astronaut theme park, Mystery World, filed for bankruptcy just a few years after it opened give us reason to be optimistic, at least in the long view. A few years ago it was virtually impossible to turn on the TV and not see yet another documentary about the lost continent of Atlantis. Now, lost continents in deep time appear to be passé and ancient astronauts/ancient aliens have cycled back to the top of the pseudoarchaeology heap, right where they were 30 years ago. Perhaps, again in the long view, all such claims have a limited shelf life. Alternatively their popularity trends in a seriation-like waxing and waning, with each claim periodically garnering the public's attention, peaking, and then declining as it is replaced by yet another construct about human antiquity. It may very well be the case that pseudoarchaeology is a disease without a cure but one that can be controlled by our thoughtful, persistent responses.

So what is an archaeologist to do? It certainly is not a viable response to surrender public discourse about the human past to the pseudos. Instead, let's heed the recommendations made by Glyn Daniel in his 1979 remarks to the Royal Anthropological Institute. He concluded his speech with suggestions about how the discipline should best respond to the nonsense that dogs it: "We should set out our considered and well argued views about man and his past as clearly, as simply and as cogently as we can in all ways—in books, lectures, broadcasts, museum displays, television programmes. . . . We should not shrink from pinpointing and exposing false bullshit archaeology in every way we can." I think if, to Daniel's list, we add websites, blogs, and tweets, we still have a pretty good strategy for responding to the challenges addressed by the contributors to this book.

Notes

1. "The Bermuda Triangle: Uncovering the Mystery of a Watery Graveyard," *Nova: Adventures in Science* (WGBH, 1988).

Works Cited

Aaronovitch, David

2009 *Voodoo Histories: The Role of the Conspiracy Theory in Shaping Modern History*. University of Wisconsin Press, Madison.

ABC

2006 Bosnian Pyramid! ABC Houston coverage. YouTube.com. Electronic document, http://www.youtube.com/watch?v=xzDYoEBvCbU, uploaded on May 8, 2007, accessed October 15, 2013.

Abercrombie, Thomas A.

1998 *Pathways of Memory and Power: Ethnography and History among an Andean People*. University of Wisconsin Press, Madison.

Adams, Richard N.

2005 The Evolution of Racism in Guatemala: Hegemony, Science, and Antihegemony. In *Histories of Anthropology Annual Volume 1*, edited by Regna Darnell and Frederic W. Gleach, pp. 132–177. University of Nebraska Press, Lincoln.

Allen, Catherine J.

2002 *The Hold Life Has: Coca and Cultural Identity in an Andean Community*. 2nd ed. Smithsonian Institution Press, Washington, D.C.

Altschul, Jeff, Charles Ewen, Andrew Moore, Monica Heller, Friedrich Lüth, and Noel B. Salazar

2014 Letter to National Geographic Channel. March 31. Electronic document, http://www.saa.org/Portals/0/SAA/GovernmentAffairs/Nazi%20War%20Diggers-V5.pdf, accessed June 10, 2015.

Amazon.com

2013 They Came before Columbus: The African Presence in Ancient America: Ivan Van Sertima: 9780812968170: Amazon.com: Books. Electronic document, http://www.amazon.com/They-Came-Before-Columbus-Presence/dp

/0812968174/ref=sr_1_1?ie=UTF8&qid=1381863243&sr=8-1&keywords=they +came+before+columbus, accessed October 15, 2013.

American Anthropological Association
1998 Statement on "Race." *American Anthropological Association*. Electronic document, http://www.aaanet.org/stmts/racepp.htm, accessed October 18, 2015.

Andersson, Axel
2010 *A Hero for the Atomic Age: Thor Heyerdahl and the Kon-Tiki Expedition*. Peter Lang, Oxford.

Andersson, Pia
2012 Alternative Archaeology: Many Pasts in Our Present. *Numen* 59:125–137.

Andrews, Anthony P.
1985 The Role of Trading Ports in Maya Civilization. In *Vision and Revision in Maya Studies*, edited by Flora S. Clancy and Peter D. Harrison, pp. 159–168. University of New Mexico Press, Albuquerque.

Ankh Amen, Nur
2001 *The Ankh: African Origin of Electromagnetism*. EWorld Inc.

Anson, Jay
1977 *The Amityville Horror*. Prentice-Hall, Englewood Cliffs, N.J.

Appiah, Kwame Anthony
2006 *Cosmopolitanism: Ethics in a World of Strangers*. W. W. Norton, New York.

Archibald, Priscilla
2011 *Imagining Modernity in the Andes*. Bucknell University Press, Lanham, Md.

Argüelles, José
1987 *The Mayan Factor: Path beyond Technology*. Bear, Santa Fe, N.M.

Arnold, Bettina
2006 Pseudoarchaeology and Nationalism: Essentializing Difference. In *Archaeological Fantasies: How Pseudoarchaeology Misrepresents the Past and Misleads the Public*, edited by Garrett G. Fagan, pp. 154–179. Routledge, London.

Asante, Molefi Kete
1996 *African Intellectual Heritage*. African American Studies. Temple University Press, Philadelphia.

Ascher, Robert
1960 Archaeology and the Public Image. *American Antiquity* 25:402–403.

Ashurst-McGee, Mark
2001 Mormonism's Encounter with the Michigan Relics. *BYU Studies* 40(3):175–209.

Asma, Stephen T.
2001 *Stuffed Animals and Pickled Heads: The Culture and Evolution of Natural History Museums*. Oxford University Press, Oxford.
2011 Risen Apes and Fallen Angels: The New Museology of Human Origins. *Curator* 54(2):141–163.

Atwood, Roger
2006 Guardians of the Dead. In *Archaeological Ethics*, edited by Chip Colwell-Chanthaphonh and Karen D. Vitelli, pp. 34–41. 2nd ed. AltaMira Press, Lanham, Md.

2007 *Stealing History: Tomb Raiders, Smugglers, and the Looting of the Ancient World*. Macmillan, London.

Austin, John Langshaw

1962 *How to Do Things with Words*. Oxford University Press, Oxford.

Bader, Christopher D., F. Carson Mencken, and Joseph O. Baker

2010 *Paranormal America: Ghost Encounters, UFO Sightings, Bigfoot Hunts, and Other Curiosities in Religion and Culture*. New York University Press, New York.

Ballinger, Dean

2011 *Conspiratoria—The Internet and the Logic of Conspiracy Theory*. Ph.D. dissertation. Department of Screen and Media Studies, University of Waikato. Electronic document, http://researchcommons.waikato.ac.nz/bitstream/handle/10289/5786/thesis.pdf?sequence=3, accessed June 10, 2015.

Baram, Uzi, and Yorke Rowan

2004 Archaeology after Nationalism: Globalization and the Consumption of the Past. In *Marketing Heritage: Archaeology and the Consumption of the Past*, edited by Rowan Yorke and Uzi Baram, pp. 3–26. AltaMira Press, Walnut Creek, Calif.

Barkun, Michael

2003 *A Culture of Conspiracy: Apocalyptic Visions in Contemporary America*. University of California Press, Berkeley.

Barnard, Charlotte (editor)

1987 *The Last Explorer: The Autobiography of Michael Terry, FRGS, FRGSA*. ANU Press/Northern Territory Research Unit, Canberra.

Barnhart, Terry A.

1986 Curious Antiquity? The Grave Creek Controversy Revisited. *West Virginia History* 48(1–4):103–124.

Barstad, Jan

2007 The Newport Tower Project: An Archeological Investigation into the Tower's Past. Unpublished manuscript. Chronognostic Research Foundation. Electronic document, http://www.chronognostic.org/pdf/tower_project_report_2007.pdf, accessed August 25, 2014.

Bartholomew, Robert E., and Brian Regal

2009 From Wild Man to Monster: The Historical Evolution of Bigfoot in New York State. *Voices: The Journal of New York Folklore* 35(3–4):13–15.

Bastien, Joseph

1985 *Mountain of the Condor: Metaphor and Ritual in an Andean Ayllu*. Waveland Press, Lake Zurich, Ill.

Baudrillard, Jean

1988 Simulacra and Simulations. In *Jean Baudrillard, Selected Writings*, edited by Mark Poster, pp. 166–184. Stanford University Press, Stanford.

Bauer, Henry H.

1984 *Beyond Velikovsky: The History of a Public Controversy*. University of Illinois Press, Urbana.

Bauval, Robert

2011 *Black Genesis: The Prehistoric Origins of Ancient Egypt*. Bear, Rochester, Vt.

Baxandall, Michael

1991 Exhibiting Intention: Some Preconditions of the Visual Display of Culturally Purposeful Objects. In *Exhibiting Cultures: The Poetics and Politics of Museum Display*, edited by Ivan Karp and Steven D. Lavine, pp. 33–41. Smithsonian Institution, Washington, D.C.

BBC

2006 Dig for Ancient Pyramid in Bosnia. BBC News. Electronic document, http://news.bbc.co.uk/1/hi/world/europe/4912040.stm, accessed June 10, 2015.

Beaudry, Mary C.

1998 Farm Journal: First Person, Four Voices. *Historical Archaeology* 32(1):20–33.

Begley, Christopher T.

1992 *Ideology and Cultural Affiliation in Eastern Honduras: Mesoamerican Ballcourts in Lower Central America*. Master's thesis, Department of Anthropology, University of Chicago. Proquest/UMI, Ann Arbor.

1999 *Elite Power Strategies and External Connections in Ancient Eastern Honduras*. Ph.D. dissertation, Department of Anthropology, University of Chicago. Proquest/UMI, Ann Arbor.

2004 Intercambio Interregional, Conexiones Externas, y Estratégias de Poder en el Oriente de Honduras durante Periódos V y VI. In *Memoria VII Seminario de Antropología de Honduras "Dr. George Hasemann."* Instituto Hondureño de Antropología e Historia, Tegucigalpa.

Begley, Christopher T., and Ellen Cox

2007 Reading and Writing the White City: Allegories Past and Future. *Southwest Philosophy Review* 23(1):179–186.

Behar, Doron M., Michael F. Hammer, Daniel Garrigan, et al.

2004 MtDNA Evidence for a Genetic Bottleneck in the Early History of the Ashkenazi Jewish Population. *European Journal of Human Genetics* 12:355–364.

Bell, Michael Mayerfeld

1997 The Ghosts of Place. *Theory and Society* 26(6):813–836.

Benjamin, Walter

1968 [1955] *Illuminations: Essays and Reflections*. Schocken Books, New York.

Benson, Elizabeth P., and Anita G. Cook (editors)

2001 *Ritual Sacrifice in Ancient Peru: New Discoveries and Interpretations*. University of Texas Press, Austin.

Bernal, Martin

1991a *Black Athena: The Afroasiatic Roots of Classical Civilization*, Vol. 1. The Fabrication of Ancient Greece 1785–1985. Rutgers University Press, New Brunswick, N.J.

1991b *Black Athena: The Afroasiatic Roots of Classical Civilization*, Vol. 2. The Archaeological and Documentary Evidence. Rutgers University Press, New Brunswick, N.J.

Bernstein, Arnie
2013 *Swastika Nation: Fritz Kuhn and the Rise and Fall of the German-American Bund*. St. Martin's Press, New York.
Bialecki, Jon
2009 Disjuncture, Continental Philosophy's New "Political Paul," and the Question of Progressive Christianity in a Southern Californian Third Wave Church. *American Ethnologist* 36(1):110–123.
Bielo, James S.
2009 *Words upon the Word: An Ethnography of Evangelical Group Bible Study*. New York University Press, New York.
Binns, Ronald
1984 *The Loch Ness Mystery Solved*. Prometheus Books, Buffalo, N.Y.
Bintliff, John L.
1984 Structuralism and Myth in Minoan Studies. *Antiquity* 58:33–38.
Bird, S. Elizabeth
1992 *For Enquiring Minds: A Cultural Study of Supermarket Tabloids*. University of Tennessee Press, Knoxville.
Blavatsky, H. P.
1893 *The Secret Doctrine: The Synthesis of Science, Religion, and Philosophy*, Vol. 2. Anthropogenesis. Theosophical Publishing House, London.
Blea, Irene I.
1980 Brujeria: A Sociological Analysis of Mexican American Witches. In *Work, Family, Sex Roles, Language: Selected Papers*, edited by Mario Barrera, Alberto Camarillo, and Francisco Hernández, pp. 177–193. Tonatiuh-Quinto Sol, Berkeley, Calif.
Blum, Deborah
2006 *Ghost Hunters: William James and the Search for Scientific Proof of Life after Death*. Penguin, New York.
Boas, Franz
1928 *Anthropology and Modern Life*. Dover, New York.
Boddy, Janice
1994 Spirit Possession Revisited: Beyond Instrumentality. *Annual Review of Anthropology* (23):407–434.
Bohannon, John
2006 Mad about Pyramids. *Science Magazine* 313:1718–1720.
Bolnick, Deborah, Kenneth L. Feder, Bradley T. Lepper, and Terry A. Barnhart
2012 Civilizations Lost and Found: Fabricating History. Part 3: Real Messages in DNA. *Skeptical Inquirer* 36(1):48–51.
Bolnick, Deborah A., and David G. Smith
2007 Migration and Social Structure among the Hopewell: Evidence from Ancient DNA. *American Antiquity* 72:627–644.
Bosnian Pyramid of the Sun Foundation
2009 *Official Website of the Archaeological Park: Bosnian Pyramid of the Sun Foun-*

dation. Electronic document, http://www.piramidasunca.ba/eng/home-en.html, accessed October 15, 2013.

BosnianPyramids.org

2006 Exclusive Interview with Semir Osmanagic. Electronic document, http://www.bosnianpyramids.org/index.php?id=6&lang=en, accessed October 15, 2013.

Bourdieu, Pierre

1977 [1972] *Outline of a Theory of Practice*. Cambridge University Press, Cambridge.

2001 Television. *European Review* 9(3):245–256.

Boyd, Colleen E., and Coll Thrush

2011 Introduction: Bringing Ghosts to Ground. In *Phantom Past, Indigenous Presence: Native Ghosts in North American Culture & History*, edited by Colleen E. Boyd and Coll Thrush, pp. vii–xl. University of Nebraska Press, Lincoln.

Brandes, Stanley

1997 Sugar, Colonialism, and Death: On the Origins of Mexico's Day of the Dead. *Comparative Studies in Society and History* 39(2):270–299.

Brandon, Jim

1978 *Weird America: A Guide to Places of Mystery in the United States*. E. P. Dutton, New York.

Brasseur de Bourbourg, Charles Étienne

2001 [1869] Lettre à M. Léon de Rosny. Written in 1869. In *The Decipherment of Ancient Maya Writing*, edited by Stephen Houston, Oswaldo Chinchilla Mazariegos, and David Stuart, pp. 60–67. University of Oklahoma Press, Norman.

Brier, Bob, and Jean-Pierre Houdin

2008 *The Secret of the Great Pyramid*. Harper, New York.

Brittain, Marcus, and Timothy Clack

2007 Introduction: Archaeology and the Media. In *Archaeology and the Media*, edited by Timothy Clack and Marcus Brittain, pp. 11–65. Left Coast Press, Walnut Creek, Calif.

Broad, William, and Nicholas Wade

1983 *Betrayers of the Truth: Fraud and Deceit in the Halls of Science*. Simon and Schuster, New York.

Brockman, Andy

2014 Springtime for Hitler and "Nazi War [Death Porn] Diggers." *Heritage Daily*. 31 March. Electronic document, http://www.heritagedaily.com/2014/03/springtime-for-hitler-and-nazi-war-death-porn- diggers/102632, accessed March 31, 2014.

Brown, Alan

2006 *Ghost Hunters of the South*. University Press of Mississippi, Jackson.

Brown, Erica, and Ellen Uchimiya

2015 Ben Carson's Unusual Theory about Pyramids. *CBS News*, November 4, 2015, http://www.cbsnews.com/news/ben-carsons-unusual-theory-about-pyramids/, accessed December 18, 2015.

Brown, Michael D., Seyed H. Hosseini, Antonio Torroni, et al.

1998 MtDNA Haplogroup X: An Ancient Link between Europe/Western Asia and North America? *American Journal of Human Genetics* 63:1852–1861.

Brunhouse, Robert L.
1975 *Pursuit of the Ancient Maya: Some Archaeologists of Yesterday*. University of New Mexico Press, Albuquerque.

Bryman, Alan
2006 *The Disneyization of Society*. Sage, London.

Buechler, Hans
1980 *The Masked Media: Fiestas and Social Interaction in the Bolivian Highlands*. Mouton, The Hague.

Buhs, Joshua Blu
2009 *Bigfoot: The Life and Times of a Legend*. University of Chicago Press, Chicago.

Burcaw, G. Ellis
1997 *Introduction to Museum Work*. 3rd ed. Alta Mira Press, Walnut Creek, Calif.

Burgess, Don
2009 Romans in Tucson? The Story of an Archaeological Hoax. *Journal of the Southwest* 51(1):3–135.

Burkhart, Louise M.
1989 *The Slippery Earth: Nahua-Christian Moral Dialogue in Sixteenth-Century Mexico*. University of Arizona Press, Tucson.

Burton, Dan, and David Grandy
2004 *Magic, Mystery, and Science: The Occult in Western Civilization*. Indiana University Press, Bloomington.

Butler, Ella
2010 God Is in the Data: Epistemologies of Knowledge at the Creation Museum. *Ethnos* 75(3):229–251.

Card, Jeb J.
n.d. *Spooky Archaeology*. In preparation. University of New Mexico Press, Albuquerque.

Carey, Thomas J., and Donald R. Schmitt
2009 *Witness to Roswell: Unmasking the Government's Biggest Cover-Up*. Foreword by Edgar Mitchell. Afterword by George Noory. Career Press, Franklin Lakes, N.J.

Carlotto, Mark J.
1997 *The Martian Enigmas: A Closer Look*. 2nd ed. North Atlantic Books, Berkeley, Calif.

Carnochan, W. B.
2006 *The Sad Story of Burton, Speke, and the Nile, or, Was John Hanning Speke a Cad: Looking at the Evidence*. Stanford University Press, Stanford, Calif.

Carpenter, Joel
2001 The Lockheed UFO Case. *International UFO Reporter* 26(3):3–9, 33–34. Electronic document, http://www.nicap.org/reports/lockufoinc htm, accessed June 10, 2015.

Carroll, Noel
1981 Nightmare and the Horror Film: The Symbolic Biology of Fantastic Beings. *Film Quarterly* 34(3):16–25.

Carrott, James H., and Brian David Johnson

2013 *Vintage Tomorrows*. O'Reilly Media, Sebastopol, Calif.

Carter, Bill

2012 TV Digs Will Harm Patrimony, Scholars Say. *New York Times*, 21 March:C1. New York.

Caso, Alfonso

1965 Existío un Imperio Olmeca? *Memoria del Colegio Nacional* 5(3):11–60.

Cerkez-Robinson, Aida

2005 Scientist: Bosnian Hill May Have Pyramid. *USA Today*. Electronic document, http://www.usatoday.com/tech/science/discoveries/2005–12-04-bosnia-pyramid_x.htm, accessed June 10, 2015.

Channel 4

2013 Was Russian "Bigfoot" Actually an African Slave? *Channel 4 Press*, 1 November. Electronic document, http://www.channel4.com/info/press/news/was-russian-bigfoot-actually-an-african-slave, accessed June 10, 2015.

Chapman, Anne M.

1957 Port of Trade Enclaves in Aztec and Maya Civilizations. In *Trade and Market in the Early Empires*, edited by Karl Polanyi, Conrad M. Arsenberg, and Harry W. Pearson, pp. 114–153. Free Press, New York.

Chronognostic Research Foundation

2008a Discovery over Touro Park. Electronic document, http://www.chronognostic.org/over_touro_park.html, accessed October 11, 2014.

2008b Rhode Island U-Haul Truck Unveiling at Touro Park. Electronic document, http://www.chronognostic.org/daily_logs.php?id=7, accessed October 11, 2014.

Churchward, James

1921 *The Origin and Evolution of the Human Race*. George Allen & Unwin, London.

Clack, Timothy, and Marcus Brittain (editors)

2007 *Archaeology and the Media*. Left Coast Press, Walnut Creek, Calif.

Clarke, Roger

2012 *Ghosts, a Natural History: 500 Years of Searching for Proof*. St. Martin's Press, New York.

Clayton, Jay

2003 *Charles Dickens in Cyberspace: The Afterlife of the Nineteenth Century in Postmodern Culture*. Oxford University Press, New York.

Clow, Barbara Hand

1992 Foreword to *Long before Columbus: How the Ancients Discovered America*, by Hans Holzer, pp. xi–xxi. Bear, Santa Fe.

Coe, Michael D.

1965 The Olmec Style and Its Distribution. In *Archaeology of Southern Mesoamerica, Part Two*, edited by Gordon R. Willey, pp. 739–775. Handbook of Middle American Indians, Vol. 3, Robert Wauchope, general editor. University of Texas Press, Austin.

2012 *Breaking the Maya Code*. 3rd ed. Thames and Hudson, New York.

Colavito, Jason

2005 *The Cult of Alien Gods: H. P. Lovecraft and Extraterrestrial Pop Culture.* Prometheus Books, Amherst, N.Y.

2014 Scott Wolter Calls for Congressional Investigation of the Smithsonian; Brien Foerster Discusses Alien DNA. Blog post, *Jason Colavito*, 7 February. Electronic document, http://www.jasoncolavito.com/blog/scott-wolter-calls-for-congressional-investigation-of-the-smithsonian-brien-foerster-discusses-alien-dna, accessed June 10, 2015.

Cole, John R.

1980 Cult Archaeology and Unscientific Method and Theory. *Advances in Archaeological Method and Theory* 3:1–33.

Coleman, Loren, and Jerome Clark

1999 *Cryptozoology A to Z: The Encyclopedia of Loch Monsters, Sasquatch, Chupacabras, and Other Authentic Mysteries of Nature.* Fireside (imprint of Simon and Schuster), New York.

Coleman, Simon, and Leslie Carlin

2004 The Cultures of Creationism: Shifting Boundaries of Belief, Knowledge, and Nationhood. In *The Cultures of Creationism: Anti-Evolutionism in English-Speaking Countries*, edited by Simon Coleman and Leslie Carlin, pp. 1–28. Ashgate, London.

Colley, Sarah

2013 Social Media and Archaeological Communication: An Australian Survey. *Archäologische Informationen* 46:65–80.

Colwell-Chanthaphonh, Chip, T. J. Ferguson, Dorothy Lippert, Randall H. McGuire, George P. Nicholas, Joe E. Watkins, and Larry J. Zimmerman

2010 The Premise and Promise of Indigenous Archaeology. *American Antiquity* 75(2):228–238.

Conrad, Geoffrey W., and Arthur A. Demarest

1984 *Religion and Empire: The Dynamics of Aztec and Inca Expansionism.* New Studies in Archaeology. Cambridge University Press, New York.

Conzemius, Eduard

1928 *Los Indios Payas de Honduras.* Société des Americanistes de Paris, Paris.

1932 *Ethnographical Survey of the Miskito and Sumu Indians of Honduras and Nicaragua.* Smithsonian Institution Bureau of American Ethnology Bulletin 106. U.S. Government Printing Office, Washington, D.C.

Cook, Nick

2001 *The Hunt for Zero Point: Inside the Classified World of Antigravity Technology.* Broadway Books, New York.

Cook, Ryan Jonathan

2004 *Weather-Workers, Saucer Seekers, and Orthoscientists: Epistemic Authority in Central Mexico.* Ph.D. dissertation, Department of Anthropology, University of Chicago. UMI/Proquest, Ann Arbor.

Cooper, Lawrence Andrew, Jr.

2005 *Gothic Realities: The Emergence of Cultural Forms of Representation of the Un-*

real. Ph.D. dissertation, Department of English, Princeton University. UMI/ Proquest, Ann Arbor.

Coppens, Philip

2006 Europe's Pyramid History Unveiled. *phillipcoppens.com*. Electronic document, http://www.philipcoppens.com/euro_pyrs.html, accessed October 15, 2013.

Cosminsky, Sheila

1976 The Evil Eye in a Quiché Community. In *The Evil Eye: Outgrowth of a Symposium on the Evil Eye Belief Held at the 1972 Meeting of the American Anthropological Association*, edited by Clarence Maloney, pp. 163–174. Columbia University Press, New York.

Covarrubias, Miguel

1942 Origen y Desarrollo del Estilo Artístico Olmec. In *Mayas y Olmecas*, pp. 46–49. Reuniones de la Mesa Redonda. Sociedad Mexicana de Antropología, Mexico, D.F.

1957 *Indian Art of Mexico and Central America*. Alfred A. Knopf, New York.

Cremo, Michael A.

2012 An Insider's View of an Alternative Archaeology. In *From Archaeology to Archaeologies: The "Other Past,"* edited by Anna Simandiraki-Grimshaw and Eleni Stefanou, pp. 14–19. BAR International Series 2409. Archaeopress, Oxford.

Cusack, Carole M.

2012 Charmed Circle: Stonehenge, Contemporary Paganism, and Alternative Archaeology. *Numen* 59:138–155.

Daniel, Glyn

1979 The Forgotten Mile Stones and Blind Alleys of the Past. *Royal Anthropological Institute News* 33:3–6.

Davidson, Linda K., and David M. Gitlitz

2002 *Pilgrimage: From the Ganges to Graceland: An Encyclopedia*, Vol. 1. ABC-CLIO, Santa Barbara, Calif.

Davidson, William Van

1991 Geographical Perspectives on Spanish-Pech (Paya) Indian Relationships, in Sixteenth-Century Northeast Honduras. In *Columbian Consequences*, Vol. 3, edited by David Hurst Thomas, pp. 205–226. Smithsonian Institution Press, Washington D.C.

Davies, Douglas J.

2002 [1997] *Death, Ritual, and Belief: The Rhetoric of Funerary Rites*. Reprint. Continuum, London.

Day, Jasmine

2006 *The Mummy's Curse: Mummymania in the English-Speaking World*. Routledge, New York.

Deal, David Allen

2010 The Ohio Decalogue: Its Origins in Eastern Anatolia at Mt. Mashu, the Landing Place of Noah's Ark. *Ancient American* 86:22–27.

Deetz, James

1998 Discussion: Archaeologists as Storytellers. *Historical Archaeology* 32(1):94–96.

Deloria, Vine, Jr.
1995 *Red Earth, White Lies: Native Americans and the Myth of Scientific Fact*. Scribner's, New York.
Dennett, Carrie
2007 The Rio Claro Site (AD 1000–1530), Northeast Honduras: A Ceramic Classification and Examination of External Connections. Unpublished master's thesis, Trent University, Peterborough, Ontario.
Denzler, Brenda
2001 *The Lure of the Edge: Scientific Passions, Religious Beliefs, and the Pursuit of UFOs*. University of California Press, Berkeley.
De Pastino, Blake
2006 Photo in the News: Pyramid Discovered in Bosnia? *National Geographic*. Electronic document, http://news.nationalgeographic.com/news/2006/04/0420_060420_pyramid.html, accessed June 10, 2015.
Derricourt, Robin
2012a Pseudoarchaeology: The Concept and Its Limitations. *Antiquity* 86:524–531.
2012b Pyramidologies of Ancient Egypt: A Typological Review. *Cambridge Archaeological Journal* 22(3):353–363.
Derry, D. E.
1956 The Dynastic Race in Egypt. *Journal of Egyptian Archaeology* 42:80–85.
Desmond, Lawrence Gustave, and Phyllis Mauch Messenger
1988 *A Dream of Maya: Augustus and Alice Le Plongeon in Nineteenth-Century Yucatan*. Foreword by Jaime Litvak King. University of New Mexico Press, Albuquerque.
Diab, Osama
2011 Sacking Zahi Hawass Is a Sign of Egypt's Ongoing Revolution. *Guardian*, 22 July. Electronic document, http://www.theguardian.com/commentisfree/2011/jul/22/sacking-zahi-hawass-egypt-revolution, accessed June 10, 2015.
Dietler, Michael
1994 "Our Ancestors the Gauls": Archaeology, Ethnic Nationalism, and the Manipulation of Celtic Identity in Modern Europe. *American Anthropologist* 96(3):584–605.
Digital Atlas Pty Ltd.
2010 *Bonzle.com digital atlas data sources*. Electronic document, http://www.bonzle.com/c/a?a=ds, accessed September 6, 2013.
Diop, Cheikh Anta
1974 *The African Origin of Civilization: Myth or Reality*. Translated by Mercer Cook. Lawrence Hill Books, Chicago.
di Peso, Charles C.
1953 The Clay Figurines of Acambaro, Guanajuato, Mexico. *American Antiquity* 18(4):388–389.
Dochuk, Darren
2010 *From Bible Belt to Sunbelt: Plain-folk Religion, Grassroots Politics, and the Rise of Evangelical Conservatism*. W. W. Norton, New York.

Dodwell, Charles R.
1993 *Pictorial Arts of the West, 800–1200*. Yale University Press, New Haven, Conn.

Doleman, William H., Thomas J. Carey, and Donald R. Schmitt (contributors)
2004 *The Roswell Dig Diaries*. Foreword by New Mexico Governor Bill Richardson. Edited by Mike McAvennie. A Sci-Fi Channel Book. Pocket Books, New York.

Donovan, Art
2011 Introduction to *The Art of Steampunk: Extraordinary Devices and Ingenious Contraptions from the Leading Artists of the Steampunk Movement*, pp. 24–29. Foreword by Dr. Jim Bennett. Fox Chapel Publishing, East Petersburg, Pa.

Drower, Margaret S.
1999 Sir William Matthews Flinders Petrie (1853–1942). In *Encyclopedia of Archaeology: The Great Archaeologists*, edited by Tim Murray, Vol. I, pp. 221–232. ABC-CLIO, Santa Barbara, Calif.

Dunn, David
2009 *The Successful Treasure Hunter's Secret Manual: Discovering Treasure Auras in the Digital Age*. True Treasure Books, Whitstable, U.K.

Eberhart, George M.
2002 *Mysterious Creatures: A Guide to Cryptozoology*. ABC-CLIO, Santa Barbara, Calif.

Edwards, I. E. S.
1964 The Early Dynastic Period in Egypt. In *The Cambridge Ancient History*, Vol. 1, pp. 1–70. Cambridge University Press, Cambridge.

Ellis, Richard
1998 *Imagining Atlantis*. Alfred A. Knopf, New York.

Emery, Walter B.
1954 *Excavations at Saqqara: Great Tombs of the First Dynasty*, Vol. 2. Government Press, Cairo, Egypt.

Engelke, Matthew
2013 *God's Agents: Biblical Publicity in Contemporary England*. University of California Press, Berkeley.

Ewen, Charles
2013 National Geographic Diggers: Is It Better? *Society for Historical Archaeology Blog*, 1 February, revision undated. Electronic document, http://www.sha.org/blog/index.php/2013/02/national-geographics-diggers-is-it-better/, accessed August 15, 2014.

Fagan, Brian M.
2005 *A Brief History of Archaeology: Classical Times to the Twenty-First Century*. Pearson Prentice Hall, Upper Saddle River, N.J.

Fagan, Garrett
2003 Seductions of Pseudoarchaeology: Far Out Television. *Archaeology* 56(3). Electronic document, http://www.archaeology.org/0305/abstracts/tv.html, accessed October 15, 2013.
2006b Diagnosing Pseudoarchaeology. In *Archaeological Fantasies: How Pseudo-*

archaeology Misrepresents the Past and Misleads the Public, edited by Garrett G. Fagan, pp. 23–46. Routledge, London.

Fagan, Garrett G. (editor)

2006a *Archaeological Fantasies: How Pseudoarchaeology Misrepresents the Past and Misleads the Public*. Routledge, London.

Fagan, Garrett G., and Kenneth L. Feder

2005 Crusading against Straw Men: An Alternative View of Alternative Archaeologies. *World Archaeology* 38(4):718–729.

Fara, Patricia

2009 *Science: A Four Thousand Year History*. Oxford University Press, Oxford.

Feder, Kenneth

1980 Foolsgold of the Gods. *Humanist* 40(1):20–23.

1984 Irrationality and Popular Archaeology. *American Antiquity* 49(3):525–541.

2010 *Encyclopedia of Dubious Archaeology: From Atlantis to the Walam Olum*. Greenwood Press, Santa Barbara, Calif.

2014 *Frauds, Myths, and Mysteries: Science and Pseudoscience in Archaeology*. 8th ed. McGraw-Hill, New York.

Feder, Kenneth L., Bradley T. Lepper, Terry A. Barnhart, and Deborah Bolnick

2011 Civilizations Lost and Found: Fabricating History; Part One: An Alternate Reality. *Skeptical Inquirer* 35(5):38–45.

Feilberg, H. F.

1895 Ghostly Lights. *Folk-lore* 6:288–300.

Fell, Barry

1976 *America B.C.: Ancient Settlers in the New World*. Pocket Books, New York.

1989 *America B.C.: Ancient Settlers in the New World*. Newly revised and updated edition. Pocket Books, New York.

Fennell, Christopher C.

2007 *Crossroads and Cosmologies: Diasporas and Ethnogenesis in the New World*. Cultural Heritage Studies. University Press of Florida, Gainesville.

Festinger, Leon, Henry W. Riecken, and Stanley Schachter

1956 *When Prophecy Fails: A Social and Psychological Study of a Modern Group That Predicted the Destruction of the World*. Harper and Row, New York.

Fetveit, Arlid

2002 Reality TV in the Digital Era: A Paradox in Visual Culture? In *Reality Squared: Television Discourse on the Real*, edited by James Friedman, pp. 119–137. Rutgers University Press, New Brunswick, N.J.

Flannery, Kent V., and Joyce Marcus

2000 Formative Mexican Chiefdoms and the Myth of the "Mother Culture." *Journal of Anthropological Archaeology* 19:1–37.

Foer, Joshua

2007 Love Triangles. *Outside Magazine*, 24 April. Electronic document, http://www.outsideonline.com/adventure-travel/Love-Triangles.html, accessed June 10, 2015.

Forman, D. J.

1972 *1:250 000 Geological Series—Explanatory Notes—Petermann Ranges Northern Territory*. Department of National Development, Bureau of Mineral Resources, Geology and Geophysics, Australian Government Publishing Service, Canberra.

Fowler, William R, Jr.

1989a *The Cultural Evolution of Ancient Nahua Civilizations: The Pipil-Nicarao of Central America*. University of Oklahoma Press, Norman.

1989b Nuevas Perspectivas sobre las Migraciones de Los Pipiles y Los Nicaraos. *Arqueologia* 1:89–98.

Freeman, Michael

2004 *Victorians and the Prehistoric: Tracks to a Lost World*. Yale University Press, New Haven, Conn.

Friedlander, Michael W.

1995 *At the Fringes of Science*. Westview Press, Boulder, Colo.

Friedman, Stanton T.

2002 UFOs: Challenge to SETI Specialists. Electronic document, http://www.stantonfriedman.com/index.php?ptp=articles&fdt=2002.05.13, accessed September 2, 2014.

Friedman, Stanton T., MSc., and Kathleen Marden

2007 *Captured! The Betty and Barney Hill Experience: The True Story of the World's First Documented Alien Abduction*. New Page Books, Franklin Lakes, N.J.

Fuchs, Christian

2013 *Social Media: A Critical Introduction*. Sage Publications, London.

Gaddis, Vincent H.

1994 *Mysterious Fires and Lights*. Borderland Sciences, Garberville, Calif.

Gallivan, Martin D., and Danielle Moretti-Langholtz

2007 Civic Engagement at Werowocomoco: Reasserting Native Narratives from a Powhatan Place of Power. In *Archaeology as a Tool of Civic Engagement*, edited by Barbara J. Little and Paul A. Shackel, pp. 47–66. Alta Mira Press, Lanham, Md.

Gann, Thomas

1926 *Ancient Cities and Modern Tribes: Exploration and Adventure in Maya Lands*. Duckworth, London.

Gardner, Eriq

2012 "Indiana Jones" Lawsuit Seeks Hollywood Profits from Alleged Crystal Skull Theft. *Hollywood Reporter*, 7 December. Electronic document, http://www.hollywoodreporter.com/thr-esq/indiana-jones-lawsuit-seeks-hollywood-399236, accessed June 10, 2015.

Gates, Henry Louis

2011 *Life upon These Shores: Looking at African American History, 1513–2008*. Alfred A. Knopf, New York.

Gates, William

1978 [1931] *An Outline Dictionary of Maya Glyphs, with a Concordance and Analysis of Their Relationships*. Dover, New York.

Genzlinger, Neil
2010 The Pharaoh of Egyptian Antiquities. *New York Times*, 13 July C4. New York.

Gibson, Walter (writing as Maxwell Grant)
1949 The Magigals Mystery. Electronic document, http://www.searchengine.org.uk/ebooks/59/85.pdf, accessed June 10, 2015.

Gilroy, Rex, and Heather Gilroy
2003 *Mysterious Australia*. 2nd ed. URU Publications, Katoomba.

Gladwin, Harold Sterling
1947 *Men Out of Asia*. Foreword by Earnest A. Hooton. Illustrated by Campbell Grant. Whittlesey House, New York.

Godfrey, William S.
1951 The Archaeology of the Old Stone Mill in Newport, R.I. *American Antiquity* 17:120–129.

Gojak, Denis
2007 Two Hundred Years of Secret Visitors: The History of a Pseudo-Archaeological Concept. Paper presented at New Ground: Australian Archaeology Conference, University of Sydney.

Goodenough, Ward H.
1966 The Tale of Pupily-Eyeballs-Thing: A Truk Ghost Story. *Expedition* 8(2): 23–29.

Gordin, Michael D.
2012 *The Pseudoscience Wars: Immanuel Velikovsky and the Birth of the Modern Fringe*. University of Chicago Press, Chicago.

Gosden, Chris
2001 Postcolonial Archaeology: Issues of Culture, Identity, and Knowledge. In *Archaeological Today*, edited by Ian Hodder, pp. 241–261. Polity Press, Cambridge.

Gould, Stephen Jay
1981 *The Mismeasure of Man*. W. W. Norton, New York.

Green, Andrew M.
1973 *Ghost Hunting: A Practical Guide*. Garnstone Press, London.

Griffiths, Nicolas, and Carlos Balinas
1998 *La Cruz y la Serpiente: La Represion y el Resurgimiento Religioso en le Peru*. Fondo Editorial PUCP, Lima, Perú.

Grove, David C.
1981 The Formative Period and the Evolution of Complex Culture. In *Archaeology*, edited by Jeremy A. Sabloff, pp. 373–391. Supplement to the Handbook of Middle American Indians, Vol. 1, Victoria R. Bricker, general editor. University of Texas Press, Austin.

Haddon, Alfred Cort
1910 Note on Mr. Lawrence Hargrave's Paper on Lope De Vega. *Journal and Proceedings of the Royal Society of New South Wales* 44:79–84.

Hadjikhani, Nouchine, Kestutis Kveraga, Paulami Naik, and Seppo P. Ahlfors
2009 Early (N170) Activation of Face-Specific Cortex by Face-like Objects. *Neuroreport* 20(4):403–407.

Halsey, John R.
2004 Forgeries, Fakes and Frauds. *Michigan History* 88(3):20–27.
Hamilakis, Yannis
1999 La trahison des archéologues: Archaeological Practice as Intellectual Activity in Postmodernism. *Journal of Mediterranean Archaeology* 12(1):60–79.
Hancock, Graham
1995 *Fingerprints of the Gods*. Three Rivers Press, New York.
Hancock, Graham, and Robert Bauval
1996 *The Message of the Sphinx: A Quest for the Hidden Legacy of Mankind*. Crown, New York.
Handler, Richard, and Eric Gable
1997 *The New History in an Old Museum: Creating the Past at Colonial Williamsburg*. Duke University Press, Durham, N.C.
Hanen, Marsha R., Margaret J. Osler, and Robert G. Weyant
1980 Preface to *Science, Pseudo-science and Society*, edited by Marsha R. Hanen, Margaret J. Osler, and Robert G. Weyant, pp. viii–x. Wilfred Laurier University Press, Waterloo.
Hanks, Michele
2011 *Between Belief and Science: Paranormal Investigators and the Production of Ghostly Knowledge in Contemporary England*. Ph.D. dissertation, Department of Anthropology, University of Illinois at Champaign-Urbana. UMI/Proquest, Ann Arbor.
2014 Redefining Rationality: Paranormal Investigator's Humour in England. *Ethnos* 1–28.
2015 *Haunted Heritage: The Cultural Politics of Ghost Tourism, Populism, and the Past*. Left Coast Press, Walnut Creek, Calif.
Hansen, Richard D.
2005 Perspectives on Olmec-Maya Interaction in the Middle Formative Period. In *New Perspectives on Formative Mesoamerican Cultures*, edited by Terry G. Powis, pp. 51–72. BAR International Series, 1377. Archaeopress, Oxford.
Hapgood, Charles H.
2000 *Mystery in Acambaro: An Account of the Ceramic Collection of the Late Waldemar Julsrud in Acambaro, Gto., Mexico*. Adventures Unlimited Press, Kempton, Ill.
Harding, Anthony
2007 The Great Bosnian Pyramid Scheme. *British Archaeology* 92:40–44.
Harding, Susan F.
2000 *The Book of Jerry Falwell: Fundamentalist Language and Politics*. Princeton University Press, Princeton, N.J.
Hargrave, Lawrence
1909 Lope de Vega. *Journal and Proceedings of the Royal Society of New South Wales* 43:412–425.
Harlow, Ilana
1993 Unravelling Stories: Exploring the Juncture of Ghost Story and Local Tragedy. *Journal of Folklore Research* 30(2–3):177–200.

Harris, James Wallace

2008 The Science Fiction Event Horizon. Blog post on *Stephen Hunt's SF Crowsnest*, 2 January. Electronic document, http://www.sfcrowsnest.com/articles/features/2008/The-science-fiction-event-horizon-12191.php, accessed October 24, 2013.

Harris, Olivia

1982 The Dead and the Devils among the Bolivian Laymi. In *Death and the Regeneration of Life*, edited by Maurice Bloch and Jonathan Parry, pp. 45–73. Cambridge University Press, New York.

Harrold, Francis B., and Raymond A. Eve (editors)

1995 *Cult Archaeology and Creationism: Understanding Pseudoscientific Beliefs about the Past*. Expanded edition. University of Iowa Press, Iowa City.

Haslip-Viera, Gabriel, Bernard Ortiz de Montellano, and Warren Barbour

1997 Robbing Native American Cultures: Van Sertima's Afrocentricity and the Olmecs. *Current Anthropology* 38(3):419–441.

Hawton, Nick

2006 Indiana Jones of the Balkans and the Mystery of a Hidden Pyramid. *Times-Online*, 15 April. Electronic document, http://www.thetimes.co.uk/tto/news/world/europe/article2601894.ece, accessed October 15, 2013.

Healy, Paul F.

1984a The Archaeology of Honduras. In *The Archaeology of Lower Central America*, edited by F. W. Lange and D. Z. Stone, pp. 113–161. University of New Mexico Press, Albuquerque.

1984b Northeast Honduras: A Precolumbian Frontier Zone. In *Recent Developments in Isthmian Archaeology*, edited by Frederick W. Lange, pp. 227–241. BAR International Series 212, Oxford.

Herlihy, Peter H.

1997 Indigenous Peoples and Biosphere Reserve Conservation in the Mosquitia Rain Forest Corridor, Honduras. In *Conservation through Cultural Survival*, edited by Stanley F. Stevens, pp. 99–129. Island Press, Washington, D.C.

Herlihy, Peter H., and Laura Hobson Herlihy

1991 La Herencia Cultural de la Reserva de la Biosfera del Rio Platano: Un Area de Confluencias Etnicas en la Mosquitia. In *Herencia de Nuestro Pasado: La Reserva de la Biosfera Del Rio Platano*, edited by Vincente Murphy, pp. 9–15. Ventanas Tropicales, Tegucigalpa.

Hertz, Robert

1960 *Death and the Right Hand*. Translated by Rodney and Claudia Needham. Free Press, Glencoe, Ill.

Heuvelmans, Bernard

2003 *The Kraken and the Colossal Octopus: In the Wake of Sea-Monsters*. Kegan Paul, London.

2007 *The Natural History of Hidden Animals*. Edited by Peter Gwynvay Hopkins. Kegan Paul, London.

Heyerdahl, Thor

1971 *The Ra Expeditions*. Doubleday, Garden City, N.J.

Hill, Annette

2005 *Reality TV: Audiences and Popular Factual Television*. Routledge, London.

Hill, Sharon

2010 *Being Scientificial: Popularity, Purpose, and Promotion of Amateur Research and Investigation Groups in the U.S.* Master's thesis, Department of Learning and Instruction, University of Buffalo, State University of New York. UMI/Proquest, Ann Arbor.

2013 Bigfoot DNA Study: Making an End Run around Science. *Skeptical Inquirer* 27(3):12–14.

Hirst, K. Kris

2007 Digging for the Truth: An Interview with Josh Bernstein. *About: Archaeology*. Electronic document, http://diggingforthetruth.net/articles/aboutarcheologyarticle.pdf, accessed April 11, 2012.

Hirth, Kenneth

1989 Observations about Ecological Relationships and Cultural Evolution in a Prehistoric Tropical Subsistence System. In *Archaeological Research in the El Cajon Region, Volume 1: Prehistoric Cultural Ecology*, edited by Kenneth Hirth, Gloria Lara Pinto, and George Hasemann, pp. 233–251. University of Pittsburgh, Department of Anthropology, Pittsburgh.

Hiscock, Peter

1996 The New Age of Alternative Archaeology in Australia. *Archaeology in Oceania* 31(3):152–164.

Hobsbawm, Eric

1983 Mass-Producing Traditions: Europe, 1870–1914. In *The Invention of Tradition*, edited by Eric Hobsbawm and Terrence Ranger, pp. 263–307. Cambridge University Press, Cambridge.

Hodder, Ian

1989 Writing Archaeology: Site Reports in Context. *Antiquity* 63:268–274.

2004 *Archaeology beyond Dialogue*. University of Utah Press, Salt Lake City.

2008 Multivocality and Social Archaeology. In *Evaluating Multiple Narratives beyond Nationalist, Colonialist, Imperialist Archaeologies*, edited by Junko Habu, Clare Fawcett, and John M. Matsunaga, pp. 196–200. Springer, New York.

Hodzic, Tarik (director)

2007 MUSTE DEDIC—Bosanska piramida [Music Video]. Visoko, Bosnia-Herzegovina. *YouTube.com*. Electronic document, http://www.youtube.com/watch?v=5TaLLJf7vFo, accessed October 15, 2013.

Hoffman, Michael A.

1979 *Egypt before the Pharaohs*. 1993 Barnes & Noble reprint ed. Alfred A. Knopf, New York.

Holloway, Marguerite

2007 Bigfoot Anatomy. *Scientific American*. Electronic document, http://www.scientificamerican.com/article/bigfoot-anatomy/?page=1, accessed June 10, 2015.

Hollowell, Julie

2012 [2006] Moral Arguments on Subsistence Digging. In *Archaeological Sites: Conservation and Management*, edited by Sharon Sullivan and Richard Mackay, pp. 202–228. Getty Publications, Los Angeles.

Holtorf, Cornelius

2005 Beyond Crusades: How (Not) to Engage with Alternative Archaeologies. *World Archaeology* 37(4):544–551.

2007 *Archaeology Is a Brand!: The Meaning of Archaeology in Contemporary Popular Culture*. Left Coast Press, Walnut Creek, Calif.

2010 Meta-stories of Archaeology. *World Archaeology* 42(3):381–393.

2012 The Colours of the Past. In *From Archaeology to Archaeologies: The "Other Past,"* edited by Anna Simandiraki-Grimshaw and Eleni Stefanou, pp. 102–105. BAR International Series 2409. Archaeopress, Oxford.

Holtorf, Cornelius, and Tim Schadla-Hall

1999 Age as Artefact: On Archaeological Authenticity. *European Journal of Archaeology* 2:229–247.

Holzer, Hans

1991 *America's Haunted Houses: Public and Private*. Longmeadow Press, Stamford, Conn.

1992 *Long before Columbus: How the Ancients Discovered America*. Bear, Santa Fe, N.M.

Hoopes, John W.

2005 The Emergence of Social Complexity in the Chibchan World of Southern Central America and Northern Colombia, AD 300–600. *Journal of Archaeological Research* 13(1):1–47.

Hooton, Earnest A.

1937 *Apes, Men, and Morons*. G. P. Putnam's Sons, New York.

1947 Foreword and Hindthoughts. In *Men Out of Asia*, by Harold S. Gladwin, pp. ix–xii. Whittlesey House, New York.

Howell, Neil, Christy Bogolin Smejkal, D. A. Mackey, et al.

2003 The Pedigree Rate of Sequence Divergence in the Human Mitochondrial Genome: There Is a Difference between Phylogenetic and Pedigree Rates. *American Journal of Human Genetics* 72:659–670.

Hubbard, Paul, and Robert S. Burrett

2012 A Clash of Ideologies: Zimbabwean Archaeology at the Fringe. In *From Archaeology to Archaeologies: The "Other Past,"* edited by Anna Simandiraki-Grimshaw and Eleni Stefanou, pp. 45–55. BAR International Series 2409. Archaeopress, Oxford.

Humes, Cynthia Ann

2012 Hindutva, Mythistory, and Pseudoarchaeology. *Numen* 59:178–201.

Hunter, W. Lester

1983 Cult Archaeology Strikes Again: A Place for Pre-Columbian Irishmen in the Mountain State? *West Virginia Archaeologist* 35:48–52.

Huttinger, Robert (director)

2006 *Pyramids of Bosnia* [documentary]. Vienna. 9 September. Electronic document, http://pyramidsofbosnia.blogspot.com/2006/09/breaking-news-documentary-film-wrap.html, accessed October, 15, 2013.

ICBP

2008 *The First International Scientific Conference about the Bosnian Pyramids*. Electronic document, http://www.icbp.ba/2008/, accessed October 15, 2013.

Ingstad, H., and A. S. Ingstad

2000 *The Viking Discovery of America: The Excavation of a Norse Settlement at L'Anse Aux Meadows*. Breakwater Books, St. John's, Newfoundland.

Irna

2009 *Le site d'Irna* [blog]. Electronic document, http://irna.lautre.net/, accessed October 27, 2009.

Isbell, William H.

1997 *Mummies and Mortuary Monuments: A Postprocessual Prehistory of Central Andean Social Organization*. University of Texas Press, Austin.

James, M. R.

1987 [1930] Ghost Story Competition. In *Ghosts and Scholars: Ghost Stories in the Tradition of M. R. James*, edited by Richard Dalby and Rosemary Pardoe, pp. 141–147. Crucible, Wellingborough.

Jesús Lanza, Rigoberto de, and Marcio Tulio Escobar

1986 *Los Pech (Payas): Una Cultura Olvidado*. Editorial Guaymaras, Tegucigalpa.

Joralemon, Donald, and Douglas Sharon

1993 *Sorcery and Shamanism: Curanderos and Clients in Northern Peru*. University of Utah Press, Salt Lake City.

Jordan, Paul

2001 *The Atlantis Syndrome*. Thrupp, Sutton.

Joseph, Frank

2002 *The Lost Pyramids of Rock Lake: Wisconsin's Sunken Civilization*. 2nd ed. Galde Press, Lakeville, Minn.

Journal of African Civilizations

2013 Dr. Ivan van Sertima. *Journal of African Civilizations*. Electronic document, http://www.journalofafricancivilizations.com/page/9048, accessed October 14, 2013.

Jung, Hwa Yol

1998 Bakhtin's Dialogical Body Politics. In *Bakhtin and the Human Sciences*, edited by Michael Bell and Michael Gardiner London, pp. 95–111. Sage, London.

Kampschror, Beth

2006 Pyramid Scheme. *Archaeology* 59(4):22–28.

Kehoe, Alice B.

2005 *The Kensington Runestone: Approaching a Research Question Holistically*. Waveland Press, Long Grove, Ill.

2007 Archaeology within Marketing Capitalism. In *Archaeology and Capitalism: From Ethics to Politics*, edited by Yannis Hamilakis and Philip Duke, pp. 169–178. Left Coast Press, Walnut Creek, Calif.

2008 *Controversies in Archaeology*. Left Coast Press, Walnut Creek, Calif.

Kemp, Arthur

2006 *March of the Titans: The Complete History of the White Race*. Ostara Publications, Burlington, Iowa.

2012 *The Children of Ra: Artistic, Historical, and Genetic Evidence for Ancient White Egypt*. Ostara Publications, Burlington, Iowa.

Kemp, Barry J.

2006 *Ancient Egypt: Anatomy of a Civilization*. 2nd ed. Routledge, London.

Kemp, Brian M., and Theodore G. Schurr

2010 Ancient and Modern Genetic Variation in the Americas. In *Human Variation in the Americas*, edited by Benjamin M. Auerbach, pp. 12–50. Center for Archaeological Investigations, Occasional Paper No. 38. Southern Illinois University, Carbondale.

Kenyon, J. Douglas

2005 Exposing a Scientific Cover-Up: *Forbidden Archaeology* Coauthor Michael Cremo Talks about the "Knowledge Filter" and Other Means for Cooking the Academic Books. In *Forbidden History: Prehistoric Technologies, Extraterrestrial Intervention, and the Suppressed Origins of Civilization*, edited by J. Douglas Kenyon, pp. 22–28. Bear, Rochester, Vt.

Ketchell, Aaron

2007 *Holy Hills of the Ozarks: Religion and Tourism in Branson, Missouri*. Johns Hopkins University Press, Baltimore.

Kilborn, Richard

2003 *Staging the Real: Factual Programming in the Age of Big Brother*. Manchester University Press, Manchester.

Kingsley, Patrick

2014 Former Egyptian Antiquities Minister Faces Questions over Theft from Pyramid. *Guardian*, 22 November. Electronic document, http://www.theguardian.com/world/2014/nov/12/egypt-former-antiquities-minister-questions-theft-pyramid-fragment, accessed June 10, 2015.

Kirschenblatt-Gimblett, Barbara

1995 Theorizing Heritage. *Ethnomusicology* 39:367–380.

Kirsten, Sven A.

2003 *The Book of Tiki*. Taschen, Köln.

Knight, Eric

2013 *Why We Argue about Climate Change*. Redblack, Melbourne.

Knowlton, Timothy

2012 Ethnicity, God Concepts, and the Indigenization of a Guatemalan Popular Saint. *Journal of Anthropological Research* 68:223–247.

Kohl, Philip L.

1998 Nationalism and Archaeology: On the Constructions of Nations and the Reconstructions of the Remote Past. *Annual Review of Anthropology* 27:223–246.

2004 Making the Past Profitable in an Age of Globalization and National Ownership: Contradictions and Considerations. In *Marketing Heritage: Archaeology and the Consumption of the Past*, edited by Yorke M. Rowan and Uzi Baram, pp. 295–301. AltaMira Press, Walnut Creek, Calif.

Kosso, Peter

2006 Introduction: The Epistemology of Archaeology. In *Archaeological Fantasies: How Pseudoarchaeology Misrepresents the Past and Misleads the Public*, edited by Garrett G. Fagan, pp. 3–23. Routledge, London.

Krassa, Peter

1978 *Disciple of the Gods: A Biography of Erich von Däniken*. Translated by David B. Koblick. W. H. Allen, London.

Kripal, Jeffrey J.

2010 *Authors of the Impossible: The Paranormal and the Sacred*. University of Chicago Press, Chicago.

Kruse, Corinna

2010 Producing Absolute Truth: CSI Science as Wishful Thinking. *American Anthropologist* 112(1):79–91.

Kuhn, Thomas S.

1970 *The Structure of Scientific Revolutions*. 2nd ed, enlarged. International Encyclopedia of Unified Science Vol. 2, No. 2. University of Chicago Press, Chicago.

Kulik, Karol

2007 A Short History of Archaeological Communication. In *Archaeology and the Media*, edited by Timothy Clack and Marcus Brittain, pp. 111–124. Left Coast Press, Walnut Creek, Calif.

Küng, Lucy, Robert G. Picard, and Ruth Towse (editors)

2008 *The Internet and the Mass Media*. Sage, Los Angeles.

Kusche, Lawrence David

1975 *The Bermuda Triangle Mystery Solved*. Warner Books, New York.

Lafollette, Marcel Chotkowski

2013 *Science on American Television: A History*. University of Chicago Press, Chicago.

Lara Pinto, Gloria, and George Hasemann

1988 La Sociedad Indigena del Noreste de Honduras en El Siglo XVI: Son La Ethnohistoria y La Arqueologia Contradictorias? *Yaxkin* 11(2):5–28.

1992 Leyenda Y Arqueología: Cuantas Ciudades Blancas Hay en la Mosquitia? In *La Reserva de la Biosfera del Río Plátano: Herencia de Nuestro Pasado*, edited by Vicente Murphy, pp. 16–19. Ventanas Tropicales, Tegucigalpa.

Larson, Edward J.

1997 *Summer for the Gods: The Scopes Trial and America's Continuing Debate over Science and Religion*. Basic Books, New York.

Lee, Penny

1996 *The Whorf Theory Complex: A Critical Reconstruction*. Amsterdam Studies in the Theory and History of Linguistic Science, Vol. 81. John Benjamins, Amsterdam/Philadelphia.

Lekson, Stephen H.
2008 *A History of the Ancient Southwest.* School for Advanced Research, Santa Fe, N.M.

Lepper, Brad T.
2005 *Ohio Archaeology: An Illustrated Chronicle of Ohio's Ancient American Indian.* Orange Frazer Press, Wilmington, Ohio.

Lepper, Bradley T., Kenneth L. Feder, Terry A. Barnhart, and Deborah A. Bolnick
2011 Civilizations Lost and Found: Fabricating History. Part Two: False Messages in Stone. *Skeptical Inquirer* 35(6):48–54.

Lepper, Bradley T., and Jeff Gill
2000 The Newark Holy Stones. *Timeline* 17(3):16–25.

Lewis, David
2005 Evolution vs. Creation: Is the Debate for Real? In *Forbidden History: Prehistoric Technologies, Extraterrestrial Intervention, and the Suppressed Origins of Civilization*, edited by J. Douglas Kenyon, pp. 14–21. Bear, Burlington, Vt.

Lewis, James R.
2012 Excavating Tradition: Alternative Archaeologies as Legitimation Strategies. *Numen* 59:202–221.

Lewis, James R., and Pia Andersson
2012 Introduction to special issue "Alternative Archaeologies." *Numen* 59(2/3):119–124.

Lewis, Kenneth E.
2000 Imagination and Archaeological Interpretations: A Methodological Tale. *Historical Archaeology* 34(2):7–9.

Lewis, Laura A.
2003 *Hall of Mirrors: Power, Witchcraft, and Caste in Colonial Mexico.* Duke University Press, Durham, N.C.

Lewis, Theodore H.
1886 The "Monumental Tortoise" Mounds of De-Coo-dah. *American Journal of Archaeology* 2:65–69.

Lieberman, Leonard, Rodney C. Kirk, and Alice Littlefield
2003 Perishing Paradigm: Race 1931–99. *American Anthropologist* 105(1):110–113.

Limp, Frederick A.
2012 Letter to the National Geographic Channel. 27 February. Electronic document, http://saa.org/Portals/0/SAA/Press/Diggers.pdf, accessed June 10, 2015.

Lindeman, Marjanna
1998 Motivation, Cognition and Pseudoscience. *Scandinavian Journal of Psychology* 39(4):257–265.

Lindeman, Marjanna, and Kia Aarnio
2007 Superstitious, Magical, and Paranormal Beliefs: An Integrative Model. *Journal of Research in Personality* 41:731–744.

Little, Barbara J.
2000 Compelling Images through Storytelling: Comment on "Imaginary, But By

No Means Unimaginable: Storytelling, Science, and Historical Archaeology." *Historical Archaeology* 34(2):10–13.

Liu, Jiangang, Jun Li, Lu Feng, Ling Li, Jie Tian, and Kang Lee
2014 Seeing Jesus in Toast: Neural and Behavioral Correlates of Face Pareidolia. *Cortex* 53(April):60–77.

Long, Burke O.
2003 *Imagining the Holy Land: Maps, Models, and Fantasy Travels*. Indiana University Press, Bloomington.

Lothrop, Samuel Kirkland, and Joy Mahler
1957 *A Chancay-Style Grave at Zapallan, Peru: An Analysis of Its Textiles, Pottery, and Other Furnishings*, Vol. 50. Papers of the Peabody Museum of Archaeology and Ethnology, Harvard University, Cambridge, Mass.

Loudon, Irvine
2006 A Brief History of Homeopathy. *Journal of the Royal Society of Medicine* 99(12): 607–610.

Lovata, Troy
2007 *Inauthentic Archaeologies: Public Uses and Abuses of the Past*. Left Coast Press, Walnut Creek, Calif.

Love, Dean (producer)
2000 *Cave of the Glowing Skulls*. Documentary. DVD. Dean Love films, New York.

Loxton, Daniel, and Donald R. Prothero
2013 *Abominable Science: Origins of the Yeti, Nessie, and Other Famous Cryptids*. Columbia University Press, New York.

Mace, Carroll Edward
1973 Charles Etienne Brasseur de Bourbourg, 1814–1874. In *Guide to Ethnohistorical Sources, Part Two*, edited by Howard F. Cline, pp. 298–325. Handbook of Middle American Indians, Vol. 13, Robert Wauchope, general editor. University of Texas Press, Austin.

Magnusson, Magnus, and Hermann Paulsson (translator)
1965 *The Vinland Sagas*. Penguin, New York.

Mainfort, Robert C., and Mary L. Kwas
2004 The Bat Creek Stone Revisited: A Fraud Exposed. *American Antiquity* 69(4): 761–769.

Majewski, Teresita
2000 "We Are All Storytellers": Comments on Storytelling, Science, and Historical Archaeology. *Historical Archaeology* 34(2):17–19.

Marshall, David
1997 *Celebrity and Power: Fame in Contemporary Culture*. University of Minnesota Press, Minneapolis.

Martin, Simon, and Nikolai Grube
2008 *Chronicle of the Maya Kings and Queens: Deciphering the Dynasties of the Ancient Maya*. 2nd ed. Thames and Hudson, London.

Mashberg, Tom
2014a TV Series Is Criticized in Handling of Deceased. *New York Times* 29 March:C1. New York.

2014b National Geographic Pulls "Nazi War Diggers" Series. *New York Times*, 31 March. Electronic document, http://artsbeat.blogs.nytimes.com/2014/03/31/national-geographic-channel-pulls-nazi-war-diggers-series/, accessed June 10, 2015.

Massey, Gerald

1907 *Ancient Egypt: The Light of the World*. T. Fisher Unwin, London.

Massoulard, Emile

1949 *Préhistorie et Protohistoire d'Égypte*. Travaux et mémoire Vol. 53. Institut d'Ethnologie, Paris.

Mathews, Robert Hamilton

1910 Some Rock Engravings of the Aborigines of New South Wales. *Journal and Proceedings of the Royal Society of New South Wales* 44:401–445.

Matthews, Keith J.

2002 Archaeology and the Extraterrestrial: Blair Cuspids, Martian Monuments and beyond the Infinite. In *Digging Holes in Popular Culture: Archaeology and Science Fiction*, edited by Miles Russell, pp. 129–160. Bournemouth University School of Conservation Sciences Occasional Paper 7, Oxbow Books, Oxford.

Mayer, Gerhard

2013 A Phenomenology of the Ghosthunting Scene in the USA and in Germany. In *The Ashgate Research Companion to Paranormal Cultures*, edited by Olu Jenzen and Sally R. Munt, pp. 363–376. Ashgate, Farnham, Surrey.

McDaniel, Stanley V., and Monica Rix Paxson (editors)

1998 *The Case for the Face: Scientists Examine the Evidence for Alien Artifacts on Mars*. Adventures Unlimited Press, Kempton, Ill.

McGarry, Molly

2008 *Ghosts of Futures Past: Spiritualism and the Cultural Politics of Nineteenth-Century America*. University of California Press, Berkeley.

McIntyre, Kenneth Gordon

1977 *The Secret Discovery of Australia: Portuguese Ventures 200 Years before Captain Cook*. Souvenir Press, Medindie.

McKusick, Marshall

1982 Psychic Archaeology: Theory, Method, and Mythology. *Journal of Field Archaeology* 9:99–118.

Melgar y Serrano, José María

1869 Antiguedades Mexicanos. *Boletin de la Sociedad Mexicana de Geografia y Estadistica* 2(1):292–297.

1871 Estudio sobre la Antiguedad y el Origen de la Cabeza Colosal de Tipo Etiópioc que Existe en Hueyapan, del Canton de los Tuxtla. *Boletin de la Sociedad Mexicana de Geografia y Estadistica* 2(3):104–109.

Mellart, James

1967 *Çatal Hüyük: A Neolithic Town in Anatolia*. McGraw-Hill, New York.

Melton, J. Gordon

2011 The Amityville Horror. In *Encyclopedia of Occultism and Parapsychology*, Vol. 1 A–L, edited by J. Gordon Melton, p. 44. 5th ed. Gale Group, Detroit.

Messenger, Lewis C., Jr.

1991 Climatic Settings and Prehistoric Social Complexity: The Central American Isthmus. In *The Formation of Social Complexity in Southeastern Mesoamerica*, edited by William Fowler, pp. 237–275. CRC Press, Boca Raton, Fla.

Messenger, Troy

1999 *Holy Leisure: Recreation and Religion in God's Square Mile*. Temple University Press, Philadelphia.

Meyers Emery, Katy, and Lynne Goldstein

2014 Student View: Apparitions and Archaeology. *Michigan State University 360 Perspective: Voices and Viewpoints*, 31 October. Electronic document, http://socialscience.msu.edu/about-us/news/?p=620, accessed June 10, 2015.

Miller, Michael E.,

2015 Ben Carson Believes Joseph Built Egypt's Pyramids to Store Grain—and It Just Might Get Him Some Votes. *Washington Post,* 5 November. https://www.washingtonpost.com/news/morning-mix/wp/2015/11/05/ben-carson-believes-joseph-built-egypts-pyramids-to-store-grain-and-it-just-may-get-him-some-votes/, accessed December 18, 2015.

Mills, Lisa

2003 Mitochondrial DNA Analysis of the Ohio Hopewell of the Hopewell Mound Group. Unpublished Ph.D. dissertation, Department of Anthropology, Ohio State University, Columbus.

Moody, Lance

2012 The Lockheed UFO Case Revisited. Blog post at *What the Hell Was That? A Skeptical Look at the Paranormal*, 20 March. Electronic document, http://www.notaghost.com/2012/03/a-prosaic-explanation-for-a-famous-ufo-case.html, accessed June 10, 2015.

Moore, R. Laurence

1994 *Selling God: American Religion in the Marketplace of Culture*. Oxford University Press, Oxford.

Moorehead, Warren King

1904 *The Field Diary of an Archaeological Collector*. Andover, Mass.

Morant, G. M.

1936 A Morphological Comparison of Two Crystal Skulls. *Man* 36:105–107.

Morrison, Richard

2009 Staggering Beauty from a Dark Age. *Times* [London, England] 30 September:13. Infotrac Newsstand.

Morrison, Tonya P.

2006 Josh Bernstein: Explorer and Anthropologist—Yes, Indiana Jones—No. *Quest Magazine*. Electronic document, http://www.questmagazine.com/z_tonya_morrison_qm200607_s2-digging-for-the-truth-josh-bernstein-history-channel.html, accessed April 11, 2012.

Moses, Wilson Jeremiah

1998 *Afrotopia: The Roots of African American Popular History*. Cambridge Studies in American Literature and Culture. Cambridge University Press, Cambridge.

Moshenska, Gabriel

2006 The Archaeological Uncanny. *Public Archaeology* 5:91–99.

2012 M. R. James and the Archaeological Uncanny. *Antiquity* 86:1192–1201.

Muckle, Robert

2012 Archaeology and Bigfoot. *Anthropology News* 53(10):s12. Electronic document, http://onlinelibrary.wiley.com/doi/10.1111/j.1556-3502.2012.531001_s.x/abstract, accessed June 10, 2015.

Muniz, Albert M., and Thomas C. O'Guinn

2001 Brand Community. *Journal of Consumer Research* 27:412–428.

Museo Nacional de Antropolgía

1956 *Official Guide to the Museo Nacional de Antropología.* Instituo Nacional de Antropología e Historia, México, D.F.

National Geographic Society and National Geographic Channel

2012 Meeting on Archeological Preservation, Avocational Metal Detecting, Ethics of Archeology. Minutes of meeting on 4 May. Electronic document, http://www.saa.org/Portals/0/SAA/new/NGSConference%20onNGS%20Minutesl.pdf, accessed August 21, 2014.

Nelson, Kit, and Arturo Ruiz Estrada

2004 Proyecto de Investigación Arqueológica: Valle de Huaura, Perú. Unpublished report submitted to the Instituto de Nacional de Cultura, Peru. April.

2010 The Chancay Tomb of Rontoy, Peru. *Antiquity* 84(323). Electronic document, http://www.antiquity.ac.uk/projgall/nelson323/, accessed June 10, 2015.

Neudorfer, Giovanna

1980 *Vermont's Stone Chambers: An Inquiry into Their Past.* Vermont Historical Society. Electronic document, http://accd.vermont.gov/sites/accd/files/Documents/strongcommunities/historic/VermontsStoneChambers.pdf, accessed June 10, 2015.

Nevins, Jess

2008 Introduction: The 19th-Century Roots of Steampunk. In *Steampunk*, edited by Ann VanderMeer and Jeff VanderMeer, pp. 3–11. Tachyon Press, San Francisco.

New South Wales [NSW] Government

2015 Correspondence and email policy. Electronic document, http://www.nsw.gov.au/correspondence-and-email-policy, accessed February 10, 2015.

New York Times (NYT)

1928 Explorer Loses Libel Suit. 15 February:5. New York.

1930 Museum Here Gets Rare Indian Finds. 29 December:59. New York.

1931a Excavations in Ur Verify Book of Daniel. 10 January:3. New York.

1931b Seeks Cradle of Race in American Jungle. 24 January:1. New York.

1931c Museum Endorses F. A. Mitchell-Hedges. 25 January:29. New York.

1931d Science Confirms Noah's Great Deluge. 15 February:128. New York.

Nickell, Joe
2007 *Adventures in Paranormal Investigation.* University Press of Kentucky, Lexington.
Noll, Mark A.
1999 Science, Theology, and Society: From Cotton Mather to William Jennings Bryan. In *Evangelicals and Science in Historical Perspective*, edited by David N. Livingstone, D. G. Hart, and Mark A. Noll, pp. 99–119. Oxford University Press, Oxford.
Numbers, Ronald L.
1992 *The Creationists: The Evolution of Scientific Creationism.* University of California Press, Berkeley.
Olsen, John
2006 Review of "The Crystal Skull." *The Shadow in Review*, 11 August. Electronic document, http://home.comcast.net/~deshadow/reviews/shadow323.html, accessed June 10, 2015.
2014 Review of "The Magigals Mystery." *The Shadow in Review*, 30 May. Electronic document, http://home.comcast.net/~deshadow/reviews/shadow323.html, accessed June 10, 2015.
Orser, Charles E., Jr.
2004 *Race and Practice in Archaeological Interpretation.* Archaeology, Culture, and Society. University of Pennsylvania Press, Philadelphia.
Ortiz de Montellano, Bernard
1995 Multiculturalism, Cult Archaeology, and Pseudoscience. In *Cult Archaeology & Creationism: Understanding Pseudoscientific Beliefs about the Past*, edited by Francis B. Harrold and Raymond A. Eve, pp. 134–151. Expanded edition. University of Iowa Press, Iowa City.
Ortiz de Montellano, Bernard, Gabriel Haslip-Viera, and Warren Barbour
1997 They Were NOT Here before Columbus: Afrocentric Hyperdiffusionism in the 1990s. *Ethnohistory* 44(2):199–234.
Osmanagić, Semir
2005 *The World of the Maya.* Gorgias Press (Euphrates Imprint), Piscataway, N.J.
2006 The Formula to Understand the Bosnian Pyramids! *World Pyramids.* Electronic document, http://world-pyramids.com/russia/Bosnia/formula.html, accessed October 15, 2013.
2007a Bosnian Pyramids. Unpublished presentation, Bosnian Embassy, London.
2007b *Bosnian Valley of Pyramids: Scientific Evidence about the Existence of Bosnian Pyramids*, digital document. Archaeological Park, Bosnian Pyramid of the Sun Foundation, Visoko.
2009 *ODBRANA DOKTORSKE DISERTACIJE.* Electronic document, http://www.semirosmanagic.com/ba/odbrana.html, accessed October 15, 2013.
Ostara Publications
2013 About. Electronic document, http://ostarapublications.com/about/, accessed October 14, 2013.
Otto, Martha
1984 Masterworks in Pipestone: Treasure from Tremper Mound. *Timeline* 1:18–33.

Ouellette, Laurie, and Susan Murray
2009 Introduction to *Reality TV: Remaking Television Culture*. 2nd ed., edited by Susan Murray and Laurie Ouellette, pp. 1–22. New York University Press, New York.
Pappas, Stephanie
2012 Indiana Jones Crystal Skull Lawsuit Raises Questions of Hoax. *LiveScience*, 10 December. Electronic document, http://www.livescience.com/25410-indiana-jones-crystal-skull-lawsuit-hoax.html, accessed June 10, 2015.
Park, Robert L.
2000 *Voodoo Science: The Road from Foolishness to Fraud*. Oxford University Press, New York.
Parsons, Steve
2005 The Perils of Planetary Amnesia: As Evidence of Ancient Cataclysm Mounts, the Legacy of a Rejected Genius Is Reconsidered. In *Forbidden History: Prehistoric Technologies, Extraterrestrial Intervention, and the Suppressed Origins of Civilization*, edited by J. Douglas Kenyon, pp. 61–68. Bear, Rochester, Vt.
Patton, Phil
1998 *Dreamland: Travels inside the Secret World of Roswell and Area 51*. Villard, New York.
Pauketat, Timothy R.
2004 *Ancient Cahokia and the Mississippians*. Cambridge University Press, Cambridge.
Pauwels, Louis, and Jacques Bergier
1963 [1960] *The Morning of the Magicians*. Translated by Rollo Myers. Avon, New York.
Pearson, Michael, and Michael Shanks
2001 *Theatre/Archaeology*. Routledge, London.
Pedraza, Cristobal de
1544 Relacion de la Provincia de Honduras y Higueras. In CDID (1868). Tomo XI, pp. 379–434. Madrid.
Peebles, Curtis
1994 *Watch the Skies! A Chronicle of the Flying Saucer Myth*. Smithsonian Institution Press, Washington, D.C.
Pelligrini, Ann
2007 "Signaling through the Flames": Hell House Performance and Structures of Religious Feeling. *American Quarterly* 59(3):911–935.
Pellot, Brian
2014 Five Religious-Themed Apps Banned from iTunes. *Washington Post*, 10 January. Electronic document, http://www.washingtonpost.com/national/religion/five-religious-themed-apps-banned-from-itunes/2014/01/10/de980502-7a3b-11e3-a647-a19deaf575b3_story.html, accessed June 10, 2015.
Penn Museum
2010 What in the World. Electronic document, http://www.penn.museum/what-in-the-world.html, accessed October 10, 2014.

Petrie, W. M. Flinders

1896 *Koptos*. Quaritch, London.

1901 *Diospolis Parva: The Cemeteries of Abadiyeh and Hu*. Egypt Exploration Fund, London.

1939 *The Making of Egypt*. Sheldon Press, London.

Petrie, W. M. Flinders, and J. E. Quibell

1896 *Naqada and Ballas*. Quaritch, London.

Pezzati, Alex

2005 Mystery at Acámbaro, Mexico. *Expedition* 47(3):6–7.

Phelan, Matthew

2014 Bigfoot Field Research Organization Head Calls DNA Study "Meaningless." *Black Bag*, 15 July. Electronic document, http://blackbag.gawker.com/bigfoot-field-research-organization-head-calls-dna-stud-1605135585, accessed June 10, 2015.

Pidgeon, William

1858 *Traditions of De-coo-dah and Antiquarian Researches*. Horace Thayer, New York.

Pigliucci, Massimo

2002 *Denying Evolution: Creationism, Scientism and the Nature of Science*. Sinauer Associates, Sunderland, Mass.

2012 Nonsense on Stilts about Science: Field Adventures of a Scientist-Philosopher. In *Between Scientists and Citizens: Proceedings of a Conference at Iowa State University, June 1–2 2012*, edited by Jean Goodwin, pp. 19–28. Great Plains Society for the Study of Argumentation, Ames, Iowa.

Pitblado, Bonnie L.

2014 An Argument for Ethical, Proactive, Archaeologist-Artifact Collector Collaboration. *American Antiquity* 79(3):385–400.

Pool, Christopher A.

2007 *Olmec Archaeology and Early Mesoamerica*. Cambridge University Press, Cambridge.

Potter, Parker B., Jr.

1981 *Public Archaeology in Annapolis: A Critical Approach to History in Maryland's Ancient City*. Smithsonian Institution Press, Washington, D.C.

Powell, John Wesley

1881 On Limitations to the Use of Some Anthropologic Data. In *First Annual Report of the Bureau of Ethnology to the Secretary of the Smithsonian Institution 1879–80*, edited by John Wesley Powell, pp. 73–86. U.S. Government Printing Office, Washington, D.C.

Preston, Douglas

2013 The El Dorado Machine: A New Scanner's Rain-forest Discoveries. *New Yorker*, 6 May.

2015 Exclusive: Lost City Discovered in Honduran Rain Forest. *National Geographic*, 2 March. Electronic document, http://news.nationalgeographic.com/2015/03/150302-honduras-lost-city-monkey-god-maya-ancient-archaeology/, accessed June 10, 2015.

Prickett, Stephen

2005 *Victorian Fantasy*. 2nd revised and expanded ed. Baylor University Press, Waco, Tex.

Priest, Josiah

1833 *American Antiquities and Discoveries in the West*. 3rd ed., revised. Hoffman and White, Albany, N.Y.

Pringle, Heather

2006 *The Master Plan: Himmler's Scholars and the Holocaust*. Hyperion, New York.

Pruitt, Tera C.

2009 Contextualising Alternative Archaeology: Socio-politics and Approaches. *Archaeological Review from Cambridge* 24(1):55–75.

2011 *Authority and the Production of Knowledge in Archaeology*. Ph.D. dissertation, Department of Archaeology, University of Cambridge.

Putnam, Charles E.

1887 The Davenport Tablets. *Science* 7(157):119–120.

Putnam, Frederic Ward

1883 Archaeological Frauds. *Science* 1:99.

1887 Report of the Curator. Sixteenth Report for 1882, signed February 17, 1883. In *Reports of the Peabody Museum of American Archeology and Ethnology, in Connection with Harvard University*, Vol. 3, 1880–1886, pp. 184–185. Cambridge, Mass.

Radford, Benjamin

2011 *Tracking the Chupacabra: The Vampire Beast in Fact, Fiction, and Folklore*. University of New Mexico Press, Albuquerque.

Raff, Jennifer A., Deborah A. Bolnick, Justin Tackney, and Dennis O'Rourke

2011 Ancient DNA Perspectives on American Colonization and Population History. *American Journal of Physical Anthropology* 146:503–514.

Ramos, Gabriela

2010 *Death and Conversion in the Andes: Lima and Cuzco, 1532–1670*. University of Notre Dame Press, Notre Dame, Ind.

Randi, James

2013 Australian Skeptics Divining Test. *Australian Skeptics*. Electronic document, http://www.skeptics.com.au/publications/articles/australian-skeptics-divining-test/, accessed November 12, 2013.

Rathje, William L.

1978 The Ancient Astronaut Myth: An Archaeologist Analyses the Impact of Von Däniken. *Archaeology* 31(6):4–7.

Read, Matthew Canfield

1888 The Archaeology of Ohio. *Western Reserve Historical Society Tract 73*. Cleveland, Ohio.

Redfern, Nick

2010 *Final Events: And the Secret Government Group on Demonic UFOs and the Afterlife*. Anomalist Books, San Antonio, Tex.

Reece, Katherine

2006 Memoirs of a True Believer. In *Archaeological Fantasies: How Pseudoarchae-*

ology Misrepresents the Past and Misleads the Public*, edited by Garrett Fagan, pp. 96–106. Routledge, New York.

2015 *In the Hall of Ma'at*. Electronic document, http://www.hallofmaat.com, accessed June 10, 2015.

Reed, Graham

1972 *The Psychology of Anomalous Experience: A Cognitive Approach*. Hutchinson University Library, London.

Regal, Brian

2008 Amateur versus Professional: The Search for Bigfoot. *Endeavour* 32(2):53–57.

2011 *Searching for Sasquatch: Crackpots, Eggheads, and Cryptozoology*. Palgrave Studies in the History of Science and Technology. Palgrave MacMillan, New York.

2013 The Jersey Devil: The Real Story. *Skeptical Inquirer* 37(6). Electronic document, http://www.csicop.org/si/show/the_jersey_devil_the_real_story, accessed September 2, 2014

Reich, David, Nick Patterson, Desmond Campbell, et al.

2012 Reconstructing Native American Population History. *Nature* 488:370–374.

Reidla, Maere, Toomas Kivisild, Ene Metspalu, et al.

2003 Origin and Diffusion of mtDNA Haplogroup X. *American Journal of Human Genetics* 73:1178–1190.

Reiss, Wilhelm, and Alphons Stubel

1880–1886 *The Necropolis of Ancon in Peru*. Asher, Berlin.

Renfrew, Colin, and Paul Bahn

2012 *Archaeology: Theories, Methods, and Practice*. 6th ed. Thames and Hudson, New York.

Renov, Michael

1993 Introduction: The Truth about Non-Fiction. In *Theorizing Documentary*, edited by Michael Renov, pp. 1–11. Routledge, New York.

Riekki, Tapani, Marjaana Lindeman, Marja Aleneff, Anni Halme, and Antti Nuortimo

2013 Paranormal and Religious Believers Are More Prone to Illusory Face Perception than Skeptics and Non-believers. *Applied Cognitive Psychology* 27(2): 150–155.

Rivas, Ramon D.

1993 *Pueblos Indígenas y Garífuna de Honduras: Una Caracterización*. Editorial Guaymuras, Tegucigalpa.

Robles García, Nelly M.

2010 Indigenous Archaeology in Mexico: Recognizing Distinctive Histories. In *Being and Becoming Indigenous Archaeologists*, edited by George P. Nicholas, pp. 277–286. Left Coast Press, Walnut Creek, Calif.

Rockman et al.

2013 *Hands-On, Hearts-In Learning: Impacts and Outcomes of Time Team America: The Science of Archaeology*. Electronic document, http://informalscience.org

/images/evaluation/2014-03-04_TTA_Summative_Report_Final.pdf, accessed June 10, 2015.

Roggersdorf, Wilhelm

1970 [1968] About Erich von Däniken. In *Gods from Outer Space: Return to the Stars or Evidence for the Impossible*, by Erich von Däniken, translated by Michael Heron, pp. 7–8. G. P. Putnam's Sons, New York.

Romberg, Raquel

2003 *Witchcraft and Welfare: Spiritual Capital and the Business of Magic in Modern Puerto Rico*. University of Texas Press, Austin.

Ron, Amos, and Jackie Feldman

2009 From Spots to Themed Sites: The Evolution of the Protestant Holy Land. *Journal of Heritage Tourism* 4(3):201–216.

Rose, Mark

2006a The Bosnia-Atlantis Connection. *Archaeology*, 27 April. Electronic document, http://www.archaeology.org/online/features/osmanagic/, accessed October 15, 2013.

2006b More on Bosnian "Pyramids." *Archaeology*, 27 June. Electronic document, http://www.archaeology.org/online/features/osmanagic/update.html, accessed October 15, 2013.

Ross, Anamaria Iosif

2012 *The Anthropology of Alternative Medicine*. Berg, London.

Ross, Andrew

1997 *The Celebration Chronicles*. Ballantine, New York.

Roth, Ann Macy

1995 Building Bridges to Afrocentrism: A Letter to My Egyptological Colleagues. *Newsletter of the American Research Center in Egypt* 167/168.

Roth, Christopher F.

2005 Ufology as Anthropology: Race, Extraterrestrials, and the Occult. In *E. T. Culture: Anthropology in Outerspaces*, edited by Debbora Battaglia, pp. 38–93. Duke University Press, Durham, N.C.

Rowan, Yorke

2004 Repacking the Pilgrimage: Visiting the Holy Land in Orlando. In *Marketing Heritage: Archaeology and the Consumption of the Past*, edited by Rowan Yorke and Uzi Baram, pp. 249–266. AltaMira Press, Walnut Creek, Calif.

Rowe, Ann P., and John Cohen

2002 *Hidden Threads of Peru: Q'ero Textiles*. Merrell in association with the Textile Museum, Washington, D.C.

Rowe, John Howland

1966 Diffusionism and Archaeology. *American Antiquity* 31(3):334–337.

Sagan, Carl

1979 *Broca's Brain: Reflections on the Romance of Science*. Random House, New York.

Said, Edward

1979. *Orientalism*. Vintage, New York.

Samson, James R.

1997 *Indigenous Lands in a Developing Region: A Historical Ethnogeography of the Pech Indians of Eastern Honduras, with Emphasis on Recent Settlement and Land Use Changes*. Ph.D. dissertation, Louisiana State University. Proquest/UMI, Ann Arbor.

Samuel, Raphael

1994 *Theatres of Memory*, Vol. 1: Past and Present in Contemporary Culture. Verso, London.

Santino, Jack

1988 Occupational Ghostlore: Social Context and the Expression of Belief. *Journal of American Folklore* 101(400):207–218.

Sasquatch Genome Project

2013 The Myths & Facts about the DNA Study. *Sasquatch Genome Project*. Electronic document, http://www.sasquatchgenomeproject.org/myths-facts-about-dna-study/, accessed June 10, 2015.

Sax, Margaret, Jane M. Walsh, Ian C. Freestone, Andrew H. Rankin, and Nigel D. Meeks

2008 The Origins of Two Purportedly Pre-Columbian Mexican Crystal Skulls. *Journal of Archaeological Science* 35:2751–2760.

Scarborough, Isabel

2008 The Bennett Monolith: Archaeological Patrimony and Cultural Restitution in Bolivia. In *The Handbook of South American Archaeology*, edited by Helaine Silverman and William H. Isbell, pp. 1089–1101. Springer, New York.

Schadla-Hall, Tim

2004 The Comforts of Unreason: The Importance and Relevance of Alternative Archaeology. In *Public Archaeology*, edited by N. Merriman, pp. 255–271. Routledge, London.

Schnabel, Jim

1994 Puck in the Laboratory: The Construction and Deconstruction of Hoax-like Deception in Science. *Science, Technology, & Human Values* 19(4):459–492.

Schoch, Robert

2007 *Circular Times*. Electronic document, http://www.robertschoch.net, accessed on October 15, 2013.

Schuldenrein, Joseph

2014 Time Team America: Making Real Reality TV. 13 August episode of *Indiana Jones: Myth, Reality, and 21st Century Archaeology* podcast. Electronic document, http://www.voiceamerica.com/episode/79812/time-team-america-making-real-reality-tv, accessed June 10, 2015.

Scott, Eugenie C.

1997 Antievolution and Creationism in the United States. *Annual Review of Anthropology* 26:263–289.

Seal, Graham

1989 *The Hidden Culture: Folklore in Australia*. Oxford University Press, Melbourne.

7newsbelize

2012a Director of Archaeology Says He Wants No Part of Crystal Skull Lawsuit.

11 December. Electronic document, http://www.7newsbelize.com/sstory.php?nid=24166, accessed June 10, 2015.

2012b Archeology Attorney Says Jaime Awe Signed Off on Lawsuit. 12 December. Electronic document, http://www.7newsbelize.com/sstory.php?nid=24180&frmsrch=1, accessed June 10, 2015.

Shani, Amir, Manuel Antonio Rivera, and Denver Severt

2007 "To Bring God's Word to All People": The Case of a Religious Theme Site. *Tourism* 55(1):39–50.

Shanks, Michael, and Christopher Y. Tilley

2007 *Re-constructing Archaeology: Theory and Practice*. 2nd ed. Routledge, London.

Sheets, Payson, David Lentz, Dolores Piperno, John Jones, Christine Dixon, George Maloof, and Angela Hood

2012 Ancient Manioc Agriculture South of the Ceren Village, El Salvador. *Latin American Antiquity* 23(3):259–281.

Shermer, Michael

2002 *Why People Believe Weird Things*. 2nd ed. Henry Holt, New York.

Shinn, Eugene A.

2004 A Geologist's Adventures with Bimini Beachrock and Atlantis True Believers. *Skeptical Inquirer* 28(1). Electronic document, http://www.csicop.org/si/show/geologists_adventures_with_bimini_beachrock/, accessed June 10, 2015.

Shirey, David L.

1972 Museum of American Indian Displays Skull Masks. *New York Times* 4 November:30.

Shlush, Liran I., Doron M. Behar, Guennady Yudkovsky, et al.

2008 The Druze: A Population Genetic Refugium of the Near East. *PLoS ONE* 3(5):e2105.

Silberman, Neil Asher

2007 "Sustainable" Heritage? Public Archaeological Interpretation and the Marketed Past. In *Archaeology and Capitalism: From Ethics to Politics*, edited by Yannis Hamilakis and Philip Duke, pp. 179–194. Left Coast Press, Walnut Creek, Calif.

Silverberg, Robert

1986 *The Mound Builders*. Ohio University Press, Athens.

Silverblatt, Irene

1987 *Moon, Sun and Witches: Gender Ideologies and Class in Inca and Colonial Peru*. Princeton University Press, Princeton, N.J.

Silverman, Irene

2002 Touring Ancient Times: The Present and Presented Past in Contemporary Peru. *American Anthropologist* 104(3):881–902.

Simandiraki-Grimshaw, Anna, and Eleni Stefanou

2012 From Archaeology to Archaeologies: Themes, Challenges, and Borders of the "Other" Past. In *From Archaeology to Archaeologies: The "Other" Past*, edited by Anna Simandiraki-Grimshaw and Eleni Stefanou. BAR International Series 2409. Archaeopress, Oxford.

Sitchin, Zecharia

1976 *The 12th Planet: Book I of the Earth Chronicles*. Harper Collins, New York.

Smith, G. Elliot

1923 *The Ancient Egyptians and the Origin of Civilization*. Harper & Brothers, London.

Smith, Michael A.

2005 *Peopling the Cleland Hills: Aboriginal History in Western Central Australia, 1850–1980*. Aboriginal History Monograph 12. Aboriginal History Incorporated, Canberra.

Soares, Pedro, Luca Ermini, Noel Thomson, et al.

2009 Correcting for Purifying Selection: An Improved Human Mitochondrial Molecular Clock. *American Journal of Human Genetics* 84:740–759.

Sobel, Dava

2000 *Galileo's Daughter: A Historical Memoir of Science, Faith, and Love*. Penguin, New York.

Southwell, Ben (producer)

2001 *Trips Money Can't Buy with Ewan McGregor*. British Broadcasting System. Documentary. DVD.

Spitulnik, Debra

1993 Anthropology and Mass Media. *Annual Review of Anthropology* 22:213–315.

Spivak, G. C.

1995 Can the Subaltern Speak? In *The Post-Colonial Studies Reader*, edited by Bill Ashcroft, Gareth Griffiths, and Helen Tiffin, pp. 24–28. Routledge, London.

Squier, Ephraim George

1871 Alleged Discovery of the Arch among the Aboriginal Remains of New Mexico. *Proceedings of the Lyceum of Natural History in the City of New York* (Series 1):91–92.

Stamps, Richard B.

2001 Tools Leave Marks: Material Analysis of the Scotford-Soper-Savage Michigan Relics. *BYU Studies* 40(3):211–238.

Starn, Orin, Carlos Ivan Degregori, and Robin Kirk

2005 Introduction to *The Peru Reader: History, Culture, Politics*, edited by Orin Starn, Carlos Ivan Degregori, and Robin Kirk, pp. 1–12. 2nd ed. Duke University Press, Durham, N.C.

Stebbins, Robert A.

1992 *Amateurs, Professionals and Serious Leisure*. McGill-Queens University Press, Montreal.

Sterling, Bruce

1986 Preface to *Mirrorshades: The Cyberpunk Anthology*, edited by Bruce Sterling, pp. ix–xvi. Ace Books, New York.

Stewart, Christopher

2013 *Jungleland: A Mysterious Lost City, a WWII Spy, and a True Story of Deadly Adventure*. HarperCollins, New York.

Stiebing, William H., Jr.

1995 The Nature and Dangers of Cult Archaeology. In *Cult Archaeology and Crea-*

tionism: Understanding Pseudoscientific Beliefs about the Past, edited by Francis B. Harrold and Raymond A. Eve, pp. 1–11. Rev. ed. University of Iowa Press, Iowa City.

Stone, Doris Z.

1941 *Archaeology of the North Coast of Honduras*. Memoirs of the Peabody Museum of Archaeology and Ethnology, Vol. 9, No. 1. Harvard University Press, Cambridge, Mass.

Stone, Peter, and Robert MacKenzie (editors)

1990 *The Excluded Past: Archaeology in Education*. One World Archaeology, Vol. 17. Routledge, London.

Story, Ronald

1976 *The Space-Gods Revealed: A Close Look at the Theories of Erich von Däniken*. New English Library, London.

Stromberg, Peter

2009 *Caught in Play: How Entertainment Works on You*. Stanford University Press, Stanford, Calif.

Strong, Steven, and Evan Strong

2014 Forgotten Origin: Steven and Evan Strong's New Theory of Human Civilization. Electronic edition, http://www.forgottenorigin.com, accessed March 1, 2014.

Strong, William D.

1934 Hunting Ancient Ruins in Northeastern Honduras. In *Smithsonian Institution Explorations and Fieldwork, 1933–34*, pp. 44–48. Smithsonian Institution, Washington, D.C.

Sutherland, Patricia

2000 The Norse and Native Americans. In *Vikings: The North Atlantic Saga*, edited by William F. Fitzhugh and Elisabeth I. Ward, pp. 238–247. Smithsonian Institution Press, Washington, D.C.

Sykes, Bryan C., Rhettman A. Mullis, Christophe Hagenmuller, Terry W. Melton, and Michel Sartori

2014 Genetic Analysis of Hair Samples Attributed to Yeti, Bigfoot and Other Anomalous Primates. *Proceedings of the Royal Society B* 281(20140161):1–3.

Taussig, Michael, and Nathan Wachtel

1998 *Pathways of Memory and Power: Ethnography and History among an Andean People*. University of Wisconsin Press, Madison.

Taylor, Brian

1995 Amateurs, Professionals and the Knowledge of Archaeology. *Journal of Sociology* 46(3):499–508.

Taylor, Kate

2011a Egyptian Antiquities Chief Says He Will Resign. *New York Times*, 3 March. Electronic document, http://artsbeat.blogs.nytimes.com/2011/03/03/egyptian-antiquities-chief-resigns/, accessed June 10, 2015.

2011b Egyptian Antiquities Minister Returns Less than a Month after Quitting. *New York Times*, 30 March. Electronic document, http://artsbeat.blogs.nytimes.com/2011/03/30/egypts-antiquities-minister-rehired-less-than-a-month-after-leaving/, accessed June 10, 2015.

Taylor, Timothy
2007 Screening Biases: Archaeology, Television, and the Banal. In *Archaeology and the Media*, edited by Timothy Clack and Marcus Brittain, pp. 187–200. Left Coast Press, Walnut Creek, Calif.

Teruel, Luis
2010 [1617] Vichama. In *La Historia Primigenia de la Mitologia Vichama*. Red de Museos del Norte Chico, Peru.

Terry, Michael
1974 *War of the Warramullas*. Rigby, Adelaide.

Thiering, Barry, and Edgar Castle (editors)
1972 *Some Trust in Chariots: Sixteen Views on Erich von Däniken's Chariots of the Gods?* West Books, Perth.

Thomas, Cyrus
1894 *Report on the Mound Explorations of the Bureau of Ethnology*. Smithsonian Institution, Washington, D.C.

Thomas, David H.
1989 *Archaeology*. 2nd ed. Holt, Rinehart and Winston, New York.

Thomas, Mark G., Tudor Parfitt, Deborah A. Weiss, et al.
2000 Y Chromosomes Traveling South: The Cohen Modal Haplotype and the Origins of the Lemba—the "Black Jews of Southern Africa." *American Journal of Human Genetics* 66:674–686.

Tilley, Christopher
2004 *The Materiality of Stone: Explorations in Landscape Phenomenology*. Berg, Oxford.

Tilley, Virginia Q.
2005 *Seeing Indians: A Study of Race, Nation, and Power in El Salvador*. University of New Mexico Press, Albuquerque.

Timms, Joanna
2012 Ghost-Hunters and Psychical Research in Interwar England. *History Workshop Journal* 74:88–104.

Tomoeda, Hiroyasu, and Luis Millones
1998 *Religion Oficial y Tradicion Verdadera: Historia y Función de Los Rituales Andinos en Los Pueblos Ayacuchanos*. Universidad Nacional de San Cristóbal de Huamanga, Ayacucho, Perú.

Toumey, Christopher
1994 *God's Own Scientists: Creationists in a Secular World*. Rutgers University Press, New Brunswick, N.J.
1996 *Conjuring Science: Scientific Symbols and Cultural Meanings in American Life*. Rutgers University Press, New Brunswick, N.J.

Trento, Salvatore Michael
1978 *The Search for Lost America: The Mysteries of the Stone Ruins*. Contemporary Books, Chicago.

Trigger, Bruce G.
1984 Alternative Archaeologies: Nationalist, Colonialist, Imperialist. *Man* 19:355–370.

1996 *A History of Archaeological Thought*. 2nd ed. Cambridge University Press, Cambridge.

Tucker, Elizabeth

2005 Ghosts in Mirrors: Reflections of the Self. *Journal of American Folklore* 118(468):186–203.

Van Sertima, Ivan

1976 *They Came before Columbus: The African Presence in Ancient America*. Random House Trade Paperbacks, New York.

1985 *African Presence in Early Europe*. Journal of African Civilizations. Transaction Publishers, New Brunswick, N.J.

1987a *African Presence in Early America*. Journal of African Civilizations. Transaction Publishers, New Brunswick, N.J.

1987b *African Presence in Early Asia*. Journal of African Civilizations. Transaction Publishers, New Brunswick, N.J.

1988 *Black Women in Antiquity*. Journal of African Civilizations. Transaction Publishers, New Brunswick, N.J.

1995 *Egypt: Child of Africa*. Journal of African Civilizations. Transaction Publishers, New Brunswick, N.J.

1998 *Early America Revisited*. Journal of African Civilizations. Transaction Publishers, New Brunswick, N.J.

Velasquez, Orlando

2001 *Los muertos viven en el norte del Peru*. Universidad Ricardo Palma, Lima, Perú.

Vescelius, Gary S.

1956 Excavations at Pattee's Caves. *Bulletin of the Eastern States Archaeological Federation* 15:13–14.

Von Däniken, Erich

1969 *Chariots of the Gods?* Corgi, North Blackburn, Victoria.

Wahlgren, Erik

1958 *The Kensington Stone: A Mystery Solved*. University of Wisconsin Press, Madison.

Wallace, Mike

1996 *Mickey Mouse History and Other Essays on American Memory*. Temple University Press, Philadelphia.

Walsh, Jane McLaren

2008 Legend of the Crystal Skulls. *Archaeology* 61(3). Electronic document, http://archive.archaeology.org/0805/etc/indy.html, June 10, 2015.

Watkins, Joe E.

2012 Public Archaeology and Indigenous Archaeology: Intersections and Divergences from a Native American Perspective. In *The Oxford Handbook of Public Archaeology*, edited by Robin Skeates, Carol McDavid, and John Carman, pp. 659–672. Oxford University Press, Oxford.

Wauchope, Robert

1962 *Lost Tribes and Sunken Continents: Myth and Method in the Study of American Indians*. University of Chicago Press, Chicago.

1965 *They Found the Buried Cities: Exploration and Excavation in the American Tropics*. University of Chicago Press, Chicago.

Wertheim, Margaret
2011 *Physics on the Fringe: Smoke Rings, Circlons, and Alternative Theories of Everything*. Walker, New York.

White, Peter
1974 *The Past Is Human: Debunking Von Daniken's Gee-Whiz Theories*. Angus & Robertson, Sydney.

Whittlesey, Charles
1876 Archaeological Frauds. *Historical and Archaeological Tracts of the Western Reserve and Northern Ohio Historical Society* 33:1–7.

Wicks, Robert S., and Roland H. Harrison
1999 *Buried Cities, Forgotten Gods: William Niven's Life of Discovery and Revolution in Mexico and the American Southwest*. Texas Tech University Press, Lubbock.

Wilkinson, Toby A. H.
1999 *Early Dynastic Egypt*. Routledge, London.

Willey, Gordon R., and Jeremy A. Sabloff
1993 *A History of American Archaeology*. 3rd ed. W. H. Freeman, New York.

Williams, Chancellor
1987 *Destruction of Black Civilization: Great Issues of a Race from 4500 B.C to 2000 A.D.* Third World Press, Chicago.

Williams, Stephen
1991 *Fantastic Archaeology: The Wild Side of North American Prehistory*. University of Pennsylvania Press, Philadelphia.

Winer, Richard
1974 *The Devil's Triangle*. Bantam Books, New York.

Witzel, Michael
2006 Rama's Realm: Indocentric Writings of Early South Asian Archaeology and History. In *Archaeological Fantasies: How Pseudoarchaeology Misrepresents the Past and Misleads the Public*, edited by Garrett G. Fagan, pp. 203–232. Routledge, London.

Wolter, Scott
2014 The Smithsonian Responds to *America Unearthed*—"Lost Relics of the Bible" Episode. Blog post, *Scott Wolter Answers*, 6 February. Electronic document, http://scottwolteranswers.blogspot.com/2014/02/the-smithsonian-responds-to-america.html, accessed June 10, 2015.

Woodard, Colin
2007 The Great Pyramids of . . . Bosnia? *Chronicle of Higher Education*, 30 March. Electronic document, http://chronicle.com/weekly/v53/i30/30a01201.htm, accessed October 15, 2013.

Woodson, Carter Goodwin
1933 *The Mis-Education of the Negro*. Associated Publishers, Washington, D.C.

Woolheater, Craig
2014 Moneymaker on Sykes' Yeti DNA Study. *Cryptomundo*, 18 July. Electronic

document, http://cryptomundo.com/bigfoot-report/moneymaker-on-sykes-yeti-dna-study/, accessed June 10, 2015.

Woolley, Leonard, Sir
1960 [1954] *Digging Up the Past.* Rev. ed. Penguin, Harmondsworth, Middlesex.

Xie, Julie
2011 DP Reporter Explores the Secrets of Penn Museum: Paranormal Stories Are Passed Down from Generation to Generation. *Daily Pennsylvanian*, 30 October. Electronic document, http://www.thedp.com/article/2011/10/dp_reporter_explores_the_secrets_of_penn_museum, accessed June 10, 2015.

Yates, Donna, and Neil Brodie
2012 Subsistence Digging. *Trafficking Culture*, 17 August. Electronic document, http://traffickingculture.org/encyclopedia/terminology/subsistence-digging/, accessed June 10, 2015.

Zhelyazkova, Antonina
2004 *Bosnia: Tolerant Hostility.* Bulgaria: IMIR, May. Electronic document, http://pasos.org/wp-content/archive/Bosnia+2004+-+Tolerant+Hostility.pdf, accessed October 15, 2013.

Zusne, Leonard, and Warren H. Jones
1982 *Anomalistic Psychology: A Study of Extraordinary Phenomena of Behaviour and Experience.* Lawrence Erlbaum Associates, Hillsdale, N.J.

Contributors

David S. Anderson is an assistant professor of anthropology at Roanoke College. He is the coeditor of *Constructing Legacies of Mesoamerica: Archaeological Practice and the Politics of Heritage in and beyond Mexico.*

Terry Barnhart is a professor of history at Eastern Illinois University. He was an associate curator at the Ohio History Society from 1983 to 1994. He is the author of *Ephraim George Squier and the Development of American Anthropology* and numerous essays on the history of American archaeology. His new book is *American Antiquities: Revisiting the Origins of American Archaeology.*

Christopher Begley is an associate professor of anthropology at Transylvania University in Lexington, Kentucky. His current research focuses on 3D imaging in underwater archaeology. He is the author of a forthcoming monograph on the archaeology of the Mosquito Coast of Honduras.

April M. Beisaw is an assistant professor of anthropology at Vassar College. She received the Gordon R. Willey Prize from the Archaeology Division of the American Anthropological Association for her article "Memory, Identity and NAGPRA in the Northeastern United States." She is also the author of *Identifying and Interpreting Animal Bones: A Manual.*

James S. Bielo is an assistant professor of anthropology at Miami University in Ohio. He is the author of *Words upon the Word: An Ethnography of Evangelical Bible Study* and *Emerging Evangelicals: Faith, Modernity, and the Desire for Authenticity* and the editor of *The Social Life of Scriptures: Cross-Cultural Perspectives on Biblicism.*

Deborah A. Bolnick is an associate professor of anthropology at the University of Texas at Austin. She is a molecular anthropologist who uses ancient DNA to help reconstruct Native American population history, and her work has been published in a variety of scientific journals, including the *American Journal of Physical Anthropology*, *American Antiquity*, and *Science*.

Jeb J. Card is a visiting assistant professor of anthropology at Miami University in Ohio. He was a postdoctoral visiting scholar at Southern Illinois University at Carbondale and is the editor of *The Archaeology of Hybrid Material Culture*.

Stacy Dunn is a doctoral student in anthropology at Tulane University and an instructor at Edinboro University. She has completed a dissertation titled "Architecture and Power in the Expansion of a Small Polity: A Study of Chancay Rural Elite Residences" on the archaeology of the central coast of Peru.

Kenneth L. Feder is a professor of anthropology at Central Connecticut State University. He is the director of the Farmington River Archaeological Project and the author of *Frauds, Myths, and Mysteries: Science and Pseudoscience in Archaeology* and *The Encyclopedia of Dubious Archaeology: From Atlantis to the Walam Olum*, among other works.

Denis Gojak is a doctoral candidate in anthropology at the University of Sydney, where he is documenting the belief that Australia was visited, mapped, or settled by other explorers before the accepted seventeenth-century discoveries by the Dutch. He is also the Senior Heritage Specialist at New South Wales Roads and Maritime Services, based in Sydney, Australia.

Bradley T. Lepper is the curator of archaeology at the Ohio Historical Connection. He is the author of *Ohio Archaeology: An Illustrated Chronicle of Ohio's Ancient American Indian Cultures* and writes a column on archaeology for the *Columbus Dispatch*.

Evan A. Parker is a doctoral student in anthropology at Tulane University. He is completing his dissertation, "Cooperation, Community, and the Ballgame in an Early Maya Village: Archaeological Investigations at Preclassic (900 B.C–250 A.D.) Paso del Macho, Yucatán, México."

Tera C. Pruitt researches authority and the politics of display in archaeology and heritage management. She worked as a postdoctoral researcher at the Department of Information Studies at UCLA on a National Science Foundation project called "Creating Collaborative Catalogs" after finishing her Ph.D. at the University of Cambridge.

Index